Auto-Anthropology
Anthropological Autobiography &
Autobiographical Anthropology
Or Destruction of the Self in the World of the Non-
Reflexive Other

Hugh M. Lewis

2005

Copyright 2005
Hugh M. Lewis

ISBN
9798416330774

The points of view presented in this text are those only of the
original author, Hugh M. Lewis, and do not represent the opinion
or position of any other person or entity in the world.

Indie Anthropology
Poor Hugh's E-Press
Lewis Micropublishing

Table of Contents

Foreword
There and Back Again in Hobbit World

I have been engaged in anthropology, in research, reading, and writing, for over forty years. And yet I cannot call myself an anthropologist in the full blown, Academically tenured sense of the term.

So I've been blessed in my lifetime making something called Alternative Anthropology work for myself at least, mostly in the solitude of my own writer's garret, and remaining yet otherwise an "invisible man" in the larger world.

At least part of this writing and work over the years has engaged alternative anthropology subjects in other directions and ways than the standard approach that it has long been, as the main course curricula of most American anthropology programs.

In hindsight, I do not regret for a second my engagement in alternative and applied anthropology in the world, as it has opened other doors I could not have ever imagined as a young veteran the first day of my first anthropology class more than forty years before.

I offer this and other texts, in a "brand" of anthropological writing I now refer to as "Indie" (Independent) Anthropology, as something both more and other than a standard academic course, or more than a highly hacked website or blog, as well as also being something (ambivalently) much less than a formal paper in a prestigious professional journal, much less a well-published book complete with an index and running heads.

I have made my way in the larger world, a world many ways much stranger than Middle Earth, well outside of the many small fields and meadows of Academic Anthropology.

Auto-Anthropology

In hindsight, I cannot now completely separate or segregate in my mind and memory where my own sense of narcissistic self-interest, sometimes writ larger than life in my surrounding world, has left off, and a more genuine sense of self-survival and social solidarity has taken over in me, especially in terms of some kind of "anthropological identity" that, beyond the Academy at least, most people do not even know, much less understand or care, about.

Preface: On Auto-Anthropology

Anthropological understanding rests upon the principle of relationship between the familiar self and the strange other, with the idea of making the strange familiar at the cost of self-estrangement. Auto-Anthropology derives from the implications and applications of this principle to the real world, by means of the deliberate Anthropological self-seeking of greater social understanding, the so-called anthropological moment, within the larger world. Such a process entails inevitable self-estrangement

We have come upon an age of truly global anthropology. It is now less a story of once proud but vanishing tribes of humankind, and increasingly more a story about emerging national varieties and sub-national tribes and mosaic ethno-tiles of a global humanity. It is a New Old World built not of place but of time, in which people become forgotten in huge crowds, largely more as a result of digital literacy, than just because they were lost tribes without literacy or written record.

Traditional anthropology occupied a transitional anthropological moment in its brief history, marked by a period of European colonization of the rest of the world, and the attempt to capture on record the vestiges and stories of disappearing and now lost tribes. It represented itself more as anthropology of place than one of period, even if period of time may always have been a critical background consideration.

Auto-Anthropology has its place in the contemporary anthropological moment, which is now post-traditional and post-colonial, but global in scope and perspective. Auto-Anthropology shares connections with many other "Anthropological varieties" including in my experience the study of ethnoculture and ethno-history, the anthropology of knowledge and its potential applications, alternative anthropology and various forms of applied anthropology, as well as the anthropology of human systems, or, in short, anthropological systems theory.

Auto-Anthropology

Contemporary Anthropology, including its fringes like Auto-Anthropology, has a fitting place in the modern global world order that is now emergent with the continuing development of human-kind, especially everywhere that old traditions are becoming challenged by new ways, customs and norms of modern living and worldview.

As we rapidly lose traditional ethno-linguistic ethos to the importation of globalization, Anthropologos and Anthropologia loses its received sense of legitimacy and its perceived purpose and relevance in a contemporary world that is changing ever more rapidly, ever more globally.

Witnessing Anthropology
1992-1999

Hugh M. Lewis

Part One

This manuscript has been in a very real sense a "living" (or at least a "never-ending") document. It will truly only end once I myself have ended as but a final epitaph (Perhaps, "Dr. Lewis was here, once upon a time.")

As it now sits primarily in ephemeral electronic digits, it is a concatenation and compilation of a handful of different texts, each covering a different period and phase of my life, overlapping here and there, and yet missing gaps elsewhere.

Most of these texts were written some twenty to thirty years ago, when I was a bit younger and far more naïve and disillusioned about my life. Much has happened to the world since then. Much has happened to us, and to others in the world, who have also shared some common sense of a history or biography.

I consider now history and biography to be interdependent extensions of one another—biography is a form of focused history written usually in terms of the life of the subject of focus. History is usually written in some larger brush-stroke that incorporates many multicolored biographies.

Most that I have written in this text was written many years ago. Whether or not I write a reworking or more updated biography about myself remains yet to be seen. Much I would now choose rather not to write about as in hindsight a lot seems so sordid and somewhat redundant by now in my sixties.

From my previous experiences, American (mostly academic) anthropology (and by extension, British, French and other variants of anthropology) seems not to have changed that much since my undergraduate days when we watched primarily videos of Napoleon Chagnon performing in native garb and face-paint.

Of course, at the time the big debate that raged across the anthropology departments was not the question of Chagnon's professional character, ethos and ethics. It was a time when New Zealand wannabe Socio-biological Anthropologist Derek Freeman somewhat belatedly challenged directly the implied paradigm and received anthropological authority of Margaret Mead in Samoan Coming of Age.

Anthropology probably by then did not realize it, but as leaders of the cultural dialog and dialectics, they fell unwittingly into the middle of the emerging culture wars and political and social correctness, which for myself at least was always a disguised way of saying tongue-in-cheek—do as I say, and not as I do. We may be forced to fake demonstrations of tolerance of designated others, but we cannot expect that forced sense of tolerance to be necessarily reciprocated upon ourselves.

The individual academic response to this shifting American climate of enforced social equality seems to have been a mix between indifference and dismissal, or else a signal to a new politically-approved and vouchsafed approach that allowed the reintroduction to economic and political Marxism; the ideological definition of feminism as more than a sociopolitical cause for female equality, thus becoming a banner-carrier for a transformed feminist world.

In hindsight now, it is unfortunate that the legacy and implications of Chagnon's anthropological work could not now be more objectively assessed for what worked, what went wrong, and how it may have been done better next time.

Whatever was to be thrown up, if not in agreement with the correct paradigm, merely provided a common target of resentment and intellectual rebellion against new correctness norms, and becoming a spur for the promotion of a hardened scientific approach. I can only imagine such meetings, met with odd body language signifying a kind of non-verbal rejection. I can imagine the self-imposed silence of one side versus the exaggerated loudness of the professional "Other."

Throughout my school career, I stalked the halls of several different anthropological departments across the country, but I never joined in any camps. If I spoke out, as I sometimes did, it was from my own point of view and no one else's, generally.

As my wife (still very much an anthropological "Other" or native) now reminds me in hindsight, I was probably always too much of an individualist. Being in the middle in the corridor was not always the best

Auto-Anthropology

or easiest place to be positioned in departments that were split clearly but zigzagging down the "no person's land" in middle of these corridors.

The manner of professional fighting was not with spears, arrows, clubs and machetes, as with Chagnon's Yanomamo, but as fighting it could sometimes be just as vicious in its own manner. As my wife reminded me today, civilized ways of killing a person is to attack their identity, their ego, they spirit, and their social authority. The Yanomamo may have just been more direct and honest in this regard, if human civilization is indeed an elaboration of the war of all against all.

I have to see the anthropological dynamics of anthropology departments within an ever-unfolding historical context, interpreting what I have long construed as modern social class dynamics, either as "American-Style" or "Other" style complete with its implication of alien-ness.

At times these organizational dynamics became quite vicious when seemingly frustrated careers led to the deliberate if ill intentioned effort to criticize and attack the careers of others, to marginalize, alienate and eventually ostracize others. The paradox is that in all these ego-politics, the so-called "genuine Other" seems to become lost between the cracks of the woodwork.

In long hindsight, I do not nor cannot regret my own "failed" career in Anthropology, as I see that, having so long been an independent Anthropologist, my professional identity as an anthropologist has not failed but only progressed in its own independent direction through the years. Failure as a result of systematic interference competition and social discrimination is merely social discrimination--denial of opportunity and strangling of potential for development.

I have since realized no significant "voice" in anthropology and I have few formal publications to my name, particularly within received professional anthropological forums, and especially after I was anonymously accused of using an apparently trite (if not tripe) trope.

To this day I am not exactly sure what a "trope" is as the criticism seemed to have been intended except it must have been something truly dangerous and threatening to the highest academic standards of anthropological literature.

My own brand of anthropology, if you could call it a "kind," is derived from and thus constitutes a core part of general system theory (human or anthropological systems theory) that has not precluded the extension to applied systems of research-design development. Furthermore, systems theory has little tolerance for narrowly restricted points of view built on the professional investment to a critical paradigm of practice.

Systems approaches in theory, methodology and application, have much to recommend themselves in anthropological praxis—they are broad enough that radically contraposed and seemingly inimical points of view may be readily reconciled. Of course, anthropological systems theory lacks in relative stylistic sophistication what it makes up for in the challenges of complexity and normative uncertainty.

I have by and large found the main part and socio-political realities of especially American Anthropology to be historically invested. But it has been also a-historical, politically and socially hypocritical and sometimes vicious, as well as being largely classist and class conscious in social orientation, idealism and ideologies, and somewhat pretentious in core professional values.

The representation of the "Other" as an a-historical, but evolutionary, entity, stuck in a frozen cultural ecology, is not just misleading of objective reality but dangerous in the surreptitious promotion of ideology pretending itself as a kind of science that does not otherwise know what to call or do with itself.

People of the earth may have been with or without a sense of history (depending on whether they were literate, took notes and kept records) but they were never without an important sense of the past.

In all of this the proverbial "Other" has been treated primarily as a counter-reference projection of the anthropologists' own needs, insecurities, and as a target for all manner of other potential behavioral and symbolic projections and externalizations.

In all of this I must yet take greater hope that the genuine "Other" in historic-biographical context, can be brought back into the larger picture as something of greater interest than theoretical validation, or as the means to a fulfilled academic career or "special people" (i.e., anything other than people interesting for their own sake.)

Auto-Anthropology

I might suggest in relation to theoretical debates on Yanomamo ferocity and proclivity to warfare or conflict, is that it is at its base probably not inherently different from the kinds of warfare and resource competition occurring between anthropologists and programs across different departments. If we presuppose the base of this to be natural, innate aggression, or something learned and acquired as a part of socialization in a competitive, conflict prone world, it probably makes little net difference.

We must recognize Napoleon Chagnon in the late sixties and early 70s for the kind of Anthropological cultural icon that he became through the success of his publications and films. When Derek Freeman about a decade later proposed a "rape gene" for Samoans in direct challenge to Margaret Mead's iconic work in "Coming of Age in Samoa," the ideological wars between Feminist-Marxist-Structuralist left and socio-biological right were begun—Freeman just managed to publish his controversial thesis after Mead's demise.

It has long struck me that the solution to the anthropological problem of human complexity is a greater sense of objectivity achieved through a more honest representation of the self with the fully humanized (and quite imperfect) other.

A lot of people have over the years told me I couldn't write (well at least) and few have ever told me to write. But write I did, mostly in my own way, and if not stylistically then at least somewhat prolifically if also it seems too prosaically for most people's taste.

I did write a lot, but I didn't edit so much, and doing a good job editing is also more important than learning to write well. I have been those years a fairly distracted fellow. Much I have written about I would now rather choose not to have written.

Some things I have written about I have laterr redlined out for one reason or another. A lot of it seems simply so sordid in long hindsight. Let's just say names have been changed to protect the innocent, and where relations couldn't be disguised by pseudonyms, then those small ugly or boring parts of the larger story were usually excised. But overall I have stuck faithfully to the dictum of truth in honesty and openness.

It has been more than forty years now since my first acquaintance with anthropology. I never gave up on anthropology, though anthropology in the conventional sense long ago gave up on and forgot about me. I feel that over the years I've gleaned the best and have come to recognize the worst of anthropological thought and theory.

For myself anthropology is both a science and humanity, in fact it is the science of humanity as well as of humankind. We cannot separate where sense of being human leaves off and sense of humanity takes over, but we understand this humanity from the perspective of comprehending the differences in others with whom we share this world.

It is not merely a science of human systems, but human systems themselves are inveterately knowledge systems, and thus anthropology is the study of both humankind and the knowledge produced and used by humankind.

The main reasoning auto-anthropology is important not only to myself but to the greater interests of humankind are that the denial of the subjective reality that leads to lack of empathy and from there to antipathy, is that it is only in the understanding and tolerance of the differences of the other, subjectively expressed in terms of their inveterate humanity, that we can create a more humanized system and better prevent the rise of fascist-style orientations that thrive on the denial and inevitable destruction of subjective others in the world.

Our subjectivity however framed is important to the expression and greater progressive social realization of our innate humanity, with the profound realization that however alone in the universe we may be, however distant from other beings in the universe who may be somewhat akin to ourselves at least in terms of intelligence, we in the end have only one another to depend upon by which to realize greater meaning in our shared collective world. We need an authentic anthropology now, disinvested of cultural politics and policies, more than ever before in our past.

As members of a common single human species, we are all time-travellers from our separate pasts toward a common wide future stream. We all had our beginnings and endings, our entrances, roles and parts to play, as well as our exits. Certainly, we do not all share the same local stage, but we have always been of one global theater.

Auto-Anthropology

Collectively, together, we travel this space-ship earth through the vast infinitely empty ocean of deep space. The lines we draw in the ground will never hold up and endure the blowing, erosive sands of time.

I still believe strongly in a broad and inclusive (and non-exclusive) anthropology, and I think its dialectics can transcend the false dichotomy of nature versus nurture, and can move on to more sophisticated and interesting theoretical arguments of human behavior and social patterning.

But alternative anthropology, the "post academic" anthropology of my own career, did not follow or find itself overly constrained by considerations of correctness and ideological conformity to ultimately narrow and unproven theoretical paradigms and their presuppositions.

I believe anthropology has yet the potential to render itself the premier science of humankind in all its many and complex facets, but only once it can satisfactorily reconcile for mutual gain and benefit the dichotomous "nature versus nurture" arguments.

WITNESSING THE ANTHROPOLOGY OF THE WORLD
Destruction of the Self in the World of the Non-reflexive Other
1993

Anthropology and Authoritarian Power Structures: An American Anthropological Alliterative Autobiography

> Whatever the type, there is a deep-seated craving common to almost all men of words which determines their attitude to the prevailing order. It is a craving for human recognition, a craving for a clearly marked status above the common run of humanity. (Eric Hoffer, Between the Devil and the Dragon 1982: 269)

I have nothing to prove my words that follow except a firm faith in my own basic honesty. I speak for myself and for no one else, and I offer but one possible interpretation, but one eyewitness testimony to the events of my experience. One must pay a price for honesty and openness to one's own experiences. Often it is a price of self-security. Sometimes it is a price of self-credulity—or of worthiness and merit in the eyes of others.

It is honesty, particularly self-honesty, that most dispels the "necessary" illusions of life that sustain our belief in our actions and our worldview. Such honesty rests upon a common ground of human weakness and frailty, and upon a healthy skepticism that while people of the world may sometimes admire a good hater, no one ever loves a chronic doubter or a selfless critic.

Witnessing one's faith in terms available to and relevant of one's own experience is sometimes the prelude to one's confirmation of that faith. It is an unveiling, an expose', and forging of one's own character in the fires of life.

<u>Auto-Anthropology</u>

Indeed, all people are by the achieved wisdom of their lived experiences 'authentic anthropologists' of the world. And anthropology has been a peculiar preoccupation of all of humankind, and an ancient profession of all people to understand themselves in disillusioned ways.

The need for professed self-honesty derives from the inability to live well with the deceit and contradictions that normally sustain most of our illusions and actions. Deceit begets ever-greater darkness and deceit, and the path of wisdom lies through the disillusionment that only honesty can hope to bring.

There is no human being who is not untransformed by experience and whose pathway through life does not twist and turn in unexpected directions, and who is not, sooner or later, forced to walk in someone else's footsteps.

I witness six different sets of experiences drawn from six different periods of my life. The events, which framed these experiences, were biographically and historically real, though the interpretation I now give to them remains my own fiction, my own mythical illusion.

The only common theme uniting these six different episodes is my own autobiographical impression formed by these various experiences that have long been bound together by my existential need for self-identity. It is a common theme composed of threads of aggression, authority and authoritarianism, being American and trying to become an 'Authentic Academic Anthropologist,' and, last but not least, my own obsessive preoccupation with authorial credibility.

We are all actors with our parts to play however minor they may really be. And we all have our own voices with which to witness the world.

We grow old only to learn the lesson more and more that we really didn't always need for our own best welfare others in the world to speak or act or intercede upon our own behalf.

Buddha

14

Whether in visible or mysterious garb,
Buddha is neither one nor divisible.
If you need to distinguish his aspects,
Imagine a Lotus blooming in a fire.

Dao Hue

I do not remember well my father's face. I remember him walking through the front door. I remember him arguing with my mother. I remember his hairy hands turning the pages while I sat in his lap trying to read with him. I remember his long interminable absences, his unexpected visits in his old gray Plymouth. I remember him working in the garage on his boat, helping bring him his tools. I remember going fishing with him, becoming sea sick, and his catching barracuda, halibut and bass. I remember riding in the car with him on his journeys, and him waiting to pick me up after school.

I loved my father and missed him sorely when he would go away without warning or telling us when he would return. I would sit in his lap while reading to him, and while he smoked a cigar or a pipe he would have me knock out for him. He would tell us stories about his having been a naval fighter pilot in the Korean War.

One day, the first of December in 1965, I walked home from school to find his car not parked beside the curb. I looked for him and waited. But he never, ever came again. Eventually my grandpa pulled up in his Chevy pickup truck, and he took me silently to my aunt's house on the other side of town.

I asked my grandpa where my father was, but he was strangely quiet. I was told at my aunt's that something had happened. My father had a 'heart attack' but that's all I found out from them. Finally the phone rang and then my aunt drove me back to my house. On the way home that day I remembered the Goodyear Blimp flying high overhead.

My mother and older sister met me at the door. They both had tears in their eyes as they told me he had died. I said: "I was told he had a heart attack." They did not say anything. I did not understand death very well at the time, for I smiled in embarrassment, not knowing what else to do.

Auto-Anthropology

My older brother had red eyes for about three days, and then that was
the last time I ever saw him cry in my life. My father had been very hard
on my brother, punishing him very fiercely when he neglected his duties
like taking out the trash.

We then had a big family reunion at my Grandma and Grandpa's house.
Family came from all over. A big long black limousine with fold-up back
seats picked us up and took us uptown to the memorial service. The
coffin was open, but as we filed by I could not see who was in it because
I was too short and I was too shy by the ceremony to ask my mother or
sister to pick me up to look inside.

We drove a long way to the funeral in a long line of cars. He was buried
on a hill at the federal cemetery in San Diego (Rosecrans National
Cemetery at Point Loma). It overlooked the beautiful blue ocean and
the gray naval ships in the harbor. The flag that draped the coffin flapped
in the breeze, as the Marines standing on the hill fired their rifles
overhead and then folded up the flag into a funny triangle and handed it
to my mom.

Everyone else left the graveside except myself, my brother and sisters
and my Mom. As we stood there in an endless geometric sea of white
grave markers, my mother and oldest sister cried. My brother, my other
sister, and myself went back to the car and waited for them, laughing and
joking about their melodramatic mood. Perhaps we were trying to escape
from the overwhelming gravity of the moment in our own naive way.

My mother put the folded flag into one of her old trunks by her bed, and
I had only seen it once or twice since that day, and only after my request.
We only visited the grave two or three times over the years after that, and
have never been back to see it later on except one time when my mom
and I took my wife, Rosie, and our child, Mahala, to Sea World, and we
visited his grave-site nearby. We both wept. My father used to take us to
church and Sunday school every Sunday morning, but after his death we
never went back to church at all.

After that my growing up was mostly memories of playing, being alone,
fighting between all the members of my family, taking care of my pet
animals, watching television and walking to and back from school. All of
these events transpired against a background of the Vietnam War,

assassinations, campus protests and racial riots, the Beatles, Star Trek, Gilligan's Island, and popular now classic rock and roll music on the radio.

I remember reading the casualty reports from the second page of the LA Times to my sixth grade class every morning for current events. I remember watching Walter Cronkite on the six o'clock news telling us "and that's the way it is."

I remember Life magazine with the pictures of the TET offensive in Hue, the casualties, the young Vietcong and the women and children of My Lai. I remember the neighbor boys next door, down the streets, behind us, all going off to Vietnam and eventually returning. One boy my mother had taught in school had told us that he was a machine gunner in the Marine Corps. Another son of family friends of ours never came back. An older brother of my best friend came back, only to be killed in a car accident a few days later.

I remember a missionary friend of the family writing from Vietnam, describing how another missionary in hiding was gunned down in the middle of the night by the Cong. In my neighborhood there was no ostensible dishonor in serving in Vietnam. It was a lower working class neighborhood of mixed Mexican American and White background, and serving one's country was an expected and not dishonorable thing to do.

My family fell apart over the next few years. My mother worked all the time and went to school at night.

My younger sister became schizophrenic later on, but her strangeness always permeated the household to the point that I was afraid to bring my school friends home to visit for fear of her unexpected behavior.

It was only several years later that I had discovered the truth about my father's death. He had been suffering for several years from paranoid schizophrenia. He spent about a year in Camarillo State Hospital receiving electro-shock therapy. He had attempted suicide one day by slashing his wrists and had taken himself to a hospital for treatment. That day in December 1965, he had shot himself in the heart with a twenty-two-caliber rifle that we used to take target shooting in the desert.

<u>Auto-Anthropology</u>

I discovered the truth from a school acquaintance that had lived nearby my Grandparent's house where it had happened, and I later confronted my mother with the question, and she explained to me the whole secret that had been kept hidden from me for so long. The pieces began falling into place, and my memories began making sense.

In hindsight I can understand my mother's reluctance to tell me the truth, as I probably wouldn't have understood it very well anyway. But it has always fundamentally bothered me that my own family had deceived me when they had been the very one's to teach me always to tell the truth. Lies, white, gray or black, are still lies.

Home

No color or complexion distinguishes the way
Still its message flares up everywhere:
Of the thousands of worlds, numerous as grains of sand
Which is not home?

Thuong Chieu

Perhaps it was desperation, or perhaps it was the epitome of wisdom, that led my mother to move to another part of the city right when I was coming of age and about to enter High School. In my old Junior High, I was not just the top of the class, but the top of the whole school.

I was probably the classic example of an early over achiever in a small, poor school district that has chronically rated some of the lowest reading and math scores in the country. I found conventional schoolwork stimulating, and I was quite the perfectionist and quite frustrated and unhappy. I achieved in spite of the emotional turmoil and desperation of our family life, and perhaps because of it.

My mom had no one else to help us move. I was the only one to help her, and we made many trips across town in our old Plymouth loaded up with our possessions. We did not finish until late at night, and we left behind many things, that we could not carry with us and put into the car or the van of a friend who came to help us in the evening. I had learned to become the little 'man of the house' taking care of many of the household chores, the animals and learning to cook and clean up after myself, my sister and for my mom while she worked.

When I was ten years old, I was regularly babysitting my next-door neighbor's son who was only five years of age, so that the mother could go to her second job teaching Hula dance in the evenings. I took care of all the animals that we had seemed to always collect—the birds in a small aviary, turtles in the backyard, cats and dogs. I once had a duck and a chicken, and a rabbit.

Most nights I was mostly alone by myself as my Mom went back to school at night or often square dancing. I did homework, made dinner for myself and sometimes for my sister, watched my nightly line-up of television shows and played mostly with my toy soldiers.

High school turned out to be one of the loneliest and unhappiest times of my life. I burned out early on in the overachievement syndrome, especially as I found myself in classrooms full of students who seemed to suffer more acutely from the need for achievement and pernicious perfectionism than myself.

My mom had landed me in an upper middle class white people's school, and the common distinction made by the student body and the teachers was between those who came from 'above the Boulevard' ("Pull-overs" or "Dress Shirts") and those unfortunate few from 'below the Boulevard" (the T-shirters, or "Out-crowd" versus non-T-shirters "In-Crowd," as someone grown up in the area later explained it to me.)

I found myself not only ostracized from most social circles in the school, but also actually shunned and ostracized from many extra-curricular activities. It was apparent to us, even then, that many of the teachers had a selective preference for supporting students from "above the boulevard." I found myself the member of a lunch-time clique who called ourselves 'the odd ball group" and didn't seem to fit in anywhere.

Of this odd-assortment, about half were from above the Blvd. (Whittier Blvd) and the other half below the Blvd. Looking back, we shared one thing in common, we were none of us academic overachievers nor were any of us engaged in extracurricular school activities. We had our own lunch corner near the center quad on campus, until one older teacher took us into her room at lunch hour.

The Vietnam War still loomed in the background, only not so overshadowing as before. It was receding quickly. By the last year of my high school the first wave Vietnamese refugee children made their first appearance in our school—about twenty or thirty of them in all. They were a strange and separate group. I tried to little avail to befriend some of them during PE class. I remember one boy proclaiming proudly that he was not Vietnamese, but Chinese from Vietnam, and that a U.S. helicopter could be shot down with a forty-five-caliber pistol if it was still bigger than the size of one's thumb.

By my senior year I was working more than full time as a dishwasher at a local restaurant and a convalescent home, and on weekends I would do people's yard work and housework. I managed to save quite a lot of money, but could no longer deal very well with school. I ended up getting kicked out of a couple of classes for fighting with other students or talking back to the teacher. Though I ended up having to go to a continuation school at night, I graduated with the rest of the class of '76 on schedule. I had a relatively high GPA but zero sense of sociability, especially with girls and female students.

I left high school without any clear sense of what I was going to do next. I remember telling my mom one evening at dinner, in quite serious earnest, that I was bound and determined to leave the house, and all the nonsense, no matter what. I paid cash that I had saved for a Volkswagen, and soon found myself living alone in a single bedroom apartment in a dusty rural city in central California, attending a state college full time as a pre-vet animal science major and still working full-time as a dishwasher at a Holiday Inn.

I must have been terribly lonely in that strange city, and also terribly confused. One day I found myself walking by a military recruiter's office downtown and saw a poster of Marines in uniform—it read 'The Few, the Proud, the Marines.' Next thing I knew I found myself inside, signing all the forms for an enlistment that was delayed only long enough to go home and say goodbye to my Mom.

I had a choice of either becoming an enlisted man, or else being sent back to college, eventually becoming an officer. I was attracted by the two thousand-dollar bonus then being offered for the 'combat arms program' and I remember one officer telling me that he thought I would be happier driving around in tanks rather than humping it with a backpack and a rifle. My mom was quite disturbed and surprised when the recruiter phoned her to congratulate her on her son's enlistment into the Marine Corps.

I spent a Veteran's Day weekend wondering around downtown Los Angeles waiting for the AAFEE's station to open on Monday morning. The induction process took a whole day, and it wasn't until nightfall that we took our oaths and made the long and lonesome bus trip down to MCRD San Diego. My first encounter with several mad Drill Instructors even before I got off the bus taught me a lesson I would have reaffirmed many times over during and after my stint in the 'Corps'—what a fool I had been in volunteering for active duty.

Boot camp was difficult and purely physical, but it was simple and straight-ahead, and it had its affect upon myself and everyone else at the time. It had effectively turned us, in the course of three months, into blindly obedient, boot shinning, rifle drilling mad machines ready to sacrifice ourselves for our country and to kill other people in the process.

The effect of this brain washing did not begin to wear off until I actually got to the Pacific Fleet Marine Force, being stationed at Camp Schwab in north central Okinawa. I spent the entire eight weeks at the tank training school polishing boots, shinning brass, running five miles a day in any kind of weather, and then sometimes going out and getting drunk at the army EM clubs. At Okinawa I had a somewhat abrupt and rude awakening to battle hardened and battle weary Marine Corps line units that were suffering a severe hangover in a kind of 'post-Vietnam' syndrome.

Morale was severely low, field officers were frequently missing and getting drunk on duty, and many had a defeatist 'Fuck the Suck' and 'Eat the Apple, Fuck the Corp's' attitude. The Lifers were still as Gungi ("Gung ho," the Marines' favorite motto) as ever, but Vietnam had left a

Auto-Anthropology

funny cloud hanging in the back of their minds and a funny look in their eyes.

Our tank platoon was put to sea with 3/9, an infamous regiment that had been called the 'Walking Dead' in Vietnam and who apparently, so the story was told, left calling game cards on the bodies of their Vietnamese victims. As the story was told to boot ears, they had lost their standards in battle and so, as the sea-lawyers had it, the unit was not allowed to return to the mainland—being semi-permanently outcast in disgrace.

While in the Philippines, the mortar and machine gun platoons we were bunked with aboard the USS Alamo were involved in a tragic helicopter crash in which 37 young marines were chopped to pieces. When the battalion returned from its six months afloat, it began rioting out in the little base village of Henoko. Many of these riots, and a great deal of the fighting, were racial/ethnic conflicts, and ethnic relations upon the island, especially between units, were always severely strained.

I returned after thirteen months on Okinawa the veteran of more than a handful of fights and small group melees, several close calls with getting killed in accidents, as well as having a friend and sergeant crushed by a tank, and a severe problem with alcoholism. By the time it was our turn to rotate back to the States, virtually everyone in our small platoon was severely alcoholic, no matter whether they were teetotaler or drinkers when they first arrived on the 'rock.'

I was stationed next at Twenty-Nine Palms, California, the combined arms training area involving regular live fire training exercises throughout the year. I stayed there for the remaining two and a half years of my active duty. "Stumps" as we called it turned out to be not only worse than the Rock, but the very bottom of the Marine Corps barrel. It was as if the Marine Corps had a secret policy of concentrating all their worst misfits in one place.

The whole base was more or less isolated from civilization, on the edge of nowhere, and was run like a minimum-security prison with weekend liberty. Not only were people being continuously harassed by the lifers, but were very frequently being rather severely punished for the slightest infractions. Our whole company especially was managed more like a work gang than a proper tank-operating unit.

We would come back to the parade ground at evening formation only to hear the meting out of that day's punishments. Many would receive several hours a night of extra work details, while the rest of the company were frequently ordered to field-day (clean) the squad bays until 9 or 10 at night for someone in the morning forgetting to make their bed well, or neglecting to clean out the trash can after emptying it. We field-day'd the squad-bays at least two or three times a week.

Whereas alcoholism was the main problem on the 'Rock,' at 'Stumps' it was the drugs that were epidemic. In my company alone, there was a staff sergeant who was the major cocaine dealer on base; a corporal who was the main marijuana dealer; growing a patch of it somewhere secretly out in the desert, and a private in my own platoon who was the main acid dealer. A cook in our company distributed speed. Almost everyone who did not drink profusely as a matter of nightly routine, at least smoked pot. Few had the character or willpower to resist for long the many foul influences that daily slinked through the open squad bay.

For the most part, I stayed free of the drug influences. I lived only to get drunk at night, and though drinking heavily, never missed a reveille and always was one of the hardest workers on the tank ramp. We sweated out the beer by the end of the hot desert day only to be primed for the next round of beer that evening.

Because I worked hard, I was soon made a tank commander in charge of my own tank. Our units then were chronically half manpower, and the whole post Vietnam-era military was suffering critical manpower shortages. My tank was probably the oldest Vietnam vintage tank left in the Marine Corps. We could never hit anything with it because the main gun had more than twice it's maximum quota of rounds put through it, and the rifling of the barrel was severely cracked around the middle and worn out.

Nevertheless, the tank, though comparatively slow, never broke down out in the field when many newer, faster tanks were having all kinds of mechanical problems. When I first got assigned to the tank it was bereft of any of its normal consignment of tools, and had many of its nuts and bolts missing off its track and armor plating.

Auto-Anthropology

Most of the tools had found their way into private toolboxes in the cars of many of the Marines. Since nothing could be done in that state, I ended up having to become a "scrounger" and "borrow" the tools off of other tanks and vehicles when no one was around. We would leave our orders with guys of our unit who were carrying guard duty on the ramp at night, to find the tools neatly stored away inside our tanks the next morning.

Going to the field, which we did on a weekly and monthly basis, was really our only respite from our mindless, mostly monotonous, and often mind-numbing normal regimen of daily inspections and the usual harassment. I came to look forward to the field and took great pleasure in the vast rocky moonscapes of Twenty-Nine Palms. I came to volunteer for any kind of duty in the field I could get, anything to get away from the madness and tedium back on the base. It was this that eventually earned me meritorious corporal amidst a situation in which too many young men turned into hardcore drug addicts, inhabitants of psych wards, or sometimes even into criminals.

I saw the same downward trajectory repeated many times over during my time there. Naïve young men, almost always highly motivated and with a bright eyed future when they first arrived there, eventually becoming burned out, coping bad attitudes, doing drugs, going UA and getting into trouble somehow. At one time, six people in my platoon deserted within one week, four from the same tank (the entire crew.)

Our platoon, already half its normal size, looked pitifully small when represented by only a handful of guys standing in formation. It was hardest then because the ones leftover had to carry on in the usual way with the whole load.

Inspections were frequent, things still had to get done on the tanks, all the extra duties were still required of us, and when we went to the field there were often only two men instead of four on each tank—a driver and a commander. When firing on the move, while the driver made his way toward some landmark or down a road, the tank commander would have to jump down, load the next round, and get back up and fire from the commander's cupola.

It was the tank accident that I was involved in that precipitated my own burn out. We had already had a long, hot and dirty day. We were filthy with dust from head to the toes of our combat boots and were tired that night. In the afternoon I had given a class with the assistance of a couple of tank crews of how "grunts" (infantryman) up close with a tank may defeat the vehicle and crew. At night we volunteered to serve as a target tank for the TOW missile people in pretty rugged terrain.

It was late at night during a sandstorm before we found our positions. We were two crews combined into one—we left my tank behind as my driver and I joined Sgt. V.'s crew with his loader, Pvt. J. Two crews together made a full tank complement, and it was all eyes on top of the tank because of the nighttime limited visibility, the high winds, the dust and the bright searchlights. PFC H, my own driver, drove the tank while I served as a gunner.

After a week in the field, we were filthy from dust from head to toe. We were being hit by the search light of another tank about half a mile off while going up and down a prominent ridge. It was blinding light, and dark shadows were obscured by blowing dust clouds kicked up by the tank tracks. The dust was always a fine whitish, chalky powder that settled between the weave of our utilities and into every crevice and nook in our bodies.

We made two or three passes on the ridge, blinded by blowing dust and the Xenon lights of the tanks nested up in the ridges. All of a sudden a huge black hole loomed up in front of the tank, as the driver took a wrong turn going down the ridge. We were flying in space until we suddenly smashed into the bottom of the ravine in a 64 ton steel behemoth. I was thrown down on top of the standing ammunitions inside the tank, landing on the floor on my knees. The loader, Private J., who was sitting just behind me on the loader's hatch, was thrown out in front of the tank and the tank came to a stop on top of him. I got up in pain, as my knees were cut and bleeding from where I fell on the floor and on top of the ammunition.

It felt like a thousand pounds had been dropped on my body. I looked around and couldn't find the loader. I climbed outside and began running around the tank looking for him. Sgt. V., the tank commander, was bent over with some broken and bruised ribs. I got down in front and **PFC H.**, my driver with his front teeth smashed out, told me he saw J. fly down in front of the tank. I sent **PFC H.** bleeding from the mouth, off running across the desert to get help, while I tried digging J. out from beneath the tank. On his way through the darkness he fell on some rocks and cut up his knees pretty well.

J. was wedged in very tightly, bleeding from the mouth, nose and ears. He was moaning softly, but was not yet dead. The ground was too hard packed in that place to dig out with a tanker bar, and he was wedged under the weight of a broken suspension. Finally, I got in the tank, started it up and backed it off him, but it was too late. A week later I was part of a seven-man team who delivered a twenty-one-rifle salute at his funeral.

In a somewhat derealized state of mind—there immediately but like being on the edge of cliff looking down on everyone below, it dawned on me then just how much of a man eating machine the Marine Corps really was—its completely impersonal manner in which it processed death. I was just a few inches away from that coffin they were lowering in the ground. Our lieutenant, that night back on base, blamed me for what had happened in no uncertain terms, but he seemed not too sorry about J's death.

Just that day before the accident Private J. had confided in me that he was planning to get a vasectomy because he didn't want his young wife to get pregnant any more. At the scene of the accident, when help finally arrived, it became clearly apparent to me, in a way it had never before been, just how much everyone was acting out their parts, and how false and made-up it seemed in the face of death.

During that time I spent two months as corporal of the guard. One Sunday early afternoon, in the Springtime with temperatures well above 115 degrees Fahrenheit, I checked my five guards across four different posts—down near the tank ramp, the storage buildings, the armory and the motor-pool on the other side of the whole base, several miles apart.

It was totally quiet and the posts were solitary and rather peaceful in spite of the heat. I carried extra water in ice in a small one-gallon thermos container, and I made sure all of my guards, drawn from my own company and platoon, all carried canteens and their canteen cups. As I visited each of the posts, I found all my guards passed out and asleep in whatever shade they could find. I woke each up in turn, gave them ice and water, and waited for them to rouse to their job and duty.

The guard at the armory who was locked into the compound area with barbed wire surrounding with his M16, was passed out in his chair with his rifle across his lap. I quietly unlocked the gate in front of him and took his rifle while he was still passed out. I woke him back up and made sure he was still awake as I went to check the other guards who were in the same area outside of the compound. They too had found a shady side of the building and were passed out. I could have reported the incidents, and probably put most of them before a court martial, but I thought better of the extenuating circumstances, the hot stillness and loneliness, the mid-day lack of shade and sharp shadows, and they were besides members of my own platoon and company. I checked the posts a couple of hours later, during change of guard and they were all alive, awake and well. No harm was done, no memory leftover besides my own.

Some time after that a sadistic Staff Sergeant of ours, who hated prostitutes and women in general but loved to play the lifer with us, thought I needed morale up-lifting at NCO school down at Camp Pendleton. I was there all of two weeks. I figured out how to earn the minimum number of demerit points in the shortest span of time. I had earned my corporal stripes the hard way and had become too salty during my final year to be processed back through another boot camp.

All I wanted was to be left alone by the lifers and to wait out my remaining time in the Corps the shortest and easiest way possible. I left the NCO school in 'disgrace' but happy that I had achieved my goal. Later my sadistic Staff Sergeant confronted me alone inside of my tank and threatened me with court martial if I did not change my attitude to suit him. I told him to 'fuck off' to his face and to leave my tank crew alone. He was a coward at heart and would never back up his fierce words with fists.

Later I was called to an unofficial 'court martial.' They called it a competency hearing and essentially asked why I had failed out of NCO school and they then also wanted me to squeal on all the drug dealers in my company. This I could not do. One day, a lifer approached me behind the supply buildings and gave me a pair of lance corporal bars again. I was happy to be back 'on the other side' with my buddies.

But I was transferred to a new and better-managed company. I spent the last eight months of my active duty in the best platoon I had ever had. All the NCO's were black and most of the enlisted men were white, and it was the easiest going platoon I had ever seen. Even the lieutenant was pretty cool, though he really freaked out like a baby when it would come to tank maneuvers with live ammo in the field.

I had been changed that last year in the suck. The lifers screwed with me all the time, but they couldn't affect me in the slightest. Nothing they had I was interested in. They no longer tried to play mind games with me. It was then that I began going to the base library and spending all my spare time reading. I began writing my first manuscript on militarism and military mentality, based upon my experiences. I wrote any time I could between guard duty, extra details, and working on the ramp or driving tanks in the field. I wrote on my rack, sitting on my footlocker or while waiting in the driver's compartment of my tank.

I began looking at the Marine Corps in a different way, as a self-perpetuating illusion, as a 'social construction of reality' directed by its own sense of reconstructed history. It was nonetheless very real in consuming the lives of countless young men in service of a higher 'ideal' that had no substantive basis in social reality beyond its own legitimated construction.

I spent my remaining months sitting on my footlocker in an open squad bay, penning out a five hundred odd page manuscript. During the summer months the First Sergeant became angry with all of us, and crammed the whole company into only one side of the bay, turning the other side into an NCO recreation room. We had our double bunk beds spaced about a foot apart in a long line down both walls of a single large room.

The officer of the day could easily monitor all the activity in the whole building by just looking up across all the bunks from one place. We had nothing to do but to sleep in our underwear in fetal positions. One night after lights out, the whole squad bay began to riot. Someone down on one end began yelling, and it soon spread throughout. The whole squad bay was yelling and screaming, and we rampaged through the building, tipping over wall lockers and knocking over racks. It subsided about as suddenly as it began. We picked everything back up and went back to bed.

During the whole time I sat writing my manuscript, not one person ever came up to me and expressed an interest in what I was working on, though one day, a man who was on legal hold for desertion was left on watch at the squad bay while we were in the field for a couple of months straight. One day he locked all the doors, broke open all the wall lockers and stole everything he could get his hands on, tipping everything out of the wall lockers. But, though he had opened mine, he left it undisturbed.

The last few months I turned into a real 'shit bag.' I wore holey, greasy utilities all the time and pulled an unstarched cover low over my eyes. Except for all the shit details, the lifers left me well alone. I remember I did a lot of extra guard duty during that time, and was like a zombie on the base, wandering around as if in a daily trance.

I left a month early. The company commander took mercy on me and gave me my accumulated leave time. I packed up my sea bag one morning and left an empty squad bay while everyone was down on the ramp. I did not say goodbye to anyone, most of who were all working on the tanks down on the 'ramp.' I found myself now leaving finally feeling acutely as alone as I had been when I first joined.

Four rather intense years of my life were suddenly over, and though I desperately needed the freedom and the privacy, it was a severely strange feeling. No more tanks, no more guns, no more lifers, no more weird events. The thing I missed the most though, was the wide vast desert spaces and its utter silence and stillness. The desert had a serene beauty—its summer storms, its winter snow, its spring flowers and gray fall skies that I had come to love.

In hindsight, after watching the unfolding of the Gulf War on television, I came to understand many of the things that had happened to us back in the desert twelve years previously. The same units I had been in then were now the ones bearing much of the brunt of the tank action in the Gulf.

Auto-Anthropology

During the Iran hostage crisis our battalion had formed a special team.
We were to fly to a small island in the Indian Ocean and there get ready
for battle, brand new tanks that were already waiting. Army Airborne and
Ranger units all converged at El Toro Air Base and we waited around for
three days with our battle gear packed, our gas masks, etc. until we were
finally flown back to the Stumps.

We were, thirteen years ago, experimenting with the very tank
maneuvers and desert tactics that were now being employed in the Gulf.
We were first field-testing the armored reconnaissance vehicles, the
desert camouflaged uniforms, and the 'combined arms' team units that
were now being flashed on the television screen live from the Gulf.

It is not too much to conclude that more than a decade ago, the
Pentagon had set its strategic sights on the Gulf region, and was even
then preparing itself for an inevitable war in the desert. Vietnam was a
strategic failure, and it took a few years for the military to recover its
discipline, its morale, its fighting spirit and its esteem. The Pentagon
needed a new strategic focus--the vital oil pipeline to the U.S. fossil fuel
economy—and a new 'threat' to American 'Security' to perpetuate its
own commitment to the efficacy of force and the credible threat of
violence.

The Lotus

What's fairer than the lotus in a swamp?
Green leaves, white blooms, gold stamens at their hearts.
Gold stamens set amidst white blooms, green leaves-
It lives near mud yet does not smell of mud.

Anonymous (Translated by Huynh Sanh Thong)

I got out without knowing what to do next. I had it in my mind to
become an artist, and I was committed to getting done with the
manuscript I was writing. I ended up renting a one-bedroom apartment
not too far from my mom's house. It was during this time that I just
wanted to be alone and not bothered by other people. I was feeling

intense 'separation anxieties' and it was in this mood that my first collection of poems flowed out almost spontaneously.

I began learning the basics of oil painting, a practice that I ended up pursuing for the next five years, elaborating into several different media. Fortunately, in spite of my drinking during my enlistment, I had managed to save about twenty thousand dollars that supported me for the first few years out. I looked for work the first year, but could find nothing. It seemed as though no one wanted to hire a young "former-Marine."

I ended up paying five hundred bucks to attend a brief four-week bank teller vocational school. There were four women, a Mexican and myself. Even though I scored the highest on the math test at the end, everyone else was hired even before the school ended except myself. I looked in every bank in the city for the next month, and though banks were hiring, none were hiring me. I began getting discouraged and began increasingly to do my artwork. I was told afterward that a scar on my face from the Marine Corps and the fact of my having been a Marine made me unsuitable as a bank teller candidate.

One day my older sister visited me in my apartment. I remember cooking her some shrimp with red sauce on top of white rice with fresh picked green beans. She herself had just been on the rebound from a divorce. She told me to go back to school, and not to worry about finding work. It seemed like a good idea, and I ended up enrolled the next year at California State University, Fullerton.

I moved back home to live with my Mom, as living alone in an apartment without any other income was becoming increasingly expensive. I paid her a small monthly amount for rent and helped her with yard work. The first couple of years at CSUF were difficult for me. I was an undeclared major and didn't know quite what I wanted to do with school. I shopped around but was dissatisfied with different programs.

Finally I took a couple of anthropology classes. I liked the professors, had good interactions, and I began making 'A's more consistently. I realized that anthropology had closely fit the orientation that I had been pursuing in my own writing, and that the alignment may have fortuitous consequences for my intellectual development.

Auto-Anthropology

I wrote a couple of more collections of poems over the next few years, as well as a couple of more manuscripts.

I became over the next four years increasingly involved in academic work, especially in black and white photography in field methods and in video taping and editing during my last couple of years pursuing undergraduate work. I received the **GI Bill** for five years, which paid enough during the school year to help my Mom out and to support my other activities in art. It freed me from having to find work so that I could devote all my time and energy to my studies and to pursuing my other interests in art and writing.

Toward the end of my undergraduate work I had become increasingly involved in my anthropological studies. CSU Fullerton was a fairly large and impersonal kind of school. It had a very alienating social atmosphere about it. During my time there, four people had committed suicide by jumping off the humanities building.

Once while I was taking a psychology class on the same floor of the same building that it happened on. The only way of surviving the daily grind was to become basically inured to the social crowding, impersonalness and anomie. I began spending all my between time at the arboretum that offered a sense of tranquility in its relative solitude.

I went for an interview to be accepted into the graduate program at UC Riverside for the following year. The professor who interviewed me made some conclusions about me based upon my record, which were not accurate or true when he told me, but formed the basis of his presumptions about my character. He did not bother to ask me if these things were true or not, since he being the professional anthropologist, must have known better.

This was my first, but not last encounter with the kind of fallacious logic anthropologists are prone to—what I have called "inferring a probable presence from a definite absence." Since he knew more about me than I knew myself, and since obviously must not have thought much about me in the first place, and since he ignored any first hand counter evidence I could bring to the occasion, I was subsequently not accepted into his program. It is sometimes true that first impressions are final ones.

At the time not seeing any other alternative future for myself in Anthropology, I applied to the Master's program at CSU Fullerton and was readily accepted. I had already planned my thesis work to be about the Vietnamese refugee culture, because they were such a strong presence both at the school and in the surrounding area, even though I had no real leads for breaking into the culture at the time.

I fortunately participated voluntarily in a health survey of a poor slum area in the city which had a strong contingent of Vietnamese refugees, and it was primarily during the course of interviewing these families that I gained the association, and friendship of a couple of families of boat people. I began my fieldwork even before I officially began my master's program. By the time the following semester as a graduate student started, I was already well enmeshed in a whole network of Vietnamese refugees. My fifth and final year at Fullerton was my busiest and perhaps most rewarding. I did my anthropology round the clock, and when I was not in school studying I was spending time with the Vietnamese families.

I gained entry into the cultural world of Little Saigon via a key informant whom I had met during the health interview surveys. I had given her my telephone number while interviewing her friend, which was not unusual practice. I only made contact with her again when her apartment came up on the randomized list. During the interview I noticed she had taped the phone number I'd given her near her phone. She had three little boys and they lived in a small single bedroom apartment, complete with rats, dirty carpet, bars on all the windows, and kicked in front door.

Her husband had left her and she spoke very little English very poorly. She was apparently quite depressed, sleeping many hours of the day, and was suffering headaches and dizzy spells which medical physicians could not properly diagnose.

I made a deal with her that if she would help me with my ethnographic work, I would help her go to ESL classes. I finally managed to enroll her in a daily ESL program during the summer months. Her middle son was enrolled in a nearby public day care center, and I baby-sat in the park each day her other two sons.

I drove her around, taking her to the grocery store and to buy things at the stores, as well as to visit her friends and families. In this way I began meeting and befriending other Vietnamese and their families, all of whom were caught up in a quite extensive multipurpose, and, so it seemed, virtually boundless network. I did not like visiting her in the apartment, because a local Vietnamese gang was quite active, and we had problems with them a couple of times.

A family who was very close and helpful to my informant had earlier moved out to an outlying satellite community about an hour and a half drive from my house. I felt it would be better to move my informant's family to be near them, and we finally managed to help her to relocate her there. Apartment hunting for these families was especially difficult because nobody wanted large families on welfare. But the Vietnamese had their own networks that seemed to consistently come through at the last moment.

I made furniture for her new apartment, and we equipped it pretty well. I was busier than ever at school, as I had my first graduate assistantship on top of trying to complete a year's worth of course work in a single semester.

Everything seemed to click and fall into place, and I wrapped almost everything up by the last semester with very few loose ends. I entered the final summer working on my thesis full time. I completed about the fourth version by August just in time for the last deadline. My committee met one morning and signed the thesis, and after that, save for a few minor administrative details, I received my Masters degree.

Writing my thesis entailed almost a complete disassociation with the Vietnamese whom I had been involved with on a regular, everyday basis for the preceding year. I could not have finished it otherwise, and I doubt I could have written it while maintaining the relationships I had before in the same way.

One of the primary obstacles in doing the background research for the thesis was wading through so much of the recent historical literature on the Vietnamese conflict. Very few English texts on traditional Vietnamese culture and history are available, and among these many are all too sketch and superficial. But the research, combined with my own participant-observation, had been a real mind-opening and mind-blowing experience.

In rewriting a brief history of Vietnamese civilization, I came to realize how wrong the Americans had been ever to have been involved in the war at all, just how devastating our involvement had been for the Vietnamese people and their culture, and how civil war and conflict had been part and parcel of Vietnamese history for at least two thousand years.

I had concluded that our acculturative influence on Vietnam, brief but decisive, were primarily destructive. We waged a war on three fronts, against a people, their sense of history and culture, and even the very land itself upon which they depended for their autochthonous identity. "One cannot destroy a nation in order to save it." (Arthur H. Westing, <u>Ecocide in Indochina</u>, pg. 61)

This viewpoint about our own American-style presence in Vietnam left me feeling very ambivalent about the Vietnamese refugee community with whom I was becoming increasingly identified with on both a personal and a professional basis. I did not blame individual Vietnamese for who they were or what they did in Vietnam, just as I do not blame the American GI for their trying to make the best of a lousy situation.

A Vietnamese friend invited me to attend the eleventh annual celebration of the fall of the Saigon regime down at the 'Bolsa Mini Mall' in little Saigon in Westminster, California. I met him there and we had a dinner before the events. We sat in back of rows of chairs in the parking lot. A stage had been set up in front with large flags of the old South Vietnamese Republic. Candles were distributed to the crowd. Speakers came on stage dressed in the military uniforms of the fallen South Vietnamese Republic and these speakers harangued the audience against the communists and against establishing diplomatic relations with North Vietnam.

The common belief and desire of these people had been they would eventually return victoriously to Vietnam and defeat the communists. They blamed Washington D. C. for their own defeat, and felt as if the U.S. government owned them a lot in return. The candles were lit and the crowd marched up the boulevard in a thick strand of people, all the while being harangued by men with loud speakers shouting at the top of their lungs—"no communists in America," "down with North Vietnam," "no diplomatic relations with North Vietnam."

Auto-Anthropology

It was obvious to me in a way that was not apparent to my poor friend, who had tears in his eyes and was fully caught up in the feeling of the moment, just how fascist the demonstration really was in sentiment and in action, just how well planned and executed it had been by the 'leadership' of the Vietnamese refugee community, and just what they had to gain, by means of control, over the poor, dispossessed Vietnamese people in the crowd.

The Vietnamese community, with help from CIA operatives, seemed fully engaged in manufacturing its own anti-communistic, pro-South Vietnamese Republic refugee mythology and ideology that it used as an instrument of control and self-aggrandizement over its own people.

I became aware of many subtle contrasts and contradictions within the Vietnamese community—the presence of so much gold in its many shops, the general success and growing affluence of its small businesses in spite of the fact that so many were on welfare and receiving government support. Every family household I had been in, which was numerous, was receiving full welfare benefits.

At the same time, every household was also involved in an 'underground economy' of stitching piecework for the garment industry which involved both a great deal of exploitation and a great deal of profit. Every week 'care' packages were piled to the ceiling in downtown little Saigon awaiting shipment back to Vietnam. At the time, these gift remittances—cases of toothpaste and hairbrushes, were one of the only and main sources of revenue for the newly reestablished Vietnam. Though the refugee leadership and their supporters wanted no diplomatic relations with Vietnam, their remittances themselves were the primary means of external aid to Vietnam.

These were not merely simple goods to be shared by family and friends back home. These items were by the carton—electronic goods, etc.—no doubt intended for the underground market. And the community was much less than tolerant for divergent points of view. One Vietnamese man was murdered in a restaurant for expressing viewpoints sympathetic to the communist regime of Vietnam. A college professor at Fullerton was shot in the neck and killed by a Vietnamese student for similar reasons.

I found several pages in different books expressing similar points of view in the library—one a poetry collection by Ho Chi Minh—whose pages had been glued together and marked out so as to be illegible. Exploitation within the community, of Vietnamese by other Vietnamese, was not an uncommon practice of getting ahead. A common attitude and contradiction that was revealed by a questionnaire I administered in little Saigon revealed that though they fled Vietnam to escape persecution and for liberty, they believed that America suffered from too much freedom and not enough police protection. This structurally translated into their own political-economic sense of socio-structural insecurity.

In hindsight, I wished I had done a follow up study of the community or had taken a longer time, as little Saigon subsequently changed in quite dramatic ways. Returning several times in the following years, little Saigon had more than doubled in the number of its small businesses, and had increased substantially in its apparent affluence. I wish I could have followed the trajectories of assimilation and adjustment of the several families I had been involved with—trajectories that became apparent to me only after the fact of my involvement with them. I needed to get away from the Vietnamese though, as I, as a naïve American, could never figure out when they were telling me the truth.

Though I respected their culture and their people, I really did not like the Vietnamese refugees well. I felt used by them, and did not trust them very well. I felt that many had been deceitful to me in fundamental ways, and I could not reconcile this basic difference of cultural value orientation and world-view with my own need for honesty. These refugees were neither the real nor the legitimate representatives of Vietnamese civilization. Rather they were the ex-colonial cast-offs, by and large corrupted by the Western influences and their own greed.

I had finished an ethnography about the Vietnamese refugee, which, I felt; the Vietnamese had little interest in trying to understand. It seemed to me that they were mostly interested in creating their own versions of their reality to suit their own somewhat desperate needs and interests.

One woman at CSU Fullerton had done an 'ethnography' of the Vietnamese that was basically anti communist and pro-refugee. It gained not only recognition by the upper class members of the Vietnamese elite, but earned her key post in the ESL program in the state. I finished my ethnography that seemed to me much more honest and realistic, as well as much more involved and professionally written, only to be met with ignorance and cold silence.

I returned to a symposium at CSU Fullerton in 1990. A young man recognized me there and knew of my thesis. He was doing his own research on the Vietnamese, and told me he really liked my ethnography. He took me to lunch at a local Vietnamese restaurant, discussing the Vietnamese, anthropology and other things, and he treated me, since I did not have any cash at the time.

Two Wild Geese

There: wild geese swimming side by side,
Staring up at the sky!
White feathers against a deep blue,
Red feet burning in green waves.

Lie Chieu and Do Phap Thuan

I finished my MA under the wire with the deadline, and I was left in a huge anticlimactic loss at what to do next. The struggle with the thesis, which was a condensation of about a thousand pages into about 250, left me in a state of psychological exhaustion. I don't know if it was the anger or the exasperation with all the minor typographical mistakes, which never seemed to end. I was also left feeling alienated and distant from the Vietnamese whom had been such a part of my life for the preceding year and a half.

I spent the next four or five months working out in my garage, making furniture on order from my family, and working part time for an old retired handy-man who paid me five bucks an hour out of his pocket. On the side I began getting into Van Gogh studies, as well as the study of venomous snakes, and I also got back into my oil painting.

I was giving a Hindu Indian woman I had met in school panting lessons (for free) once a week. I had given up on the idea of going on in an American University, believing somewhat naively that they were all too difficult to get into. Anyway, I had set my sights on leaving the U.S. and since I wanted to pursue Southeast Asian Studies, I began doing background research into the different countries there.

I realized that Malaysia and Singapore had been British colonies and English was still widely spoken there. Besides, they seemed to have a relatively open social tourist policy that allowed foreigners to visit there for extended periods of time. I decided that Malaysia would be my destination. I planned and prepared for the trip several times over—but no amount of planning prepared me for the experiences I was about to have. I had little experience as a traveler and failed to take a friend's advice to travel 'lightly.' I bought a ticket for late January, squared away my passport, and said goodbye to my Mom once again, and caught a bus to the airport.

The plane landed in Kuala Lumpur about midnight on the same day it left LA (Los Angeles) half a world away. The "No Dada" and "Death To Drug Traffickers" signs greeted me even before debarking from the plane. It was a strange feeling. I instantly became drenched in sweat. I had made no prior hotel reservations and did not know what the going rates were. It was the beginning of Chinese New Year celebrations and many of the decent hotels were booked up. A self-appointed tourist guide offered to take me to the city and to find a hotel for a price. He eventually found me a hotel in the downtown area that was rather quite exorbitant for the area and for the standards.

I spent the first weekend with him and his family, as he took me to the zoo, to the cultural museum, downtown and to his flat to eat a curry dinner cooked by his Malay wife. The weekend had been on me, and I knew I couldn't continue for very long at that rate. The dinner at his home was eaten with our bare fingers, a custom that I never got quite used to, and which at the time almost made me vomit my chicken curry rice.

On Sunday morning he took me to the train station and I purchased a rail pass that allowed me to travel on the Malaysian Railway System for two weeks. It was a great deal, but I only used the train once during that time. I left half my extra belongings behind with my tour guide/expensive friend—a pair of shoes, a couple of books, a small brief case and some other odds and ends. I never saw my things again, and still had two bags full of useless junk to struggle with.

The train headed north to Penang. I might as well have been the dark side of the moon as far as I was concerned. The trip took more than eight hours, and did not come rolling into the Butterworth station until about ten o'clock at night. I made the acquaintance of the ex-Police Chief of K.L.—an elderly Sikh gentleman. We talked for a couple of hours and he told me to check into the YMCA on Burma Road in Penang and he warned me to stay away from drugs.

The worst thing one can do is to enter a strange city in the middle of the night. A cascade of lights and a continuous cacophony of strange noises and smells and feelings shock one into a wakened dream state. I did not realize that Penang was on an island and that the train let me off at the Ferry. I followed the crowd loaded down under my bags, sweating profusely in the humid night air. We swept along a wooden walkway and into a large deck area with rows of benches. I did not realize I was on a boat until the gate closed behind me and I settled down on top of my bags only to feel the rocking motion beneath me. We got off on the other side about twenty minutes later, and we swept down more wooden ramps to descend into a busy crowd of anxious waiters and shouting trishaw drivers and porters.

For five Malaysian dollars, a young Tamil porter carried both my bags to his trishaw. I asked him if he could take me to the YMCA. He said of course, and I, in blind faith, jumped in for the ride. The cool air was refreshing, but it was a very thrilling experience to be riding headfirst into the oncoming headlights of cars. We stopped in front of the New Asia Hotel and he said that this was the best and most reasonable place in town (he also worked under commission by the hotel manager).

He carried my bags up the steps to the second floor, and I ordered a pint of Malaysian Heineken beer and settled in under the ceiling fan of my sparsely equipped room. I had never been in a Chinese style hotel before, but I might as well have landed on Mars. I though I had really done it this time, but had extremely mixed feelings of 'Old Asia' excitement with the sudden realization of what a clumsy fool I must have been to come so far to the edge of nowhere.

The next day was spent getting lost in the midst of the city on my own foot walking tour. I found various temples and *Kong Si*'s, and an overly friendly Indian homosexual propositioned me. I witnessed a heroin transaction with a young drug addict who was following me around the city. Finally, having gotten lost, I found another Tamil trishaw driver who rode me back to the hotel.

The first ten days or so was beset with an incredible loneliness, alienation and tremendous, almost paralyzing culture shock. One early morning while happening by the gate of a *Kong Si* a young Chinese man noticed me and tagged along. He made himself my unofficial tour guide and we traveled everywhere in the city together. I paid him only a small amount, but did not trust him as I found him going through my bags and helping himself to what was inside. He was biding his time, waiting for the moment to set me up and get my money. One day on the street he was behaving very strangely toward me, and I hailed a taxi and told him to take me to the police station.

I told my tour guide who would not leave me alone to get in. As I turned around he vanished into the crowd. I had had about enough of traveling, and was extremely disoriented and depressed. I checked into a rather luxurious downtown hotel across the street from the police station and stayed there for two days. I planned to leave Penang that Monday, and to leave Malaysia as soon as possible, as it seemed to me that all anyone wanted from me was my money. I met the bartender in the hotel lounge and we began talking. His command of English for a Chinese person seemed surprising to me. I told him I was leaving the next day and he agreed to take me back to the train station. The next morning he met me with his car and his young wife. I ended up touring the island with them, and as they seemed friendly enough, they invited me to come and visit their home.

I ended up staying with this Chinese family for about a month. I paid them a little money for rent and food, and they were quite friendly to me. This is where I met Rosie, who was boarding with them. The son who had first invited me turned out to be quite untrustworthy. He too was intending to set me up for some kind of scam, and the father warned me about him. Once he realized I was on to him, it is as if I no longer existed.

Auto-Anthropology

I moved my things down to the bedroom on the end where Rosie was staying. Rosie worked during the day, and we would go out on the town at night. She told me about the son and the family she was staying with, how they were not to be trusted and had, in the past, ripped her off as well. She lived with them because she had no other family and could not afford to live alone. Before I left, I bought her an electric fan that she could never afford with her small salary, and a little gold pendant with her initials on it.

I flew back to KL and then back to LA I had been all of six weeks in Malaysia, and besides bringing home a couple of boxes of ceramic gifts and souvenirs, I had little to show for my journey.

I spent about two months back in California. I was in utter limbo. I wrote another collection of poems, but did little else. I wrote back to Rosie almost everyday, and I really missed her. One day I wrote to her and proposed marriage by letter. Almost two weeks later she called me by telephone one evening and told me yes. I made arrangements to return to Malaysia, better prepared than before. The trip went smoothly and without a hitch the second time around.

I checked into a small Chinese hotel near where Rosie was staying with the family, without realizing I had checked into a Chinese style brothel. Rosie came and visited me there each evening and we made arrangements for our marriage. There were a few legal formalities, mostly a matter of money and fees, which had to be taken care of first. A friend of Rosie's helped find me a room to rent for five Malaysian dollars a day at the Lee Kong Si.

I stayed there for about a week. The family that Rosie had been staying with became hostile, as they didn't want to lose the means of income that Rosie provided for them. Rosie's friends from work really came through for her, while the family she was staying with began spreading malicious rumors about town about me. I became a confidence trickster, a California abalone diver and a CIA operative. One day I rented a taxi and we drove to their house. No one there would let us in so I pushed the door open. The people inside pretended to themselves that we were not there. Rosie took me in and we gathered up her belongings, loaded them in the boot of the taxi and left.

We ended up renting an old-style house in a nearby village. It was a nice big place with a big compound behind it, backing a jungle on a hill, and it cost all of one hundred and fifty dollars U.S. a month to rent. Getting married in a civil ceremony, beneath a low ceiling fan, we had a no frills, no honeymoon wedding. We settled into our new home while Rosie went to work everyday.

The possibility of employment in Malaysia was zero, and even though I had married a Malaysian citizen, I gained no visa or passport privileges or residency whatsoever. I talked with all kinds of civil Malay authorities and learned that the best I could do was to put up a thousand dollars bond for a year long visa that precluded my working there. If I had married a Muslim woman, things might have been a little easier, but I was married to a Chinese woman, and there were already too many Chinese women in Malaysia.

We went to the U.S. embassy in KL and applied for Rosie's residency in the U.S. It took about four or five months to clear up the administrative paperwork, and we needed to have affidavits of support signed and completed by my family in the states. This processing was not completed before my own social tourist visa had expired, and I ended up having to exit the country twice, and almost a third time, and re-enter for a one-month extensions.

I was getting worried because each time was proving problematic to get any extension at all, as the immigration authorities would always wonder what I was doing in Malaysia. We spent one weekend in Singapore that was an interesting escape, and one weekend in *Hatyai* in southern Thailand that was interesting in another way.

I ended up staying about seven months in Malaysia. Rosie worked much of the time while I purchased some hand tools from cheap side downtown and began making furniture from wood. Malaysia is a strange country. There has a political repression and almost a social paranoia of persecution about it. One had the very real feeling that the police could walk into your home virtually anytime, and arrest you under almost any pretext. One did not speak too loudly or freely in public places, and always took care what one said and who was listening.

Auto-Anthropology

The tension between the Chinese and the Malays is very strong and apparent. The Chinese are much more industrious and entrepreneurial, the Malays devoutly religious. The discrimination and political persecution of the Chinese by the Malays was fairly blatant and open. Though the Chinese were economically prosperous and largely independent, the Malays had gained political dominance and controlled everything in a very systematic way.

No Chinese or Tamils went beyond the equivalent of the twelfth grade, while Malay students who were poorly qualified were sent abroad to the U.S. to continue their schooling. Housing, government jobs, even businesses were under control by the Malays to the systematic exclusion of the Chinese and Tamils.

On the other hand, Penang proved to be one of the most fascinating cities on earth. It is known as hawkers' paradise and as a "Pearl of the Orient." One can witness well the cycle of seasons in the year round calendar of religious celebrations. Chinese New Year consisted of all night vigils by Chinese storekeepers, who burned up huge mounds of paper in the streets, set out huge tables of roasted pigs, ducks and other Chinese delicacies for the Gods, and who lit off multiple strings of dynamite-sized firecrackers. *Thaipusam* was a Tamil celebration in which the *Kavadi* is carried by many men, women and children with hooks in their skin, shoes of nails, and spines and needles through the cheek. The streets flowed with coconut milk from all the coconut smashing done in payment to the Gods for good fortune.

Wesak Day is the equivalent of Christmas, and it went on at the Buddhist association next door to the *Lee Kong si* while we were staying there. We made the rounds of countless temples, the Sleeping Buddha, the Thai temples across the street, the *Kuan Yin* temple where we had offerings made for our marriage, *Kek Lok Si* temple set against the hillside with the huge white statue of the Goddess of Mercy. Then came the month of Ramadan and *Hari Raya Puasa*. The Christians have several shrines of local saints—a pilgrimage to the shrine of Saint Anne.

The most interesting temple is the Buddhist temple of a thousand and one steps, which almost no tourists know about and which are frequented only by a few Chinese who are willing to make the climb up Penang Hill. Rosie's friends took us there a couple of times. It is by far the most peaceful and serene place on the whole island—free of the squalid hubbub of the city directly below it.

The action on the streets of Penang is fast, cheap and dirty. It is an old, out of the way Chinese commercial city that has changed little since the pre-World War II days of the British.

There is an excitement about the place—the morning Chinese markets, the fish markets, hawkers and their stalls. It proved as cheap and more convenient to eat out than to bother buying food and cooking by the charcoal stoves at home. And we came to know the city by knowing where the best food was to be found at the most convenient times. I never cared for Malaysian society, but I grew accustomed to and quite fond of the little city of Penang.

I became quite the old Asia hand. I got to know Penang very well by walking around it almost everyday. On our periodic trips to KL, Singapore and Thailand, we would meet each time a young American tourist headed up to Penang. We would serve as their tour guide and treated them quite royally, showing them the sites that tourists do not normally see.

I missed being with Americans, talking American and it is this, which lead me to make these acquaintances. We never took advantage of these people, and they kept in touch with us when we returned to the U.S.

I think they immensely appreciated someone taking the time and care to help them in the city and to show them around a little. I also missed drinking milk while I was there, and grew quite thin. The soybean juice and coconut milk, while quite delicious, did not prove to be adequate substitutes for my craving for milk, which I never really got over.

Renting the house, I bought a young black dog from the caretaker of the Lee Kongsi where we had first stayed. The dog was kept permanently on the end of a short chain out in the open. It had worn a little brown spot on the lawn, and I would find it there day and night, rain or shine. I ended up buying the dog from the man for few Malaysian dollars, and an *ang pow* of a pound of sugar for the old man. He was quite delighted to receive an *ang pow* from a young white man.

Auto-Anthropology

The dog was quite difficult to deal with. So long on a short chain, it proved uncontrollable and hyperactive in our compound. I spent a few days trying to mend the fence to prevent him from escaping. It had ticks and I found some tick bathe at the local **RSPCA** that was just down the street. The dog liked me, but could not keep down or from biting me in the leg. It was near wild and proved too much for me to deal with everyday. I ended up taking him down to the **RSPCA** where he would be put down.

I listened to him howling all night, and the next day, walking back from town, I happened by the front gate of the **RSPCA** to find the dog shooter with the doors of his van open. I sensed something and went into the compound and found the stiff black body of the dog with its head wrapped in bloody newspapers. The Tamil shooter told me it was a beautiful dog. I agreed while stroking its flank. I left with tears in my eyes. I will never forget the look the dog gave me when I first carried it to the cage at the **RSPCA**—as if I had forsaken its loyalty. It rained very hard that day, and I felt utterly depressed. It was as if the Gods somewhere up in Heaven had been angry with me and was scolding me with the thunder and lightening in the afternoon storm that had been sent.

That evening we decided to go to a movie in town to cheer up. While waiting at the dark bus stop two young men on a motorcycle came riding straight up to us. The man on the back was about to snatch Rosie's purse. I poked out my umbrella with its metal point like a bayonet and caught him in the elbow.

They backed off and came on us again very aggressively. One was edging closer to Rosie, putting his hands on her. I interposed myself between him and Rosie and grabbed my Swiss pocket- knife I carried in my pocket. I pulled Rosie behind me, who was frightened into panic, while we retreated into the darkness.

The strangers had taken off their helmets and were intending to bash us in the head with them. Passers by just ignored the whole scene, and no one was getting involved. I became very angry at Malaysia and Malaysians. Just then a police car happened by and we waved them over. The two motorcyclists took off in a hurry. The police gave chase.

We waited and the police came back and took us to the police station where we filed a report. The two guys had been active in the area for a while—they had slashed a nun at a nearby Catholic cancer hospital while trying to steal a necklace off her. After that incident, I never felt comfortable anywhere in Malaysia again except when in the company of other people and in well-lighted places.

> The Buddha body is omnipresent.
> Each sentient being beholds it
> Through aspiration and Karma relation
> As it dwells eternally on this seat of meditation

We arrived back in LA in August of that year. Rosie wore her traditional *kerbaya* and *sarong* on the airplane. We had a hard time in customs, and were met outside in the lobby by my Mom and sister who were carrying balloons and candy.

After half a year in Penang, LA suddenly seemed like one big, endless, crowded freeway. We did not know what we would do next. But soon my brother propositioned me to help him construct a dental office for his business, as he had finished dental school a couple of years previously, was already tired of turning a huge profit for other dentists, and was anxious to strike out on his own.

After quite a bit of conflict over how to do it and who would do it, during which I quit more than once to leave him stranded, I finally convinced him that he didn't need to pay a contractor shark thirty dollars an hour and that we could do it ourselves. I ended up working almost everyday for the next six months. I did virtually everything—plastering, framing, dry-walling, electrical and plumbing installation, lighting, purchasing, building much of the office furniture, shelves and counter tops, helping to install the wall to wall carpeting, hanging all the doors, all the painting and finishing touches.

Auto-Anthropology

It turned out quite nice. I even made nice oak and walnut picture frames for his diplomas, which he hung in his front office. I worked mostly alone, with Rosie sometimes at my side to assist with the more tedious tasks.

I finished this job in January of the following year, and had earned all of about a thousand dollars for about six months full time work. I begrudged my brother for having promised to pay me four dollars an hour and for only really paying me only about fifty cents an hour, but I did it to help my mother who was bearing most of the costs of the materials for the project, and whom I owed a few thousand dollars for the trip to Malaysia anyway.

Once that ended I began seriously looking for a job with my Master's degree for the next five months. I went back to visit the chairperson of the anthropology department at CSU Downtown to get his advice. He told me to look for federal government jobs. I ended up learning how to do it on my own. I looked not only at federal level, but also at the state and local levels as well. A Master's degree is something that nobody wants to hire and pay for—one is either 'over qualified' for many kinds of jobs, or 'under qualified' for the really good jobs. It was a difficult time for us as we had little money and no future in a big expensive city where money was everything.

I followed every possible lead for jobs I could find. I became aware of how much there were screens of obfuscation, especially at the municipal and state level, that got people involved in long extensive examinations, lines and interviewing, but from which very few if any jobs were actually forthcoming. It seemed like an elaborate, systematic scam to keep the jobless preoccupied with filling out forms and standing in lines in hopes of some minimal job, when there were actually few real jobs to be had that weren't going to people through insider networks.

I ended up compiling a large notebook on getting jobs in various sectors, in teaching, in government, business, and international, and giving it to the Chairperson of the Anthropology department so that other students would not have to go through the troubles that I did in compiling information on relevant jobs. It was a notebook complete with the federal job application forms, numbers and addresses for job listings and for community college credentials.

I became increasingly depressed and not finding anything while spinning my wheels. Rosie entered a regional vocational training school in the early summertime and was quite happy in her schoolwork. I had sent an application to Northeast State University Anthropology program while filling out other job application forms without much farther thought of it. It had been sitting inside the top drawer of my desk since 1986 and it seemed just like a shot in the dark. "Why not?" I asked myself.

I had forgotten completely about it when in July, I received an acceptance letter from this anthropology department. The best I had managed to find in the way of the job was as a "recreation director" at a senior citizen's center way across the city. It was all of seven hours a week and paid four-fifty an hour. It consisted of sweeping up and picking up the chairs and tables after the old people, and doing typing for a young woman in charge who was still working on her BA in social sciences.

I worked with a young sixteen-year old Chicano gang member who was given the same job more than full time. He lasted on the job shorter than I did, getting busted by the police for ripping off the cafeteria storeroom. The time and pay made it hardly worth the time, hassle and amount of gas driving across town. It was during these months that I built a deck for my Mom in her backyard, as well as helped to finish another one for a friend. I also got into buying cheap furniture at the local thrift shops and stripping out and refinishing them.

Without much to lose, we packed up our little VW bug that I had refinished, the same one I bought brand new in 1976 and had only driven it for less than a year myself, and drove to New York in time for the Fall semester at a state university in a small city in the Northeast.

I found the anthropology department to my distaste the first week there. It was unfriendly and alienating. I had no support and spent the first year there sitting out in the hallways. Towards the end of the first school year, I was working in the empty conference room when the chairman happened by the door in the hallway, looked in at me, and told me they would have to find an office for me.

I only laughed, thinking he was a day late and about a dollar short. The first semester was the hardest. We were living miserably in a small run down single bedroom apartment. The slumlord was only interested in

Auto-Anthropology

money, and failed to fix anything. The plumbing from the bathroom upstairs leaked severely into our only closet and the water made its way to our bed. I grew less and less patient, and we finally moved to a much better place on the edge of town.

I befriended a couple of people that first semester. One was a British social anthropologist who was interested in what he called 'human behavior'. He early on warned me about the department and told me he thought I would be better to transfer to another school. He himself hated the politics of the department. He saw it having gone downhill over the years; the very people whom he himself had brought into the department were now stabbing him in the back and withdrawing departmental support for his students.

The department was very cold and had a "closed door policy." People were chronically whispering and looking over their shoulders. I also befriended another professor there, a socio-linguist from Edinburgh and Singapore who was on a one-year contract there. He also was quite alienated and ostracized in the department, and quite lonely there. People did not like him because he had cerebral palsy and people found him strange. He delighted that my wife was Malaysian Chinese and we developed an almost instant friendship. We had many dinners, many beers and many talks together,

I did not like the school, and was quite ambivalent about remaining there. I did have good interaction with a couple of professors. The students were extremely competitive and even viciously so. I only knew and liked a handful of students there; many made an obvious point of ignoring my wife as well as myself, and even of venting their sense of hostility towards us.

The second semester proved to be the best one there. I made the acquaintance of another professor, a cultural anthropologist. Rosie began baby-sitting nearly full time for her two young children. Everyday I would make the long drive to and from her home to pick up and drop off Rosie. With a little income, and better relations in the department, I became more productive.

I wrote four manuscripts during the spring and summer. It was also during that second spring semester that I decided to do ethnography of the anthropology department for the field methods class. Both students and faculty met me with mixed reactions. Many faculty members were absent and ignored whatever was going on. Many students initially expressed enthusiasm for the project. My social anthropology professor warned me against it, saying it would not be a good thing to do. I ended up interviewing about forty people in the department, about a third of the whole department.

Several aspects became apparent to me. First and foremost was the utter multiplicity and complexity of viewpoints and attitudes. Second was the degree to which such attitudes and viewpoints were largely a function of the individual's relative position within the department and the larger context, and of the individual's own distinctive biography and background experience. Third was the distinction between what people were telling me and what they were not telling me. By and large most people wanted to present a positive image of them selves to me.

An interesting aspect is that about 79% of the students reported an upper middle class background, and 79% were white, non-foreign and from the northeastern United States. I interviewed about 50% men and women, and about 79% of the men reported that they did not believe anthropology to be a male dominated field and about 79% of the women reported that they did believe anthropology was male dominated. People on either side of the coin had reasonable rationalizations for their beliefs.

Virtually everyone I spoke with made 'sense' when set in context to their own background experiences and rationalizations. I came away from the study concluding that people for the most part tried to present to me their best side during the interview, and were interested in hiding aspects of their own character that they themselves believed might detract from their anthropological identity.

There was also a clear dichotomy between people who were critical and negative about the department and those who believed that the department, though maybe having some problems, was really a good place.

Those of the former group tended to report particular instances and more specific complaints of unfairness or discrimination, while those of the latter group tended to be more general and nonspecific, and more

Auto-Anthropology

'ego-centrically' focused upon their own situations and values. They tended to see themselves and the department in which they were situated in a more unproblematic and unquestionable way.

Everyone was expecting me to publish my results, at least within the department, and many expected my results would focus upon a set of their specific suggestions on "how to improve the department."

My main objective in conducting the study in the first place was descriptive, rather than prescriptive. Because I genuinely felt that some of the information may be harmful for some, as well as for myself, if it were published, and because I did not complete a finished version of the manuscript and I could not clearly ascertain what would and what may not be harmful to people in the department, I decided not to publish it at all.

I think more than a few people felt let down by this, as if I owed them something to them for granting me the interview, and I think this may have tended to reflect negatively upon my status within the department. I already had my own ideas on how to improve things in the department, even before the study, and my results from the study only tended to reinforce rather than to disconfirm those ideas. I myself could not clearly nor concisely separate my own values and attitudes from those that I was supposed to be reporting on in the department.

During many of the interviews themselves, I became keenly aware of how my presence, my own relative position and status, and my own background experiences were critically influencing the direction and results of each interview. If the interviewee and interviewer were interested in achieving rapport, there tended to be an exclusive emphasis on things shared in common, and a de-emphasize upon exceptional differences.

If there was a block to achieving mutual rapport, as happened most often with some of the faculty, then the emphasis came to be on the differences and upon the dominance of the interviewee's own points of view, while things in common tended to be de-emphasized.

Either way, the results were considerably more biased than an ideal, disinterested study demands. Though I think this kind of bias is inevitable and must always contaminate the neutrality of any kind of ethnographic participant-observation, this does not completely negate the value or importance of such a study.

In hindsight, it has struck me how much like anyone else anthropologists really are, and how much like any other kind of corporate community an anthropology department is really like. In this regard, the expectations of reciprocity for the interview were not too unlike the demands many Vietnamese refugees made of me in return for interviewing them.

Bringing the results of such a study too close to 'home' must always have unintended and probably damaging consequences for someone within the department, as it must follow the dictum: 'knowledge is power.'

There is no such thing, in a local context, of neutral knowledge. There is also no way of being able to be completely sure that the identity of one's informants is completely protected, so that what they say may not be used against them by other people in power.

Different people were attempting not only to influence what I wrote or how it was written by representing themselves, and the department, cast in a certain light, but were indirectly via my own study attempting to exert an influence within the departmental setting. There is no knowledge, however indirect, which cannot be used to 'triangulate' upon a person's identity and to modify the local status of that individual.

This key insight brought home though an acute and critical understanding of what I now consider universal to small groups in a primary community; that is the social politics and normative influence by informal gossip and status-control in the manipulation of social identities. It gave me as well an alternative framework for analysis of cross-cultural research.

The most important thing though, was that everyone seemed to be presenting themselves and their own perceived situations in the most advantageous light possible, myself included, and were, conversely, subconsciously trying to cover over all that may have been threatening to their own sense of status identity.

Auto-Anthropology

How each person represented her/himself depended largely upon their own position and context within the department, such that what some people may have been attempting to highlight, others may have been attempting to implicitly deny.

Finally, this sense of foreground/background contrast seemed to me to relate to what I believe to be a prototypically 'American' characteristic of a kind of compartmentalization between private and public domains of existence and experience, and a kind of socially reinforced ego-centricity of orientation in which experience becomes focused by, and oriented around, one's own individual psycho-social and biographical identity.

Another interesting aspect of the study was that almost everyone believed that the interviews and the question protocol asked during the interview was the main thing of the study, when actually the main organ of the ethnography was my own participant-observation and the indirect open-endedness that the interviews with its protocols was set up to foster.

The interviews by themselves meant little, but when compared to everything else that went on alongside of and outside of the interview, tended to reveal a great discrepancy between how almost everyone presented themselves to me and the kinds of actual interactions that occurred in many other contexts. This speaks of the silent, subtle, and the sublime power, which the ethnographer carries to the field. No aspect of an ethnographer's experiences escapes notice and interpretation. There are few if any 'neutral' elements of such experience.

Setting oneself in a position of participant-observer in any setting has certain consequences. It tends to frame all experiences in a quasi-objective manner, such that every new experience becomes added to the cumulative fund of knowledge, and becomes weighed in relation to this larger fund. It superimposes degree of self-alienation in which others come to participate in and reinforce. In such a manner, one can no longer be a naïve or completely innocent participant in the ongoing production, but one's own identity and position is thus contaminated.

Furthermore, this is an irreversible process that leads not only to a permanent loss of innocence, and greater understanding, but to the relatively permanent affective separation of one's own sense of identity and the social context in which that identity becomes defined. Once achieved, such an attitude or point of view cannot be simply undone or removed from experience, though it can perhaps be redefined.

Though only one person in the department actually read what I wrote, and though only a couple expressed enough interest to actually ask me about it in any detail, everyone seemed to have formed some kind of opinion about the whole thing, for better or worse, both before, during and after it happened. For some it was seen as a threat, to others it was a weapon, and to still others it was to be a tool for change.

During the interviews, a few found my protocol not matching their own expectations, and expressed disappointment. Others found the interview fun and even enjoyable, largely because it was one of the few times they got to talk at length about what they themselves were about to someone else within the Department context. A few criticized my approach and told me how I should do it and what I should be asking.

Summer soon came, and with the semester over, the incentive to continue actively with the project waned. Other involvements quickly diverted my attention and I left the whole thing basically incomplete and unfinished. I felt like I did with the Vietnamese. I grew tired of the interviews and I grew to dislike the whole situation I was involved in.

I did not want to be construed any longer as the student doing ethnography of the department—either as a rebel or as a savior. The whole project seemed to have gained control over me, my status, my frame of mind, and identity; rather than my having control over it. I began believing that the whole thing was a mistake from the beginning, an unwise mistake, and I came to question my original motives for starting it in the first place.

Nevertheless, subsequent events, a few of which were quite unexpected, and others that seemed almost too predictable, tended afterward to confirm my understanding, and to reaffirm my basic attitude about the department and the people within it. I had set something in motion, which I no longer had the power to stop, either in myself or in the department. My own status and position within the department had become irrevocably jeopardized by the study.

Auto-Anthropology

It is interesting that during the course of the study, though I had been already into it for a couple of months, an outside set of evaluators came in to give the department a critique. They were there all of one day, and they were given the grand tour by the powers that be. Though everyone had long known what I was up to, no one even suggested the possibility that these observers might want to talk to me about the department. There was almost a feeling that I should be kept apart from them. I have always wondered what these relative strangers could learn about the department in the course of a single day that I couldn't learn in a few months.

They must be pretty good. I've learned to accept my own anthropological triviality and mediocrity—besides I did not yet have that all-important Ph.D. that would legitimate whatever I do. A similar thing had happened at CSU Fullerton. A rather politically oriented professor was appointed in charge of a program for the Southeast Asian refugees, not because of her relative lack of experience with these people, but because she had a Ph.D. Meanwhile I've remained long unemployed and essentially unemployable in spite of my anthropological experiences.

I got involved in painting the house where we lived for our landlady, and doing some carpentry during the summer. It did not earn us very much, but the gratitude and friendship of our landlady. My wife became pregnant, which tended to complicate everything else a little bit. Toward the end of summer, just about two weeks before the fall semester began one of the students in our department committed suicide.

I had met him in the hallway just a week before as he was having an interview with one of the professors—the same person who was not only implicated in his own problems in the department, which this professor was trying to apply to my problems. His suicide caught everyone including his live-in girlfriend, by surprise, and everyone was quite upset about it.

I placed flowers in the department in his name. The head of the department definitely did not want them there, as I felt he wanted to cover over the whole incident and get things back to business as quickly as possible before the new semester began.

A group of students who were his friends approached me, and asked if I would help sign a petition of complaint that would go above and outside of the department, in protest of unfair practices, which they believed, aggravated the circumstances of his death. I agreed, but didn't hear anything more about it.

Even before, I had reached the general conclusion about the department that, because it was so hierarchically top down and status oriented, it depended upon its effective ethos upon finding and persecuting abnormal difference within the department. This was a kind of groupthink phenomena in which many people seemed to be engaging in unconsciously.

Different people had been the target of this kind of "persecutory" and incriminating complex, with various consequences. It was a kind of scapegoating and ostracizing that maintained the relatively tight reign of authority, control and conformity that the more politically motivated people seemed to have over the whole department.

This formed a kind of background context that tended to predefine and precondition the individual student's own status identity, psycho-social adjustments, and their peer and official evaluations that were kept on file and that were used as a chief instrument in determining a person's eligibility for support and subsequent trajectory through the program.

One person almost experienced a nervous breakdown over the evaluations, which she read about herself by a professor, an evaluation she felt to be unfounded and unfair. Also, other students were quite aware of this, and were deliberately engaged in "impression management," not only in terms of their identity, but also in manipulating professors' opinions about other students in the department.

This involvement and influence of other students over the official and semi-official status of an individual graduate student within the department became especially marked over issues involving critical indeterminacy and greater subjectivity of evaluation.

Some people who seemed almost frightened by too much subjectivity approached and demanded from professors a more objective and authoritative standard from above. It is a paradox, that some of the most self-righteous, and most cool seeming students were the ones most implicated in this deliberate manipulation of the professor's attitudes and opinions about other students. These demands were always made in terms of greater authorial objectivity.

In regard to the professors, one facet of their authoritarianism I found particularly disgusting was their somewhat hypocritical and hypercritical paternalism toward 'their' students. Those students who manipulated the professors played up to them as if they were parental figures and they were dependent 'children' who needed to be protected and favored over and above the other students who refused to play along with the unwritten rules of the game.

This kind of paternalistic attitude toward graduate students became particularly apparent to me in the third and final semester at the department. I was finally given a Teaching Assistant-ship (TA-ship), and though I carried a heavier load, and did most of the work on schedule, some of the TAs were late even though they had only half as many students, these TAs were chronically given preferential treatment by the professor because they 'played along' with him in such a supplicating and paternalistic manner.

One professor in particular thought that she could solve my problem, which became expressed in terms of writing. I resented her paternalistic, parent-child attitude from the beginning, and refused to play along with her. I disliked not being treated like an adult, with my own sense of the world.

She backed down after I threatened to put a special note into my file complaining of her preferential treatment of some students over others in our class. Though I wrote some of the most productive papers ever for her class, she began giving me consistently lower marks for each subsequent paper. I began responding by adopting ever more outlandish styles in which to frame my essays.

I was working on the assumption that authoritarian personalities have difficulty in dealing with normal frame disruption. If one deliberately disrupts the 'normal' taken for granted frames and style of convention in one's writing, such people would not be able to deal in a tolerant way with such differences, even though such framing had little or nothing to do with the actual subject matter or content of the paper, except in terms of being 'meta-logically' framed in ways that reflected the content.

The real power a professor has over the status of the student became clearly apparent to me by the end of the semester. A group of professors who did not like me decided to withdraw departmental support I had been promised for the following Spring semester. I knew this would happen even a few months earlier.

The first response by this particular professor to my first term paper sealed my fate. I remember realizing then, in a sudden moment, that I had no more future or place in the department. I remember, two months before it ever happened, walking out to a window at the end of the hallway and looking out at the cold gray skies, and feeling the same cold inside of me.

I planned my exit from the department in a graceful fashion. I had already written to many other schools and had applied to ten programs. People whom I asked for letters of recommendation from Binghamton I either did not fully trust, or else they failed somewhat miserably to come through at the last moment for me. The key professor I was counting on, the British social anthropologist who advised me to transfer the year before, suddenly took off to Africa without completing what I requested from him. None of the schools around that time accepted me, and I ended up leaving Binghamton without anywhere else to go.

The news of the withdrawal of support and the readjustment of my status, from a Ph.D. Candidate to conditional on the basis of the letter grade of that one paper. I resented as well the fact that I had already had my MA degree that I felt I had earned the hard way. It still hit me like a ton of bricks. It happened right at Christmas time, and right before Rosie was due to have her baby. I was floored and severely depressed.

I never stepped foot back in the department, and never said goodbye to anyone except one student who had been in Brazil when all of this happened, and yet who remained a close friend in spite of it. We left there about a month after Mahala was born, packing our truck, giving away most of our possessions, and driving back to California. No one there got to see what our baby looked like, and none of my 'friends' had seemed to have the nerve to bother to find out about us.

I left the campus completely. I met another graduate student in philosophy there who came there at the same time as I and who was just leaving the school behind in the same way. He expressed to me many of the same feelings that I had felt about the place. We had both arrived there a year and a half before with high expectations of success, and we were both leaving with profound disappointment about the school.

I had been made to feel like a failure when I had really done nothing wrong, except not to conform myself to the paternalistic expectations of a few professors. Their own judgment weighed much heavier than all the years of experience and successful involvement in anthropology I had had. I would not doubt it if these same professors intentionally tried to keep me from getting into other graduate programs through insider networks and unofficial phone calls. We all still know who we are, in spite of the impersonal side of it all.

The Gateless Gate

An instant realization sees endless time.
Endless time is as one moment.
When one comprehends the endless moment
He realizes the person who is seeing it.

I arrived back in California feeling as if we had never left, as if we had gone right back to where we had begun with, nothing different except the facts that we were two years older, had a small baby, and a sour attitude towards anthropologists and anthropology in general. I anxiously awaited the news from my other applications only to receive one disappointment after another. It seemed as if no program wanted a half-baked, blacklisted anthropological reject from my Northeast program.

I was left without any sense of direction or determination, and we didn't know what to do. I felt like déjà vu all over again, like a vicious and endless cycle. I knew anthropology and felt fundamentally confident of myself and my training, and I resolved myself to apply again. I ended up applying to about 16 more schools over the summertime, for all those programs accepted applications in the off season. I cost me about a thousand dollars all in. I busied myself in the meantime with little different projects. I installed a Jacuzzi my sister had given to my mom into the deck I had built for her two years before.

I worked on another deck for a professor friend from CSU Fullerton that was located in the mountains. I later received the news that the whole cabin had burned down. I was near frantic to hear positive news from somebody, some graduate program, but was feeling in fundamental despair without any hope of anything. I believed I would only receive more rejections. I ended up pouring a concrete driveway for my mom. Then I received news of acceptance from a distinguished private university and one from a major Midwest public university at about the same time.

I couldn't make up my mind between the two, and left early to visit both departments. The Private University had offered me support for the springtime and seemed as if it had more wealth than the public school. It was perhaps one of the hardest decisions I ever made, and after visiting both places, I felt more uncertain and confused than before.

I felt literally as if I was in two places at once without being wholly in any place. The Private University soon came through with on campus housing which clenched the decision for me. We stayed about a month in a hotel room until the campus housing became available. We moved in just before Christmas time and settled in just in time for the Spring semester to begin.

It took me all of about two weeks to realize I had made a mistake in choosing Private University. It was not really, from a purely academic standpoint, a bad department. I just did not click with the people in it very well. I felt even more ostracized beginning at that program than I did finishing at my previous department. I made open comments to a lecturer in one of the classes that neither the lecturer nor any of the students appreciated very much.

Auto-Anthropology

The next day, in my office, I overheard this same professor talking out loud about it, saying how this new student was being nonconformist. I thought I had made an intellectually valid and interesting comment. Rumor spread throughout the department, the reverberations of which came back to me via other professors, and though none of the other students even made the effort to talk with me or to try to get to know me, it was as if they had already formed their own opinion and evaluation about me.

The other teaching assistant I worked with added fuel to the fire. She was an upper middle-class, middle-aged neurotic woman who drove to school everyday in a Mercedes-Benz, and seemed to have little better to do than to annoy other students and flirt with the faculty.

She thought that she should have control over my sections and my own work even though the professor in charge of both of us made it explicitly clear from the outset that we could do our own thing under the aegis of her syllabus.

She followed this professor around like a young child, and her paternalism was as strong as what I had experienced at the previous campus I attended. The Professoress though, saw through it for the most part and was a little disturbed by it. She just didn't know what to do about it. This student was a pain in more than one butt.

This individual was having an ongoing affair with another, rather neurotic looking professor, and felt as if she had some power in the department. She spread lies about me just at the time when the funding for the following semester was being decided, and tried to influence the department about me, even though she herself never bothered to ask about me or try to get to know me in any way.

She had convinced our professor that I was being too "subjective" in my evaluations of my students' essays when in fact all I was really doing was using my own system of "points" different from the other teaching assistants. It seemed pretty petty and pointless, but the effect was well designed and deliberate: that was to influence the committee decision against my further funding.

The same general kind of phenomenon I had observed going on between professor and students at the Northeast State University I observed at the Anthropology department of this prestigious private school.

It was the same paternalism and manipulation; the same kind of incriminating ostracism; the same status control and manipulation through the grapevine; and the same focusing of all these issues over the authorial problem of objectivity and subjectivity as expressed through writing and grading of students' papers in a writing intensive program.

It happened not just once, but several times at this private, fairly conservative school. I was prepared for it, having experienced it before and I knew better how to deal with it. I bowed out rather gracefully from the program by the end of the semester, though I made As in almost all my course work there, and we packed our truck and left without saying goodbye to anyone but my former Professoress who brought us a going away gift.

The case and cause at this Private University was not exactly the same as at the Northeast State School. I had made the acquaintance of one graduate student who had been six years at the Private University and he had informed me a little of the inside history of the department. The general orientation of the whole department, exceptions notwithstanding, was basically one of cultural materialism (Marvin Harris) and cultural ecology (a la Roy Rappaport and Julian Stewart.) Anything outside of that was anathema.

Any critical voice to the contrary was met with strong reaction, a mutual reaction by both order imposing professors and order seeking and conformist oriented students all of whom wanted to play at science.

Materialism formed a certain orienting, and often, hidden, agenda that to myself at least seemed something questionable, to exclusively emphasize the etic over the emic, the material over the ideal, and the positive over the evaluative. This acquaintance had been screwed over by the same strong voices of people who thought that I should be silent and obedient in class, and he was looking to transfer to another more productive program.

A Mountain Dream

Pure Void: bamboos by thousands find a home.
The brook cascades-a mirror spilling chills.
A shower of moonlight drenched the air last night.
I rode the yellow crane and joined the gods.

Nguyen Trai

I am now completing my first semester at the Mid-Western Public
Campus. We drove directly north to Mid-Missouri from Dallas. I
opened a bank account there the first day, and we deposited our
possessions in a storage rental, and drove back to California to await
news of receiving on campus housing, which I was expecting a month
later. Back at home again, I put in a new lawn, an automatic sprinkler
system and landscaped the front yard for my mom.

We drove back to the campus in a hurry when we found, a day late, that
we had to be there in person to be let into our apartment by the first,
which meant we had just one week to get ready again. We made the
move without any hitches and settled in during the hot summer months
at the University Village.

Since being here, I had dedicated myself almost exclusively to my writing
and this has proven to be one of the most productive periods of my life.
The basic cost of living here was about as cheap and affordable for poor
people as can be had in the entire US.

Though I refuse to adopt the same kind of attitude as I had at either the
Northeast State or Private University, and will not try to analyze the
social relations or power structure within the department, I will offer my
first impressions of the place. It is perhaps one of the poorest universities
on the States—making its incentive structure for graduate students less
than adequate. The people, either graduate students or faculty, are not
overly friendly. Though I've been here almost a semester now, I've only

spoken to one other graduate student at all, though I see a few almost everyday. Everyone here seems too busy or too important to take the time to chat.

The professors here, like everywhere, are always very busy juggling their schedules. But here, people seemed to behave more professionally and less paternalistically, perhaps more in spite of themselves than because of themselves. I do not know what complex set of factors make the difference between one professor who passes judgment without a complete knowledge and another who withholds such prejudgment, or at least refrains from allowing their own presentiments from being the decisive factor in their treatment of students.

The future is in deed and in word still an open, unfinished book. There is no telling what our future will bring us, whether we will reach yet another dead end, or whether my time, money and energy spent here at Mid-Town will prove rewarding and worth it. Though I am of a minority in Anthropology, I am not alone, and I know of more than a mutilated handful of others who share a little at least in my anthropological worldview and values.

I have learned one important lesson from all of my many trials and tribulations throughout my life. Though I may often be alone, I no longer feel lonely, and though I may be in the company of many others, I often feel very alone. I will not treat others in my time as others have so often treated me.

Sleeping Buddha
Dreaming of Nirvana
By the time you awaken
It will be too late

I now take my anthropology with a grain of salt. There are no complete, unfinished, impartial truths in the world—there is only half-truth that is discolored by deceit and obscured beneath the veil of illusion.

Auto-Anthropology

The truth can both empower a person and can be used against a person—it is a double-edged sword that often as not cuts both ways.

We would sometimes like to live within a world in which truth is simple and straight forward, clear-cut and concise, but it proves to be rarely, if ever, so.

There is a certain prestige power associated with the command over and control of truth in the world. Because truth is always half empty and therefore half false, there is always an unfortunate degree of uncertainty also associated with truth. Uncertainty becomes associated with falsehood and the unknown, as well as with the possibility of deceit. Such uncertainty also becomes associated with failure, especially in a society that values success, and rewards it well.

The preoccupation with success is underscored by a secret fear of failure that must be projected out upon antithetical examples in our social environment. One must sometimes pay a heavy price for non-conformity. We must find failure in our world as much as we must find success, and we must realize it projectively and semi-objectively in order that we can then persecute it.

Such fear of failure leads to an obsession with uncertainty and a compulsion for certainty and the kind of order that such certainty brings with it. Those obsessed with failure must seek out and destroy uncertainty in their lives, and they must find examples that embody such uncertainty as much as they symbolize failure.

I was never so afraid of failure that I've allowed it to dictate and control my choices. Because truth is relative, one person's certainty may be another's uncertainty, one person's success another's failure.

The power of truth involves the possession of information and the management of social impressions in order to reinforce status and social solidarity. Control over the truth amounts to control of a person's solidarity. It amounts to control of a person's status in face-to-face and group interactions. Truth and its illusion determines the measure of acceptability and legitimacy of certain forms of knowledge that in turn tends to validate such knowledge in self reinforcing cycles of belief and behavior.

Information networks—grapevines—serve the function of reinforcing status and group boundaries—augmenting the status quo of the existing power hierarchy and systematically excluding marginal members who come to represent the repressed feeling of failure and doubt that is common to the social atmosphere. Gossip and informal conversation often form the principle and often only forum for status manipulation and negotiation to be played out in otherwise strongly structured hierarchical settings.

In maintaining the power of one's truth and the system that supports it, one must deny and falsify or exclude evidence and viewpoints that are contradictory or conflicting and that cast the shadow of uncertainty over such power.

Deceit is implicit to the denial of truth. Within the circle of deception that maintains the vital lie of absolute truth, deceit comes at various levels and in various ways: as blind faith, ideological prognostication, rhetoric, etc. There are permissible kinds of everyday deceptions that are largely unconscious and mostly out of awareness, in the service of maintaining the local status of one's own ego identity. Then there are tolerable deceptions that pass unnoticed or are semi-officially acknowledged as part of the way things are.

There are also promotional deceptions, those delusions that become part and parcel of ideology and the mythoi of power. Then there are also those tactical and strategic deceptions that allow the effective user to manipulate, conceal, deny, and distort truth in effective ways, for the purposes of power.

In the circle of deception, truth becomes the vicious, unfortunate lie. Truth becomes dangerous, and becomes sanctioned to the taboo regions. In the manner of Erving Goffman and John Berreman, we can separate dramaturgical social spaces into the front regions of open, overt discourse and back regions of tacit denial and of covert dialogue in closed circles.

With the social reinforcement of the denial of truth, there comes a need not to know. If knowledge creates responsibility, then its denial constitutes an avoidance of responsibility. There is a need to avoid, ignore and discriminate against those elements of our common environment that constitute a threat to our understanding—ultimately the threat to our unknown shadows and our fear of uncertainty.

Within small communities, the social psychological phenomenon of "group think" can take control over the ethos, nomos and pathos of collective group consciousness and conscience. The desire for the kind of solidarity which comes from blind conformity and self-sacrifice to the good of the corporate interests of the collective, and the corresponding emphasis upon organizational efficiency and routine operational conformity can take control and become the over-riding imperative in the determination of an individual's status identity, relative freedom and behavioral responses.

Within such an atmosphere, truth becomes taboo, and deceit becomes routinized, habitual and an indirectly sanctioned constraint upon an individual's belief and behavior, upon one's actions and even rationalizations.

To the extent that an anthropology department provides a forum for social mobility, like any other academic forum, anthropological knowledge and understanding becomes conditioned and informed by a kind of class-consciousness that is articulated in status control, ego identity, and 'truth power' in daily, face-to-face discourse.

This is as true for graduate students who are preoccupied with their own future careers in the field as much as it is for faculty members who are concerned for the reputation and their professional recognition within the wider status hierarchy of the field. To some extent, this class-consciousness informs the mythoi of Anthropologos.

In this regard it must be seriously questioned what is the symbolic status of the anthropological other as a counter-reference significant other, as well as to what is the somewhat liminal, and anti-structural status of the field in relation to the center of anthropology as this is practiced and reproduced within the anthropology program(s) of the department of the University.

It has been my claim that, to this extent, the field has constituted by and large an officially sanctioned dumping ground in which the normally repressed subjectivities of the anthropologist can be enacted and brought to realization, while the significant, counter-reference other constitutes the unconscious, symbolic target of the anthropologist's own repressed subjectivities and feelings of weakness, inferiority and insecurity.

American culture and character reinforces this predisposition and egocentric orientation of self-aggrandizement at the expense of others by its extreme emphasis upon the values of achievement and social success.

Anthropologia, within the academic island of the department, becomes imbued with so much Americana with its implicit promotion of aggressiveness and personal acquisitiveness.

There are several related features of a kind of American complex of what might be called Academic Authoritarianism. First, besides being largely class tied and class bound consciousness of status identity, which from the standpoint of false consciousness of people preaching one thing and doing the opposite, constitutes so much legitimated and legitimating hypocrisy, academic authoritarian in general is largely paternalistic.

Besides being a male dominated, 'father knows best' kind of attitude, it promotes a parent-child identification and relationship of social dependency/dominance between the professor and the student.

This kind of relationship is mutually reinforcing and suppliant for the egos of both the professor and the student—reaffirming one another's identity vis-à-vis the significant Reference/Counter-Reference other. (1. Counter-reference other—the "Other" actors from the ethnographic field whom one studies; Reference other—the "Others" one identifies with, mentors, models, and becomes like in the Academic field.)

This relationship links knowledge and the control of truth with ego identity and situationally relative feelings of certainty/uncertainty, success/failure and with social power/prestige and status role identity.

It involves, differentially and quite variably, some measure of compartmentalization of the self between personal and subjective feelings of uncertainty and insecurity, and professional and objective attitudes of confidence and expertise.

Auto-Anthropology

These tendencies become highlighted in a field such as American anthropology when one's professional status is not as unequivocally legitimated by social values and interests as are, for instance, a medical doctor or a lawyer. This is so especially when the chances for failure are large, the consequences devastating for one's career and livelihood, and the opportunities for research and funding are increasingly fewer and further between.

This complex is central to the understanding of anthropology as a socio-cultural system with its own distinctive dialectics of discourse and power, its own professional ethos and sense of specialized community interests, values and views, and as embedded within a larger American and world society.

Serving as certain definite structural functional purposes within the larger context, as a "mode of information" that the issues of subjectivity/objectivity and of the legitimization and empowerment of one's anthropological status, such study should come to focus upon and be articulated by the power and authority of the written word. It is the literal legitimacy of the signature, the published, printed article, that the greatest power of truth becomes articulated.

One's success as a writer, in a convincing, anthropologically acceptable mode or style, dealing with 'interesting' problem sets, is what makes or breaks one's anthropological status, authenticity and authority in the world. Anthropological authority is authorial, and anthropological authoritarianism is most articulated as authorial authoritarianism (or as "*auctoritas*" (Hannah Arendt—that is achieved through acquired status and derivative authority.)

It is not by accident that most of the issues involving anthropological authority and academic authoritarianism with which I became involved in or have given autobiographical witness of, have involved the issues of the subjectivity and credibility of the student's ability and manner of writing, in which cases it is often not so much a matter of what is said rather than how it is said.

I close this extended paper with the last claim that autobiographical authority remains the most reasonable, and perhaps the most honest, form of authorial claim to the truth that the anthropologist in the world has. Whatever the experiences, the ethnographic encounters in the field remain foremost and in the final analysis the participant-observer's own, primarily subjective, personal, biographical episodes of her/his own life history.

Autobiography is not the only form of psychosocial inquiry available to anthropology. It is neither mere narcissism, nor just introspection. It involves an extended kind of reflexivity in which we do not just see ourselves as others see us, but through which we also begin to also see others as seen by ourselves, and perhaps even more importantly, to see others as we see ourselves.

All experience is first and foremost autobiographical experience, everything else is alienated from the self and restructured by others, and such experience constitutes the only available pathway to a common ground of understanding between all humankind.

Along this way we come sooner or later to our own heart of darkness that we share with so many others, and then we arrive at the realization of the possibility of our own, and others, eventual possible, or spiritual salvation.

I proffer autobiography as a legitimate, authentic mode of anthropological discourse. It is not the imperialistic 'I came, I saw, I conquered,' but it is enough: "I witnessed, It happened, We and the world became connected and transformed by the experience of interconnection."

It offers us an acceptable, anthropological alternative to the meta-logical horns of the reflexive dilemma of making the strange familiar and the familiar strange, without our having to compromise our sense of anthropological authority in the world.

Given American ego-centrism, the first person singular is perhaps the best we can do in the world. It reaffirms my faith to know that not only are anthropologists like any other people in the world, but that other people's Anthropologos are liable to be similar in basic ways to our own.

Auto-Anthropology

Without acknowledging the inherent subjectivity of human suffering in the world, there is little point or purpose in achieving anthropological wisdom or seeking anthropological experience.

The wild geese fly across the long sky above.
Their image is reflected upon the chilly water below.
The geese do not mean to cast their image on the water:
Nor does the water mean to hold the image of the geese.

Anonymous

As a point of deriving some objective value from this study, I have drawn the following conclusions based upon it:

1. The denial of human inter-subjectivity, the subjectivity of both self and others, is at the base of both authoritarianism and the positivistic 'objectivity' of the social sciences.

2. It is this inherent subjectivity and inter-subjectivity of human understanding that renders our 'Anthropologos' irremediably 'relative' and susceptible to so much bias and distortion.

3. The issues of objective/subjective in Anthropologos form a background dialectic in the production of knowledge in the field and in the social reproduction and construction of the field itself.

4. This dialectic of Anthropologos becomes focused upon the issues of writing, literacy, the written and published word, the signature, the thesis, the term paper, and the kinds of conventional and informal but common constraints placed upon such literary production,

5. Much normal and conventional discursive and literary praxis centered upon Anthropologos is oriented towards relative objectivity and implicitly denies the inherent subjectivity of anthropological truth and understanding. Autobiography is proffered as one alternative approach to such Anthropologos that has as its aim the historical/biographical excoriation of such received social subjectivity of understanding. It is a form that can be applied to and by both the self and others.

6. Issues of power, of authenticity, anthropological credulity and authority, as well as of ego-identity, come to be centered and depend crucially upon the issue of relative objectivity/subjectivity of the written word. This then becomes articulated primarily in terms of its dialectic of Anthropologos.

7. There are many corollaries to the preceding points. Issues of class-consciousness, especially as this is articulated in day-to-day, face-to-face dialectics of personal power within the departmental setting (whose word if the final one?) underlie most social relationships.

   Related issues inform these relations as well, including issues of:
   - A form of derivative 'false consciousness' legitimating a status quo of power relations in the world;
   - Of resulting hypocrisy between the said and the done;
   - Professed beliefs and actual behaviors;
   - Professional Anthropologos as a social symbolically sanctioned structural functional 'mode of information production/consumption' that has as its implicit, primary, unmarked purpose the annihilation of the subjective identity of the Other of the world and the affirmation of the objectiveness of the Self.

   The denial of the subjectivity of the Other in the world has been witnessed in terms of the denial of their sense of history, biography, time, experience, mythoi, and even their very human being, and in social programmatic settings often the source of mass destruction.

Auto-Anthropology

8. In terms of the 'professionalization' of students of
    Anthropologos and the social reproduction of the field itself, its
    measure of effectiveness, though always partial and incomplete,
    comes to depend upon the Archimedean fulcrum of the
    dichotomization and compartmentalization between the
    subjective and the objective, which by common human
    association, becomes critically connected to the separation and
    compartmentalization between the personal background and the
    tertiary socialization of a public, professional, graduate level
    foreground.

    There is a great deal of individual variability in just how this kind
    of separation and compartmentalization is achieved, depending
    upon many intermediate biographical and historical variables.
    But in whatever way it becomes expressed, its consequences are
    generally the same. What is repressed as subjective and
    personal, as weak, partial and antithetical to the public, objective
    and professional, becomes projected implicitly upon the images
    of the Counter reference significant 'Other' of the field.

    The mythoi of the field constitute a kind of theoretical, affective,
    social and methodological anti-structure to the structure and
    authoritarian praxis of the academic department.

9. Other common associations that become connected with
    subjectivity/objectivity are those of: failure/success,
    uncertainty/certainty, falsehood/truth, weak/strong, corrupt/pure,
    non-rational/rational, nonscientific/scientific, etc.

10. This set of interrelated points constitute what I would call a
    central paradigm of the mythoi, consciousness and character of
    authoritarian Anthropologos, informing the central constraints
    of the dialectic of Anthropologos as this is played out in
    anthropological forums, academic or otherwise, around the
    world.

We must somehow learn to live with the prospect and possibility that in
our dialectic of Anthropologos we must always remain remedial, un-
rehabilitated, imperfect, and partial pawns of power in the world.

Because human development, and the human world, is yet unfinished business, so also must our Anthropologos and Anthropologia remain unfinished business.

Though some of these points may seem intuitively obvious, the extent to which they inform the everyday praxis of anthropological production is somewhat less than obvious, and usually out of awareness.

Part Two

My journey in anthropology did not end with the awarding of my degrees, though life circumstances certainly often made me feel that way during the first few years. In hindsight, I can say that my lifelong road-trip in anthropology was just beginning, though no one then could have told me that.

My sense of self was isomorphic professionally with my anthropological identity during that time 30 years ago as a middle-aged man in the mid-30s with a small young family to be responsible for.

The trouble was really that my sense of ego-identity as an anthropologist was not entirely symmetrical or congruent with the lot life had cast for me as somewhat of an "invisible human being."

This marginal identity was only exacerbated and was often made to often feel acutely real by the lack of good jobs, the poor pay of part-time and inconsistent employments, interspersed with prolonged periods not just of joblessness, but of a creeping sense of existential hopelessness.

A late bloomer and a slow starter, little did I then understand that my life was only just beginning, and the best yet lay ahead. All was not lost, and relief of our chronic condition sometimes came in the most unexpected of directions.

Looking back now in older age, the larger circles in which we were living and journeying in life were not as apparent to me back then as they have become gradually since then.

In the hindsight that is older age, the time of letting go and summarizing one's net losses and gains, I can truly say without regret that I chose the correct path in my life I was meant to be upon, for the intersection of many different reasons beginning with early childhood, and extending in broad circles and cycles over the years, converging sometimes and diverging others.

My time in the **USMC**, its reasons yet elusive to me so long after my discharge, has in the long run become quite clearly evident to me by now. All was not lost back then or ever, it was always just very slow yet to be found.

REWITNESSING THE ANTHROPOLOGY
OF THE WORLD

The Anthropological Construction of American Anthropology and an Addendum and Afterward

This work has special meaning for me now because in a literal sense I have come full circle to where I began more than 25 years ago. I sit now in front of my computer, rather than at my typewriter when I first composed this work about 10 years ago, but that seems to be about the only real difference, except perhaps for the fact that I am now ten years older. I am living in the same place where I started out back then, after all our adventures and sojourns around the world and across the country.

I have come full circle to where I started out 25 years ago, and I cannot say exactly what I have gained from the experience. Very little materially was gained, so far at least, in the final accounting. We've had and we've lost, regained and given up. I am in fact poorer now than in the beginning, at least in a material sense. I am much less of a conformist than I was a quarter century ago, at least in an implicit way.

We are surprisingly unattached to material things. Funny about this, because my core character remains the same and even more conservative than I used to be about certain things that always have a conservative connotation. I tend to judge people, sometimes quite harshly, on the basis of their behavior and their values, not in terms of their status or material possession, their looks or their means.

But in a soulful and intellectual manner, I am so much richer than I used to be. If I can say I've ever had my act in one bag, it has been just in the past year that this has grown in sophistication and complexity in a way that was never before known. I am counting on it eventually becoming the prelude to a better life for us in many senses--if I can translate it finally into some material and social sense of well-being.

This second part of my story begins basically where I left off from the writing of the first part, that first year at the Midwest University, in 1992. The second part consists of about 6 different sections leading up to the current time of my writing here where I started out so long ago.

Since then, we lived in Missouri a couple of years, traveled to do fieldwork in Penang, Malaysia for about a year and a half, and then returned to Missouri to finish our dissertation, a process that required about 7 or 8 months more to complete from the "scratch" of undigested field notes and record materials. (I do not write about this period in Malaysia during the doctoral research work 'of an annual cycle of seasons' but this is highlighted in the text 'The Professional Pariah.' following the first part.)

We then returned in August of 1995, after submitting my final draft of my dissertation, to my mom's house in Southern California where I looked for work with my degree behind me. I sent off over three hundred applications that year, and received not one nibble for an interview.

In August of 1996 we got in our minivan and traveled back East, camping as we went. Our aim was an education program in Tennessee, which we found unsuitable for ourselves. We ended up with a broken down car in Rock Springs, Wyoming, where one thing led to the next until I ended up with a job conducting genealogical and historical research for a family there.

To retell the second part of my story, I must bring the last part of our recent sojourn to central China and the first part of my memories of my father together. Sitting in China about a year and a half ago, (late 1998) I had a memory (or should I say 'remembrance'?) that I had forgotten and not remembered since before the death of my father. China was our penultimate episode, before coming back to where we are now, where it all began so long ago.

China proved to be mostly a miserable experience for us. I had grand and somewhat selfish plans of recouping some of my lost research context in comparative culture that had left a huge hole in the core of my being and in my central identity as an anthropologist and therefore worthy person in the world.

Auto-Anthropology

I brought three computers to mainland central China, with the purpose of carrying forward research. Little did we know after a long train journey to the interior, that almost everything we hoped for would be systematically dashed, eroded, and finally destroyed by powers that be in China and that were totally, completely beyond my control above day to day management of our lives.

The primary individual with whom I dealt, the key foreign affairs person who by the way was one of the few good English speakers of the entire city, proved to be not only unreliable and incredibly manipulative, but also downright damned deceitful.

He, more than anyone else, who was the critical mediator of our adjustment to China, destroyed not only our research context, but also probably permanently our ability to trust Chinese. This is all another long story, for another place and time.

Our "home" in China I called the dungeon. It was a semi-subterranean basement at the backend of the guest hotel of the city. Its tiled floors were chronically damp and cold. Mildew formed overnight on all the walls and in all the dark nooks and crannies.

In the course of a year there I killed over forty centipedes within the immediate vicinity of our quarters, many of them in our bathroom and bedroom. I also killed many rats and a few mice. We were frequently without lights, even in the middle of the day, working and reading in the dark interior by the light of candles that we pushed into the openings of one-liter beer bottles.

We rarely had any hot water—only once or twice a week at first, and frequently we had no water at all. Often it was just brown water. It would be shut off on us unpredictably at any time of the day or night.

There was a good side to our being in China, because we befriended many of the students, and of these, a few proved to be very dear to us. My students would come visit with smelly feet, embarrassed to take off their shoes in our "Asian" household. Often they would not have showered for almost a week. And yet, we found many of them to be kind and caring, and they lightened our burden on a daily basis, in spite of their smelly feet, stinky bedding and bad breath.

It was in such a situation, sometime in late November or early December, with the cold of winter descended upon our abode, and with nothing but a small space heater and many blankets and layers of clothing to keep us warm.

All of us more than a little hungry for lack of good food and whole meat, that I found myself stripped bare of all my illusions about life. I had found myself, and even worse, my small family, incarcerated for a year in a place I didn't really want to be, without the compensation of being able to productively carry forward the fieldwork I expected.

In such a condition we received a surprise box of goodies from my Aunt and Uncle and my cousin's family from Chowchilla, California, where I was born. Strange it seemed that they would bother to send us such a box. It was full of snack foods, sausages, canned potato soup mix, dried mash potatoes, and many other small goodies that raised the curiosity of my students. And this box of food, close to Christmas time, made me think back very deeply to my childhood in a way that I had never thought of before.

For some odd reason, I was able to remember the day before my father died, when he took me to my Grandmother's house and I helped him in the back one-acre lot behind the house to sand on the small rowboat he had built a few years before. I remember that he had previously shown me how to sand with the grain of the wood, and in circles, using a block of wood that fit into palm of my hand. He showed me how to sand one row at a time in small sections of the downside-up bottom of the boat as it rested on saw horses.

Well, I was up on that boat with him standing on a sawhorse, and he told me that he was soon to go away again. He told me he had to go to a special place. He had, in his illness, gone so many times before, so that I in my 7-year-old naiveté and blank innocence asked him where he was going and for how long. I wondered if it would be for a couple of weeks like before. He told me he didn't know for how long, but it would be for a long time. Then I asked him if it would be for a whole month, without a clear idea of how long a month was.

In my mind I pictured something like a clinic across the street, or a hotel, done in typical 1950s So Cal.-Style architecture. It was a one-story affair with translucent glass brick walls, and palm trees in front. Then I asked him if I could come with him, but he told me no, that I must stay and look after my mom. I didn't understand what he was telling me. Soon afterward my mom came home from her teaching job to pick me up, and I remember waiting by the boat while my mom and father had an argument on the path to the back lot, out of my earshot.

That was to be the last time I ever spoke with my father or saw him alive. He killed himself the following day. He had shot himself in the heart with the .22 caliber rifle that we used to shoot old tin cans with out in the desert near Palm Springs.

I do not know why I had repressed this memory from my conscious experience for so long. I do not know why, sitting in that dark dirty room in China, looking at the box my Uncle, my father's brother, had sent to us in kindness, that I should suddenly then remember that curious experience. And it was not even clear if it was really real, or just imagined, though I believe it really did happen. It is almost as clear as the day it must have happened.

Funny, to be stripped of all life's illusions, laid bare of all familiar and comfortable attachments, and in such a miserable condition to be able to remember things that had been forgotten for almost 35 years. But I believe my life changed fundamentally from that moment. I relinquished my basic illusions about Anthropology and research that I had long maintained, and I decided henceforth on a radical change of identity and a new declaration of rugged independence.

It was a kind of early mid-life crisis, I believe, perhaps precipitated by our stressful life experiences iced by the cake of our present circumstances. It was male menopause at 41-years of age and I reevaluated all I had done before, and asked myself what it was all now worth, and then determined to myself to do it all over again, somehow.

With this digression, it is worthwhile now to backtrack to where I left off with my life in Part I, during the first semester of my time at the University of Missouri, Columbia.

The time spent at the Midwest Public University, between the summer of 1991 and the summer of 1994, were especially productive for me from the standpoint of my writing, my studies and my research. The first year we stayed at the University Village that was situated basically off the main-campus and at the head of a public trail built on an old railroad track through the city.

The apartment complex was a series of double-storied redbrick apartment buildings that dated back to the late 1940s in construction style, with black asphalt tiled floors, small refrigerators and windows with metal frames and hand-cranks. We were in these apartments for the first year, during which time we made many sets of friends within the complex. Most of these friends were young foreign families.

There was a Taiwanese family in the building across from us, and an upper class Indonesian family with their live-in Indonesian Amah whom we especially befriended.

There was a Mainland Chinese family in the block down from us, and a young white girl with a young baby on the other side. My wife babysat this young mother while she (the mother) attended classes on campus.

There was a Hungarian student and his Polish wife in the very last block of apartments that faced the forests of the trail.

There was a young white Texan who worked at Kinko's and his Mexican-American wife who was attending the law school. Most of these families had small children, just born or just a few years old.

There was a Korean family in the apartment next door to us who had lived there for seven years and whose children were already adolescent. The father worked in the English department and played golf, and though we liked the wife and daughter, we also found that the father and son were quite arrogant.

There were also quite a few single Indians living in the apartment complex—how they got to live there without having families no one ever asked or answered. The Indians always seemed to be getting special advantages others didn't have.

Auto-Anthropology

There was an African family from Rwanda who moved next door to us on the other side whom we also grew quite close to. And then there was the young white southern couple from Southeastern Texas with their small daughter. These were all our friends. We got to know each other fairly well during that year, and we would go to picnic and to the lake swimming sometimes, or take walks up the Katie trail in the evening.

During the first few months of my time there, in the first semester, I dedicated myself to writing, and I wrote probably about five or six manuscripts during that period of time, including the first part of this manuscript. Rosie earned a little money from baby-sitting.

In the first semester I sat for my Ph.D. candidacy exam, and in the second semester, I gained a teaching assistantship in an introductory course in General Anthropology with a distinguished North American archaeologist and ethnohistorian. I look back at this time as one of the better and happier periods of our life. It was marked by peace and poverty, but a washing away of the difference that poverty made by a curious kind of *Communitas* within an international set of friends.

There was a stark contrast between these families and the mostly white families at the private University in our previous campus apartment (excepting for ourselves at least a friendly Singaporean, a kind Jordanian couple, and a Turkish family.)

At first there was a little tension between Rosie and myself that did not resolve itself for about a month. I devoted myself to writing and some of my writing was the most creative I had done so far. Also, at the encouragement of one of my professors: 'don't come back to me unless you have first bought a computer,' I purchased myself a little MacIntosh Classic II computer.

It was the first computer I ever owned and it took me a couple of months how to figure out what to do with it. My introduction to computers was primarily with trying to write and print my first manuscripts, and to figure out how to build expert systems for a class.

It was a period of transition in my writing between reliance on my typewriters and reliance on my computer, keyboard and printer.

84

I would spend most days at my typewriter or computer, and in the late afternoons I would take the bicycle that I had bought at a yard-sale for $15 with a child's seat on the back, and take Mahala down the public trail. The trail was actually an old railroad line that was pulled up. It ran fairly straight with long wide curves and was mostly embanked at a level higher than the surrounding terrain. It ran more or less from the center of town, along the edge of a fairly large stream, out to the point that it intersected the country road beyond the town limit at least a few miles in the countryside, by a cornfield.

Each day we would ride further and further down a little bit. Eventually we made our way to the small lake about halfway down its length. Nearby was a river that cut a deep gorge. We would ride through the barren deciduous forest of fall and wintertime, passing by small farm fields and under the highway. Mahala would like to stop here and play at the water's edge, hunting for frogs and finding dead fish and things.

The trail stretched a total of 5 or 6 miles, winding under the main road of town, and going out through farm fields, near a lake, and then down through woods until it came to a dead-end at a T-section with a lonely country road. One day I made it all the way to the end of the trail. It was a warm day.

I was by myself, as I think Mahala had grown tired of the long rides. It was a good stress releaser for me. I reached the end of the trail, and on the way back followed a butterfly that flitted its way all the length of the last leg of the trail until it opened out near the cornfields by the lake. It flew as fast as I rode, though it could not fly in a straight line, and I was amazed by its speed and persistence to travel almost a mile in such a manner, before veering off into a neighboring field.

I returned from this bicycle trip, having found what was at the end of the trail, and parked the bike, and never took it back down the trail again. After that we would walk down the trail along the little stream that wound its way around near the trail entrance.

Our apartment backed this trail, blocked off from its deep forest growth only by a high chain link fence. There were many creatures in this forest. One night I saw two opossums and three raccoons at the same time in the same area immediately behind our apartment. Deer even ran along the edge of the trail up to the point it intersected the main highway, often stalking right by a train of bicyclists and joggers without being noticed.

Overall, I would say in hindsight that this was one of the happier and most carefree periods of our married life. Most of the students didn't have a lot of money. A few of the foreign students were from obviously wealthy backgrounds, but generally they made a point of not playing this up.

During the spring semester, when the weather started to warm up again, and the green came back to the trees and grass, I began playing baseball with a young teenage Mainland Chinese boy. His father was attending an engineering program and his mother worked at a chemistry plant outside of town. (I think she worked at the chemistry lab.)

I don't remember how we started. I started tossing the ball to him, and we began playing more and more, until it reached a point that we were playing quite regularly in the evenings after I came back from my classes.

Soon he had found some gloves and I bought a bat and some balls and then other kids and even some of the adult students began playing with us. By the end of our time there, we had organized a regular baseball game with the kids on the green area near our apartments, and even the manager who was a Puerto Rican and a good player joined in.

It happened in the second Spring semester, as I held a TA-ship and was busier at school that a young Korean couple moved into the apartment directly above us. I don't even remember who was there before them. But this couple was not very friendly. The husband beat the wife several times, as we could hear through the ceiling. They were quite noisy and disturbed me frequently, to the point that I became very annoyed and it began to ruin the peace and pleasantness of the village. To top this off, I believe they sometime made noise deliberately to annoy us, and would act very unfriendly to us whenever we met them outside.

I therefore decided to put in a request to relocate to the University Terrace apartments that were located on the other side of the campus behind the Medical Center. They did not have the trail nearby, but they had gardens behind that students could use, and they had more private arrangements that seemed better than those of the Village. So before the end of the semester we were relocating once again back to the other apartment complex. My Rwandan friend and my Taiwanese friend from across the street both helped me to move--a luxury I have seldom had either before or since.

We used my old big blue Chevy suburban, and made several trips back and forth. On one the return trips, we went in to get more furniture, and I made the mistake of leaving Mahala in the back of the truck. She crawled to the front driver's seat and must have begun playing with the shift lever on the steering column. As we came back outside the apartment with a box in our arms, we noticed the truck slowly rolling forward down the slight slope of the parking place.

I immediately let go of what we had and ran to catch up with it and saw little Mahala steering the truck, as it was rolling forward and not knowing really what was happening. I tried to get in front of the truck to slow it down a little bit, but to no avail, and it ran into the back of another car-- an Indian man's car, on the other side. It did no real obvious damage, and no one else seemed to notice the incident, so we pulled the truck back, loaded the rest of the furniture, and finished our move.

We relocated to the new apartments near the end of the second semester, just before the period of the final exams began. The complexes were made entirely of cinderblock, built in the early 60s, and they had a bigger, newer and better-organized kitchen with a real refrigerator.

They had also a private laundry facility for each four-apartment block that was easier than the central facility of the Village. I did not regret making that move, though Rosie at first did not want to do it and I basically had to do most of the work myself. But we soon made new sets of friends there, and kept most of our old friends as well.

There was especially a young Portuguese couple whose husband was finishing the veterinarian program and whose wife was a doctor who had already finished the Medical school and was doing her internship at the Cancer hospital on the North side of the town. There was a Salvadoran family who had been there a number of years, and a family from Bangladesh with a young boy, who always spit, and another family from

Auto-Anthropology

Pakistan, and a Sri Lankan family whose small girl was Mahala's age who played with her.

There was a family from Jordan with a little boy. There was a Taiwanese family directly above us whose baby was just one, and another Taiwanese family with a young girl. There were a couple of Mainland Chinese families. There was a Thai family who had a small daughter, and a couple of Indonesian families with small girls too. There was also a Korean family with two little boys.

All of these families became our friends. The playground was in a square area in the middle, surrounded by the apartment blocks, and it created a common meeting ground for children to play together safely and for the parents to get to know one another. Though there were few trees and no trail, the Terrace proved to be even better than the Village. There was a white family with two little girls whose mother was a Mormon and the husband was a Vietnam Veteran who worked at the Veterans' hospital across the parking lot and who was an Art education major.

The relocation interfered with the studies a little bit, but I remember getting down with a couple of more books during that Spring Semester. Near the end of the semester, the backfields behind the apartments were ploughed up and spaces were offered to all the students to plant gardens.

The spaces were about 10-12 feet wide by about 20 feet long. We drew numbers from a box, and I pulled a lot that landed me in the very middle of the entire field. I remember laying out my garden very carefully, stretching some yellow twine used in construction to mark the boundary and to help me level the garden a little bit as it was on the side of a gradual hill and sloped widthwise enough to make the water drain rapidly away.

As I was working out under the sun, an old Mainland Chinese grandmother came over to my garden, and twanged the taut little yellow line, and started laughing at it as if it were a big joke. I was a little annoyed but persisted in my efforts. I planted my seeds and covered the areas over with dried grass clippings from the mown lawns.

At the end of the semester, while the seeds were germinating, we decided to drive back on a vacation to Southern California to spend a couple of weeks with my mom. I paid an older Indonesian girl to water the garden for me, and we got in the Van and drove back to LA. We had a car problem in Utah, near Green River, when I lost my battery and had to get a new one. It was then that I decided we needed a newer and more reliable "used" car and we shopped about LA, and found a Toyota mini-van for about $6,000. My mom helped us from a loan she had previously taken out.

I sold the Suburban to a Mexican, a friend or family member of the Mexican who worked for George, the Japanese gardener who was doing my Mom's house. I don't remember much else about this particular trip back to Grandma's. I gathered my drip-irrigation stuff and transformed a couple of old buckets into water-containers for my garden, and I scrounged some good organic fertilizers from around the house.

We had left on our cross-country road-trip in our old blue Chevy suburban, and returned in a "new" Toyota mini-van that was quite sporty looking with its decaled racing pinstripes. We turned more than a few heads as we pulled into our parking space. My garden had been dried up, but otherwise the seeds were all just sprouting up through the dried grass clippings, which had proven effective in blocking the direct sun and keeping the moisture down in the soil. So that summertime, with little else to do, I worked mainly on my garden, installing my drip system that also caught the attention of a few people, and brought more derisive laughter from the old Chinese woman who spoke no English and smiled with a toothless grin.

I also worked on a couple of manuscripts. By mid-summer, my garden had grown up huge in the middle of the field. Most of the other gardens were dwarfed by comparison. I mulched it with some hay and manure and regular additions of grass clippings I would gather in the cool mornings. I had a trellis of beans, a row of Sunflowers, about six tomato plants, peppers, cucumbers, carrots, even some corn and potatoes. I planted the corn too late and it did not do so well. I also had some pumpkins that did quite well, and squash.

It proved to be the most outstanding garden of the entire field. The apartment manager would even take visitors to see it. The old Chinese woman never came around anymore, though one late summer's afternoon a couple of young Chinese men almost tried picking a fight with me.

By late summer time, we had more vegetables than we knew what to do with, and we ended up passing these out to the various families around us, who came to look forward to my returns from the garden. I got about 16 pumpkins from the Garden, some fairly large.

We took a trip in my mini-van with the Taiwanese family from the village in late August to St. Louis to visit my Uncle's family and to take the kids to the St. Louis zoo. We spent the day there and it was quite nice at the zoo.

During the summer I befriended a Korean friend who was finishing his doctorate in Journalism. His boy played with Mahala outside in the evenings, and I would see him out in the gardens, where he came over to ask me for some help on some minor matter. So we began to get to know each other. He was not like the other Koreans who were mostly in a closed network among themselves.

He had told me he made a commitment to living and working in the U.S. He had worked an internship program in Washington, D.C., and was trying to figure out what to do for his dissertation. He taught part-time a course in statistics.

I helped him during our discussions to formulate his ideas for the dissertation, and he came to me to inquire about how to do content analysis. I had only done a little content analysis before, but he decided on focusing on labor union strikes in the steel industry after World War I. I helped him a little bit with the evaluation of some of the articles he used in his survey, and in the end, the following semester; I helped him by editing his dissertation after class.

It was between all my classes that I got side tracked by helping the wives to organize a Halloween party. I don't know where it started, or whose idea it was, but I remember that I ended up doing most of the work in the last week to prepare for it. We arranged with the Taiwanese manager whose wife had a few airs to use a vacant apartment. At first he gave us a hard time, but a deputation of women went to talk to Judy, the administrator of the apartments, and she overruled the manager.

So at the last moment, we got an apartment and just a day before Halloween, the men and women were all in there fixing it up. We decided to convert one bedroom into a haunted house, and the other into a scary room with different activities for children.

The main room was to be the central hall for the adult guests to eat and socialize. It was to be a costume arrangement. It took more work and time than I wanted from my studies, but it turned into a big success and almost everyone from the terrace came to see it and bring their children. Even some local news television cameras from town came to take some video of the party and interview some of the guests.

That fall semester, besides the difficult A.I. class, I had to take a foreign language exam for Spanish that was the foreign language I knew best. I had hired a Cuban friend of mine to tutor me after class in the evenings, and she helped considerably to improve my oral skills of listening and pronunciation and my vocabulary. It was a crash course in a life-long language lesson plan. I put over a thousand new Spanish words on index cards and drilled myself daily until I knew most of them on the tip of my tongue.

We resumed classes in late August. A few weeks before, I got a telephone call from one of the professors in the department. I had been offered another TA-ship in a course on comparative primatology. I also decided, since it was to be our final year of graduate study, to go ahead and take out a $7,500 dollar student loan to help cover the expenses for the year. In fact, with the TA-ship, we only used about half of the amount, and put the balance to help cover the costs of fieldwork in Penang. Even now, as I write this book, I am still paying back that loan. We have since managed to knock it down to just under $2000.

Pursuing some aspects of anthropological study in knowledge representation, I decided to take a course in Artificial Intelligence being offered in the Computer Science Department. It was my first graduate course outside of the Anthropological milieu, and quite an eye-opener for me. It was from one standpoint one of the most difficult classes I ever had. It was also one of the least friendly and most competitive classes I ever sat in.

Auto-Anthropology

Many of the students, as I surmised by what I saw in class and in the corridors, were probably engaged in regular cheating. Especially, I felt, the few Mainland Chinese students who were always making the highest grades in the class but never seemed to be doing any real work. They were gaining answers from other members of their small and exclusive coterie, and even from a couple Chinese professors in that department. It proved to be my first experience with an alternate cultural pattern that was to prove itself even more evident in China six years later.

I went ABD (all but dissertation) in the spring of 1993, after two years study. I managed to take the right classes, after being notified of some special technical course requirements at the last moment, and in the end, my main mentor managed to have most of my credit hours from my previous programs transferred over to my completion of coursework for the degree. The examination consisted of a week of writing papers for questions posed by the various members of my committee, and finally an oral examination.

I had spent a great amount of time that semester writing research proposals and grant and fellowship applications. Of the many I sent out, I received only two grants. One came from the University itself. It was a travel grant for the amount of $600. The other was from the Pacific Cultural Foundation for the amount of $2000. I was a little disappointed by the amounts received, as I knew it would not get us very far in the field. Thus we finished the semester and I had nothing else to do but to go to try to get to the field. I had already submitted a request with the Malaysian government for permission to do fieldwork in Malaysia. It was supposed to take six months to get a reply.

We got rid of a great deal of our belongings that couldn't fit the small storage space that I had rented. I should have gotten a larger space. And then we ended up driving back to southern California one more time. I helped the Mormon family who was moving at the same time. He was lucky enough to land a lecturing job in art out at a California State University in his area of clay sculpting, and they rented a huge Ryder moving van and loaded all their junk into it.

Their small apartment was chock full of furniture, a piano, and new appliances that they had been acquiring. We reached California first, and when they got there, the husband called me and I went over and helped him to load all his belongings into a storage space. About a month later, he called me again, and I helped him to move his belongings to a nice new house he had found down 1-15 near Rancho California.

We had little else to do, and we decided to try to go to Malaysia early before we received our official authorization in order to try to get something started. It was a risky move, and a little expensive, costing us most of our extra loan money. But in hindsight it was probably crucial to the eventual success of the fieldwork there, as it gave us about a two-month period to break through some social barriers and get us oriented in the right direction. We came back from Penang Malaysia sometime in September, and we ended up spending the next few months working on my computer projects and putting together some of my tasks for my field methods.

I was quite intense on developing some AI type programs derived from my previous anthropological work, and I began making progress on this line of inquiry eventually. By about November, not hearing anything from the Malaysian Authorities for at least six or seven months, I decided to send another letter off, and then to make a few phone calls to the Malaysian embassy about it. It was fortunate that I did this because it was apparent that the paperwork had gotten stuck on some desk in KL, pending approval in three separate departments.

Eventually though, soon afterward, notification of permission to conduct fieldwork did arrive to me, but not the necessary paperwork that was supposed to be completed with it. Thus we were set to return to Penang, and we arrived back in mid-January just about a week before the Chinese New Year festivities were to kick off. It was a good time. It was warm but not so impossibly humid. We checked back into the Modern Hotel we had stayed at half a year before and received special rates just in time before the price-hiking season kicked in.

The plane flight over was, as usual, uncomfortable. The only saving grace of the interminable flight was a young Malaysian Chinese hostess who talked to my wife, and took a strong interest in my young daughter, even taking her up to the cockpit of the giant plane to visit the pilot. We

Auto-Anthropology

arrived in Penang having taken a hop from **KL**. We stayed in a small Malay run hotel the first night in **KL**. We woke up in the morning to find huge cockroaches crawling inside of a box of cookies we had carelessly left half open on the nightstand.

We checked back into the Modern hotel, and the management was surprised and delighted to see us back again. But the management had changed. A new rotund and gregarious middle-aged woman had won part shares in the establishment through gambling, and though she was quite friendly, she drank a lot, which was quite unseemly for a Hokkien woman to do in the first place.

Also she had two new cronies who were regulars in the hotel. It turned out that they were members of the Chinese secret society and were quite nefarious in their activities. It turned out, as the staff confided to us afterward, that they had been drilling holes through the walls of the rooms, from the back store room and other rooms, to peep at women.

Two American women had checked into the room next to ours. They were a mother and a young daughter duo who were from Southern California and who had decided to go trekking together. They were made to feel very uncomfortable in the hotel, and after the mother witnessed the rape of a woman in the field behind the hotel, which upset her greatly, they fled Penang in great culture shock without having given it a chance to have its charms sink in.

I felt sorry for them. I told them to get away from the hotel. It was obvious the two gangsters were making little holes through the plaster of the storeroom walls next to the American mother and daughter. The Americans found plaster dust on their bags and felt quite violated. Regardless of these unfolding and unfortunate circumstances, which the old management really regretted, we had a good New Year's dinner.

It was about a month into our stay there that I went to the local immigration office to see about my visa. I was concerned because I had only been granted a tourist visa on my entrance to Malaysia, and no one told me anything about what to expect.

At the immigration office I explained to the officer my situation and I showed him our papers and letters. He told me he could do nothing more for us but we would have to go back down to **K.L.** to straighten things out. That weekend we found ourselves on a flight back to **K.L.** Within two days we contacted the Prime Minister's office.

We were told there, finally, that we were supposed to have received official letters telling us of what we needed to do upon our arrival, and to have a research visa chopped with an identity card, but the letter had been mailed to the wrong address in California and therefore never reached us.

Thus we ended up taking an long and expensive taxi ride to the other side of **K.L.**, after having some passport photos and an special identity card made up, to the main immigration headquarters where we had to pay another nominal fee to have our visas chopped once again in our passports, good for one year. We got back to Penang within three days of our whirlwind tour with a severe case of diarrhea picked up from a *Maumak* hawker in the city.

I was intent on getting established in a research context, and knew that the hotel was inappropriate for this purpose. The management wanted us to stay, even to the point that they wouldn't help me to place a phone call outside, and I ended up having to go find some real estate agents in the city by myself in order to locate a decent place to rent.

We looked for several days, until we found a nice old second story of a Chinese style mansion in *Tanjung Tokong* not far from the beach. It had been owned by the deceased husband of the landlady, who was the God-mum of the young Chinese couple who lived on the bottom floor and who already had three little girls.

The main floor below us was being occupied by another older family of chicken hawkers who spoke loudly and crudely in a different dialect, and were at their job making money every day. We resided on the floor above them, and eventually, a young British couple came to reside on the top floor above us in a small one-bedroom apartment. The apartments were in a grand style with large balconies, huge cut-glass mirrors, red clay tiles and built-in closets and cupboards.

A Malay family had previously occupied the place. There was a large hall, three bedrooms, three bathrooms, a laundry room and two balconies off our own floor. There was also a kitchen. I was still receiving his mail and especially his electrical bills, which he had dutifully disregarded notifying of his relocation.

I even had to pay part of a month's bill that belonged to him, before I could get my own service established. But the apartment was filthy when we moved into it. The walls were completed covered by grim, grease, and the young Malay daughter's crayons. The kitchen looked as if it hadn't been cleaned for years.

At the bottom of the stairway leading down to the main floor, there was a two-foot heap of trash that had just been thrown down the stairs. It took us a good week to clean the place up, and I offered to the managers to paint the place to make it habitable for us, if they bought the paint. They bought the cheapest paint possible, and it was so thin it required at least two coats for to make it cover over all the dirt spots.

The aunt and uncle, the part owner of the Modern Hotel, offered to help us to clean the place, and they spent a couple of afternoons working very hard to help us. I paid them a small amount of money, but they at first refused any. It took us about a week to get it cleaned up. I was growing more and more anxious to get the research going, as we were already into our second month on the island, and beyond a few life-history interviews, had gotten little else going for the money we had spent.

But we were getting organized quickly. We enrolled our daughter into a day-care in the mornings. She at first liked this because the primary teacher was a pretty young Indian woman who had taken vows to become a Hindi nun and was always dressed in yellow. She was very nice and my daughter took to her right away. We would take her in the morning to the day-care that was at a private residence right on the coast below our house, and then take the bus downtown.

At first we began walking through the town conducting interviews with shop owners and doing surveys and census. We began mapping most of the central part of the city of Georgetown. We would return by bus early in the afternoon to the other side of the island in time to pick up our daughter and to settle in before the hottest part of the day.

After a couple of weeks of this routine we realized we were not getting very far, and I knew I needed to establish a community context for the work I was doing. One day we were down one street near Weld Quay and we noticed some tourists in trishaws going into the area of the city known as the Jetty and that was notorious for harboring criminals, gangsters and lower-class elements of Hokkien society.

On a lark we decided to follow the tourists into the area and, unlike any of the tourists, we sat at the coffee shop outside to take a break and talk to people. Soon an uncle had bought us a cup of coffee, and they took great interest in us as a mixed couple, and in the fact that my wife spoke Hokkien. In fact, my wife was born in that place not very far from that street, and her extended family probably came from the area surrounding.

We began asking and answering many questions, and then I had an idea that maybe these people would welcome us coming there to do further research work. They told us to come back the next day to talk to the leader of the community, a man whom they had called, somewhat uncomplimentary in manner, as "pig belly."

Pig belly met us at the same coffee shop the next morning and appeared quite kind and reasonable. He was a fairly large, middle-aged man, and seemed quite mild and sensible. I bought him a cup of coffee, which he acknowledged with a nod of his head. He told us it was OK if we came to do our work. He told us of a woman who had worked there a couple of years before.

I had previously tried to get permission from authorities to interview and conduct research in a local Kampong on the Island, near *Tanjung Bungah.* The old *Penghulu* welcomed us and was quite open to our presence in his community, but an UMNO party official showed up and refused us permission, explaining the intent to induce the people to relocate from the Kampong to new flats in order to make way for future development.

And so it was that we landed our primary research group during that year on Penang in 1994. We ended up going there everyday, spending most of the mornings there interviewing and talking to people. We did this for about the next eight or nine months. I started out to break the ice by

Auto-Anthropology

taking people's blood pressure and asking some basic survey questions and interviewing individuals and giving some fun color tasks. We continued on some off days and in the early afternoons, before returning to fetch our daughter, while continuing to do fieldwork also in the larger part of the town.

I came to focus on some particular aspects of the larger city pattern. We were soon invited into different people's homes and I began piecing together the facets of my study based on what I wanted to get done. One day, in one of the homes, the mother directly asked us if we could teach her kids English. I considered it, and the next day told her that I would do it if in turn those I taught would do some tasks for me. This was an acceptable arrangement and soon I was teaching three separate classes, once or twice each week, to young adults, some teenagers, and younger children on the Jetty.

In exchange for these lessons, I was provided with three groups of regular people of different age sets to do my symbolic framing tasks, and through this means I rapidly developed, tested and retested my Symbolic Framing battery and a host of other innovative tasks.

Up until that time, the problem with this level of the research was the lack of coordination and consistency in the study. People came and went and it was largely catch as catch could within the context of our limited time there. Thus I found the opportunity to teach English on a regular basis in order to gain a captive "control" group who would do the tasks for me. I also felt like I was giving something back to the community for their having given me so much time and opportunity to work there in the first place.

This work became the focus of my study for the next several months, though I carried on many other aspects of my field methods concurrently and intermittently. During that time, mostly the Spring and Summer of 1994, we lost the narrow network of friends and associates we had previously had in Penang, and we transformed in a curious way. We became much more independent there, and we reached a point that our previous connections did not have any real relevance to what we were doing.

I gained a considerable amount of self-confidence and a sense of independence in the conduct of the fieldwork itself and became quite adept at administering tasks, observing and taking notes, and giving interviews. This was an invaluable lesson, and soon we were accumulating reams of notes and assorted task papers. I had set up a little black and white photo lab in our flat, and in the afternoons would process the film from the day's work. We accumulated this way a huge dividend of photographic materials from our work there.

Our daughter was proving to have difficulty in her preschool, and we were not happy with her new primary care-giver, an Tamil Indian woman who seemed very distant, even possibly mean to the kids. We ended up cutting back her hours and days considerably, and letting her spend more time with us on the jetty. The families there all loved her very much, and she had much greater access to households than we ever managed. Soon she fit right in with the other kids of the Jetty. Because it was so hot, she ran around in her underpants only, like many of the other people there.

There soon emerged a fundamental schism in our daughter's behavior between school, where her behavior was increasingly negative, to the point of refusing to eat or do the tasks they requested of her, and on the Jetty where she knew almost no bounds and at every turn people were feeding her and shoving candy at her.

We ended up first removing her completely from the school by late summertime, and then even had to cut back taking her to the Jetty to get her straightened out. Thus it was that by October we had decided to begin phasing back our work on the Jetty, as it seemed that the people there were getting tired of answering all our interminable questions anyway.

I began putting an end to the tasks I was doing, and wrapping things up. It seemed provident that we should look at cutting our costs in the entire affair, and even return early enough to try to complete the dissertation write-up by Spring. I was in a hurry, after almost a decade of graduate study, to bring this phase of our life to a close. We had burned out on the Jetty a little ourselves, and it was growing increasingly difficult to justify to myself spending more of our limited resources in this way.

Auto-Anthropology

It was during the last phase of our work in Penang that we had gained the acquaintance of the British couple who lived above us and their coterie of British friends. They had moved in several months after us and were for a couple of months quite aloof and I considered unfriendly.

Finally, one evening, the young girl of the couple came down and asked us through the window if we knew a doctor for her boyfriend. He had been kicked in the ribs during a soccer match at the University. A couple of phone calls later and we were all soon in the back seat of my friend's car, going to the general hospital on the island.

Fortunately, my friend was acquainted with the main physician on duty, and our British acquaintance was soon taken in to be X-rayed within five minutes of our arrival. It turned out only to be a very severe and painful bruise, fortunately, and he had to pay only a small nominal fee for the x-ray and the painkillers he was given. We went back to our apartment and we ended up talking until the wee hours of the morning with our British friends.

The frosty British ice was broken, and we were soon in the middle of a network of about 18 British students, many of them paired off heterosexually, who were all attending a Malaysian language program at the University. I came to like these young British a great deal, and to admire their adventurous spirit abroad, and then took the opportunity to administer to as many of them as I could my symbolic framing study to gain a comparative sample that I had missed because of the politics of the study with the Malays and Indians on the island. A couple of them even accompanied me to the Jetty to observe what I was up to and soon were installed there with some of the more status conscious families teaching English to their children.

So it came to pass that our routines consisted mostly of getting up early in the morning and seeing our daughter off to school. We then caught the earliest bus we could downtown, always waiting dutifully for the Sri Negara bus as we had befriended most of the bus staff and learned a great deal from our daily intercourse.

We either went to the Jetty to try to finish up one end of the study or another, or else walked about on one errand or another downtown, to spend the mornings and early afternoons there, to return in the afternoon to fetch our daughter, then to settle in for the evening, frequently in the company of our new British friends.

In late October, I had given notice to our manager of our intention to vacate the apartment, and we arranged a flight out of Penang back to the U.S., which could not be secured for about a month later. Fortunately, the timing was pretty good in fact. The last month was spent constructing some crates in the afternoons and evenings to hold my research materials, and arranging for their shipment back to the U.S.

We shipped most of our materials out a couple of weeks before we left Penang, which was a week before Thanksgiving holiday back in the States. The last couple of weeks were spent in a strange kind of limbo for us. We were detached from most people there, and were growing a little homesick finally. I think to get the research done, we had put everything on hold for most of year, only to wake up at the end of it to discover that we were not at home there, and perhaps more than a little culture shocked.

Whatever is written about culture shock, I would say that it hits different people in different ways and at different times. For us perhaps, it had settled at that time deeper down in a sense of fundamental existential rootlessness--a sense of not feeling attached or like we didn't belong to anything. I gradually brought each of my English classes to a close, one after the other, and looked forward to the termination of what had become somewhat dull and routine for me. Already I was looking forward somewhat disparagingly to the next challenge of meeting more academic deadlines in the game of chasing my doctorate.

One day at the Jetty, I realized our time had come to an end, and the feeling seemed mutual, and I knew that when we left it, we would not be coming back to it. Many of the people sensed it as well, as if we did not really belong there after all.

For the first time, near the end of the study, I had begun walking around the other Jetty neighborhoods more and looking around at the larger scope of the place. I wondered why we did the things the way we did them, and not in some other way. Then, finally, we looked at the occasional tourists who sauntered down to the Quay, and we sensed that we were no longer any different—just transient beings waiting for our train to come.

The last week of our time in Malaysia in 1994, I booked a nice hotel room at the Lone Pine hotel down at *Batu Ferringhx*, the nice resort hotel along a short stretch of beach. It was the almost Northern-most outpost of world civilization on the whole island short of a set of workers flats, built just a little further up the coast. We had stayed at this hotel a couple of times previously, the first time back in 1986.

We liked it a great deal, compared to the neighboring luxury hotels. It was small, very quaint and relatively modest in price. It had the charm of having many nice Casuarina pines on the beach, with a nice lawn. It had been built in the 1950s and had wonderful *Meranti* and *Datu* wood furnishings. We took the room for about a week, and we invited as many of our Chinese friends and associates as we could. For about a week we had almost continuous visits from people, up until the last day we left.

The return to the U.S. was uneventful. I hardly even remember it now. I remember being met at the Penang airport by one of my students. They saw us off, and we were soon on the plane. We waited at the K.L. airport only a few hours before boarding the plane for the U.S.

We decided to cut short our time in Penang and booked a flight that got us back to the U.S. about a week before Thanksgiving holiday. I had previously shipped the four crates I had made full mostly of my research papers, and we went back to await their arrival. It was several weeks later and we were still waiting, when I by chance made a few phone calls to find out that the crates had already arrived and were sitting for a couple of weeks in some warehouse, ready to be claimed.

No one notified me. I went down in my minivan, and it ended up costing me another $130 dollars to pay for the warehousing of the crates and the forklift that put them at the edge of the loading dock. I had to back my van in and load the crates myself. I was very disappointed. It was apparent that a Taiwanese company had taken over and monopolized this end of shipping, and was realizing a tremendous middleman mark up for their 'services."'

Having gotten finally my notes, about three weeks overdue, I launched soon into the organization of my materials, and then into the analysis of the information, one section or set at a time. I had conceived of an overall framework for analysis, depending on type of task battery administered. I began working everyday, at least 15 hours per day, for the next four or five months in such a manner. I worked for about five weeks thus at my mom's house in Southern California, before heading back in the first two weeks of January to get settled in there before the semester began. It was my intention to have the dissertation finished by the end of the spring semester.

I was offered a TA-ship with my main advisor in his Hindu civilization class. It was yet another writing intensive course and my job of course was to read and reread all the students' written essays. I continued with the analysis of the information, into the middle of February, at which time I had begun to work on a rough draft of the dissertation.

My main advisor, kept encouraging me to submit the draft as soon as possible, as he worked on a first come first serve basis, and he had a commitment pending with some student in some other program. I got pretty pissed off at him when I finally did bring in a draft of my dissertation, only to have him refuse to look at it for several weeks so he could focus on this other student's, who was not even in our program. I could see that I would be getting no special favors from anybody, not even from my own primary mentor.

The next couple of months were spent mostly writing and rewriting the dissertation, and doing the students' essays, and continuing with the analysis of my data. Things began falling into place pretty tightly by the fourth month, and by the fifth the finished form had taken shape. It went through four successive versions, and went from about 2000 pages in total length to a finished form of about 250 pages, a not unreasonable reduction, especially when 95% of the photographs were removed. I also had problems with my committee membership, as both the external committee members from other departments were no longer available.

One was still in Malaysia on a visiting teacher program, and the other had mysteriously "left" his program because he had problems of not completing his own dissertation (no body told me about this issue beforehand.) I found a fourth and fifth committee member, both from within the program, and from without, in the department of psychology.

The cognitive psychologist was just the right individual to appreciate the work I had been conducting in cross-cultural psychology, and I had the least problems with him in this regard than with anybody else. Though he was busy, he was not unforthcoming in helping me.

I was so tied up in finishing the dissertation that I had blocked out all social relations besides counseling a few of the students for who I was a Teaching Assistant. It was not until the end of the semester, while I was waiting for my advisors to review the dissertation, that I had time to form new friendships in the Terrace.

The Taiwanese family whom we had known previously from the village was finishing his dissertation also, even before me, and he asked me to read the finished draft for English corrections. I did this for him, and when moving day came, helped them to load their things on the belated truck. I also formed a good friendship with the Argentine family that lived immediately across from us.

The wife had been a lawyer in Argentina and babysat mostly for Latin families during the day, while her husband, Roberto, was finishing his Master's Thesis in Agro-meteorology.

I defended my dissertation in July 1995. I did not consider five advisors meeting one more time and afterward never able to meet again, as one of them was leaving to Florida for a new position. In other words, we either met that afternoon or else I would never finish my doctorate. I successfully defended my dissertation. I walked outside and one after the other came out the door to shake my hand. One asked me what I intended to do next. He said I had no hope for a job in Academia because I was "a white man."

We returned to Southern California to stay once again with my mom in early August of 1995. I immediately began sending off letters of application to various academic positions, especially to one in Singapore that I was really hoping on. During the first month, I continued to finish a couple of manuscripts relating to my symbolic framing methods and inter-correlational analysis while doing applications and waiting to get some reply from them.

I think I worked so much on my little Mac power-book that I soon caused it to crash and had to rebuild my operating system, discovering in the process that the salesman I had bought the computer from back in late 1994 must have opened the box and taken the system software out, perhaps for the purpose of reselling it.

Anyway, after crashing my program, I more or less let go of the work on the research I had been doing. I read a few books in anthropology, and submitted a few of my works for publication to some journals. I mostly worked on all the job applications I could find to academic positions, high and low, far and wide. I did over two hundred such applications to schools domestically, and if I remember right, about 15% to schools abroad in one country or another. By January I was mostly watching and just waiting for all the rejections to begin coming in, one after another, while continuing to send out as many more applications as I could. I figured that I could gain at least one position.

By springtime, with my daughter in her first year of kindergarten, we were helping the teacher almost on a daily basis to put in a small garden for the kids. It was a very successful garden, installing my old drip system as well as mulching mostly with dried lawn clippings and straw hay that we had bought at a feed store in Yorba Linda.

I continued to hold out hope, but I watched one rejection after another come back to me. I applied for grants and post-doctoral fellowships, all to no avail. I even applied to a couple of Teacher's training programs in Tennessee, of all places, that looked fairly prospective. I came to learn that slightly over 300 new positions opened in Anthropology each year, though over 500 new PhDs were produced each year, with a growing backlog of anthropology graduates of some 200 per year.

Furthermore, this bottleneck had been happening for more than a decade. To top the problem off, I found out through The Chronicle of Higher Education that as much as fifty percent of these open positions were de facto reserved for students from foreign universities, thereby doubling the bottleneck produced on new American-made Ph.D.'s in

Auto-Anthropology

Anthropology each year. I figured the backlog amounted to possibly 20,000 PhD's over more than a decade with little chance at anything but a part-time or temporary adjunct position.

It was evident to me though by April that no jobs were forthcoming for me, and, besides being more than a little down about it, I decided that it was better just to get on the road by July and see where we would end up. So that was our decision.

About a week after my daughter's school had ended, we packed up our little van, had repair work done on it, bought new tires, and hit the road, not clear where we would end up. We had bought some camping equipment—new sleeping bags, utensils and a new self-supporting dome tent, with the idea of camping a little while along the way back east. I figured I would get back as far as Tennessee, to see if the program was real or not.

Not having a clear direction, clutching at tenuous straws cast from far away, we got in our small minivan in late July of 1996 and just drove away, hoping to find something better for ourselves down the road. We got up to Wyoming where we decided to put in for a day or two camping down at Flaming Gorge reservoir. It was hot, and the campgrounds were not very pleasant for us, lacking even the amenities of water or proximate toilets.

Rosie was miserable for the couple of days there, and made me know it. Finally we got in our car early and drove back up to Rock Springs. On a hill coming back, my car popped a belt. It proved to be the alternator belt. Fortunately we got into the town of Rock Springs and to a mechanic at a Texaco Station, who was willing to repair it for us, but it would take at least a day and we checked into a hotel just behind the station.

Little did we know that day that we would end up spending the next couple of years of our life there in Rock Springs. The car was not finished until early afternoon the next day, and we had already paid for a hotel room for another day. So we decided to spend another day in the city.

We saw the advertisement for the Dinosaur exhibit at the community college, and we found directions and drove up the hill to visit the exhibit. While there, we met a woman who was the curator of the museum there. We got talking to her and I told her I was a doctor of Anthropology, and next thing I know she was showing us around her collections in the back room behind the exhibition hall of the museum. She gave my daughter some small fossils and a piece of trona.

On the way out the next morning, we drove across the rest of Wyoming headed east, and by the time we had gotten into the western side of Nebraska, Rosie was crying and I had to stop. She didn't want to go on, though we drove across Nebraska, into Kansas, through Missouri, down to Southeastern Missouri where we cross the river at Cape Giradeau, and then made our way across the Southern tip of Illinois and then into Tennessee. We arrived at Johnson City in East Tennessee a couple of days later. I tried immediately accessing the program at the school, only to discover that most of my paper work had never left the desk of the admissions officer, and there was no knowledge of my intention to join the program.

A day spent fruitlessly at the school, where I was desperately pleading with one program member, finally led us to a hasty departure later that evening. The hotel we were at seemed insecure, and was run by an Indian woman. The locks on the doors were in disrepair, as was the entire room, and we were not comfortable there as there was much transience and trash coming and going. Finally, late into the night, I told Rosie to pack our things and we took off back down the road in the direction we came from. I drove most of the night, until I pulled into a truck stop somewhere in central Tennessee to sleep a couple of hours. I got up the next morning and we drove all the way back through Kentucky, Illinois and into St. Louis.

We ended up staying that night just west of Hannibal, Missouri. We decided to go back to Rock Springs and plant our flag there in that sandy ground. We rented a cheap hotel room there with a weekly rate and a kitchenette, and I commenced the job of searching for an apartment. In fact, we took the first apartment we looked at, after comparing it to a couple more. We liked the manageress, and we were soon headed back down to Southern California on a Grey Hound bus in order to rent a U-

Auto-Anthropology

Haul truck to bring our belongings back up. We had a week to get squared away, as Mahala had to begin first grade by then.

We had Mahala in school and I began looking for work. For a couple of weeks I went to interviews but had no luck. Nobody wanted to hire me, as I was 'overqualified.' I applied for a substitute teaching credential with the state and had to take a special examination to meet residency requirements.

In the meantime, our landlady, knowing I was a doctor of anthropology, told us of her friend, a restaurant owner, who had a book that he wanted us to take a look at. We went down one morning to the restaurant and left the hostess our phone number, after eating a breakfast there. About a week later the owner called us and we made an appointment to talk with him for that evening. We had dinner at the restaurant with him and his wife, who did most of the management and cooking in the restaurant.

It turned out to be a huge place, in excess of 7,000 square feet, with a large banquet hall, conference rooms, a full bar, etc. In fact, the place had a notorious reputation at one time of being the longest bar in the state of Wyoming, and a place of corruption where a federal drug agent had been assassinated by the local police just a few years prior.

They had an old book with the binding broken and in tatters. It was a story of the Robidoux. It turned out that the wife was a descendent of this family, and they asked me to do the necessary research to uncover her lineage and to figure out how the restaurant could be renovated in keeping with this story.

And so it was that I fell in with the owners of this restaurant. At first, for the first couple of months, they wanted me to plan a major renovation of the main area of the restaurant before the Holiday period. I came up with a Santa Fe style plan, in keeping with the name of the restaurant and the cultural tastes of the wife, who was part Native American. We planned new tiles, and the construction of lodge-pole columns dividing off the interior space.

We redid many of the walls, knocking out some, rebuilding the stage, retiling all the floors, painting and having the main framework of the timbers installed. We made their late November Thanksgiving deadline by just a day or two. After this was completed, they set me to work doing some carpentry work about the place, and we set up a small woodworking shop in a garage space nearby my apartment.

By that time, I had managed to get them in touch with a genealogist who had already reconstructed the majority of their family line—all they needed to do was to tie themselves and their family in at the bottom of the tree. It turned out that the wife was the direct patrilineal descendant of "Indian Joe" Robidoux, the son of the famous Joseph Robidoux of St. Joseph, Missouri. They then asked me to build an art exhibit on the theme of the Robidoux and the fur trade, and to collect art for a gallery.

Thus I built almost a hundred wooden frames, planned and executed an information exhibit incorporating about 25 information boards. I worked in that small space through the winter and early spring, sometimes when temperatures outside reached 50 below zero and all there was a small kerosene space heater. I did the matting and framing and the design of the entire exhibit.

By the time this was completed in early summer, we had more than a hundred pieces hung on their walls. At that time, the husband was unsure of which direction to proceed, and set me on the task of designing further renovations that would be suitable.

I made a couple of signs for the outside, and we put up a Teepee and I spent about a month painting this. I formulated several plans for them to consider, bringing in several outside experts to assist us. One plan consisted of a trading post/museum store distributed in nice cabinets located throughout the facility.

I set to work building a few of these cabinets—making three in all to begin with. Another plan was to have school children tour the facility and to enact shows on the stage. We hired a doctor of education local to the area that had done her work on the Mormon trail and she began writing us a script to use for such a program with small children.

She suggested that we build a Mormon handcart in keeping with the theme of the trail, and we found plans for this and found an historical Reconstructionist who had worked on Robidoux projects in Colorado.

Auto-Anthropology

He came up with a plan to renovate part of the interior to produce a
Fort/trading post. I also came up with an idea for installing a multi-media
presentation system on the central stage to incorporate normal dining
within this relatively unused area of the restaurant.

None of these ideas seemed attractive to the husband, who did not want
to invest the $10,000 or more each of the plans would have entailed. By
November, I told him that I had better just turn to on writing my book
on the Robidoux, based on all the information I had gathered during the
previous year. He was afraid of someone stealing the story or the book
or the whole thing, and grew impatient. So during the winter and spring
of 1997-8 I turned to finishing this book. I was in fact finished with it by
April of 1998, but it needed extensive editing and rewriting to be
manageable.

By then relations between the husband and myself had become strained.
I wanted to redefine our relationship in a way I thought would be
mutually better for both of us. As it was, with the amount of pay I was
receiving compared to the number of hours per week I had been
working, it came to almost a minimum wage. In December I took only
half pay from him, hoping that he would back off to a part-time position,
so that I could then gain the leverage for starting my own business.

What sealed my decision was the fact that in the second year of working
for him, the IRS took an extra eight hundred dollars of our savings, just
when we had accumulated enough to buy a CD with it or to invest in a
little parcel of land, which we were intending then to do.

They took us up on a weekend fling to Jackson Hole Wyoming, in early
spring, just as the roads had cleared enough for traffic to get safely
through. They tried to convince me to stay with them on a quasi-
permanent basis, though they could give me nothing in writing and no
sense of security. Furthermore, they were imposing a definition of my
professional identity that I found far too constraining, and in the larger
scheme of things, somewhat unrealistic.

The husband and I got into increasing arguments over copyright, as he
believed it to be a work for hire though no contracts were signed or
anything and the work was in fact a by-product of the entire project to
date. He wanted the rights to the entire book exclusively. I was afraid not

only that he would totally alienate my identity or authorship from the text, but also that he would actually take the book after I had completed it to a ghostwriter to butcher it in any way he saw fit. He asked me to research out copyright law, and when I reported to him that I felt, by law, that copyright was retainable by myself, he accused me of lying and trying to cheat him.

The husband had dreams of realizing a lot of profit from the book. I was willing to yield copyright to him, but felt very strongly that my authorship should not be alienated thus as he tried to do. I therefore quit him by May, and finished the book on my own, paying for its reproduction mostly with what little money we had managed to save from the year before.

Therefore I made about 25 copies of it myself, to distribute to archives and libraries. The husband found out and had me produce twenty more copies, and in total I made myself 51 copies of the book. We finished the book the very last day of our residence in Rock Springs, actually working the night before by the light of a drop-lamp hung from an outlet from outside because our electricity had been shut off.

We gave the husband and wife about 25 copies, and kept most of the rest for distribution. We left Wyoming in the early afternoon, just having finished packing up our few belongings. We were headed back to California before going to China, where I had managed to land a contract to teach English.

The trip back from Wyoming was very peaceful and pleasant. We were accompanied by storm clouds the entire way across the state and into Utah, which took the edge off the heat of the early summer and cast the greening landscapes in remarkable veiled vistas of shadow and clouds. Coming through Utah, we drove directly into a storm with lightening and wind swirling. We in fact drove southward on the freeway through Salt Lake City in the afternoon between three tornado wind funnels that were touching down. It was this in hindsight that I've come to miss most about Wyoming.

Auto-Anthropology

My motivation to go to China was based on two sets of factors that were only indirectly related to one another. In my deteriorating relationship with my employers, I needed a reasonable direction of escape. I did not look forward to becoming unemployed once again in Wyoming after going through what we had already done. The other issue was the unfinished agenda of my doctorate and conducting post-doctoral research in China related to some aspects of my doctoral research regarding computer-based simulation of cultural systems. Some Chinese were interested in this, and we had written a couple of grant proposals back in 1995-6, but nothing came out of it.

Thus, it was unfinished business in the background of our lives. In fact I applied to the position in China while applying to other positions in the U.S. through the Chronicle of Higher Education. I had done it on a whim, without taking it very seriously.

So I was surprised a few months later to receive an acceptance letter, and then an e-mail from a foreign affairs person in central China. At the moment, Rosie really did not look forward to going to China. Her own job was working out well for her and she was gaining status and pay, though it was hardly enough to sustain us.

In fact, I was very unsure of China myself. The first set of prospective schools there in fact refused me, after offering it to me and then offering it to somebody else. But soon I received a phone call very early in the morning, to be told that I would be teaching at a small teacher's college in central China. I agreed to this, with the proviso that I would be allowed to conduct the research I had intended to.

We had to rush through a set of medical examinations, which, in order to clear their requirements of official seals, in fact had to somewhat fraudulently use and complete the forms using only a notary public's signature. If I had known then the implications of this convoluted bureaucratic procedure, I would probably not have ventured to China at all.

We stayed in California just a few weeks. I was waiting for the Chinese embassy to finally chop our passports, which they did by the very last day of the posted period. It was getting late in August, and the semester there was supposed to begin in just a week or two. I was impatient to get my family resettled before the semester began. As it was, I had already had enough bullshit from the Chinese, between the medical exams and the embassy and their foreign affairs people. The last day, I was very uncertain about it all, and almost just got back into the car to drive back the way we came.

But the day soon came to pack up our things for China. We bought a new set of luggage, some nesting suitcases with little wheels, for only $29. I had three computers to carry with me, on the expectation that these would be used for doing some of the research and development work. The foreign affairs person with whom I was in contact was somewhat vague and sketchy about anything, and I should have taken this then as a sign that something may not be quite right.

On the eve of our departure, I had spent over $500 in faxes to China, and had almost 10 pieces of luggage loaded with our belongings and things to do field research with. I had also shipped off two sea-bags loaded with textbooks and other materials for teaching and research I was expecting to get done.

We went to China, not knowing what we were getting into, with no expectation of real pay or savings, giving up most of what little bit we had accumulated, overloaded with junk and quite ill-prepared for what we were actually getting into. We arrived in China early in the week in late August. We landed at first in Beijing. We were ushered off a plane to be greeted by a host of uniformed security officers, all looking as if they were in the military. My feelings were very ambivalent, as I am sure my wife felt strangely too. The sense of oppression greeted us at the door as much as the humidity would greet us at the door of the plane in Malaysia. It was a sense of oppression that would not leave us finally until after our departure a year later the following July.

We stayed in Shanghai for the first several days. The foreign affairs man who met us struck me from the very beginning as affable, but falsely friendly and it did not take me very long to begin not really liking this fellow very much. I will call him Mr. Z. He was tall and skinny and he brought his wife with him. She had never been to Shanghai before and she was relatively fat and short, unusual for a Mainland Chinese woman for which a history of periodic famine and cannibalism selected for thin women.

Auto-Anthropology

They were an odd couple, and I bemused about them somewhat extraordinarily. Their little boy was friendly enough, but he caged around like a monkey enough to become especially annoying to my wife. With each passing day the foreign affairs person rubbed me the wrong way worse and worse. The first night, we got in two taxi's and one got lost getting to the hotel, when it did finally arrive, an argument ensued between the waiting taxi driver and the foreign affairs person over extra payment for the half-hour spent waiting. It was already 2 or 3 in the morning and we were all too tired to stand the bullshit.

A couple of days later I bought him and his wife a nice dinner at the hotel we were at, and I became quite embarrassed by his arguing with the main hostess over the charge for the tea. I did not mind the cross-cultural aspect of it, but felt, even from a Chinese standpoint, that such vociferous argument in a nice place was a little bit embarrassing.

Going back to the train station to go to the school a day later, I was really upset when we got in two taxis but his sped off and left my wife and daughter in the rear taxi stopped at a traffic signal. We became separated in the crowded streets of Shanghai near the train station for at least an hour, and when we finally did reconnect my daughter was broken down in tears and my wife was near tears. Then he had the gall to get into another argument with some poor porters, a family, to carry our bags but refusing to pay just a few Yuan they wanted.

The train took more than twelve hours, and we arrived in *Zheng Zhou* station the next day. We had to maneuver our heavy bags into a small waiting room to wait for our connection. He never told me anything, even if I asked him, but acted impatiently with things. We waited a few hours there in a squalid and overcrowded room, with men spitting all over the floor and a couple of women in military uniforms shouting at them as if they were caged animals.

We finally got on the train for *Xinyang* and we arrived in the evening exhausted, hot and thirsty from a long trip. I noticed our foreign affairs person was buying food for his wife and himself, but would not even offer to buy us some, so before leaving for *Xinyang* I insisted that we go buy some food and drink to quench our insatiable thirst and hunger.

We were quite disappointed to find only hot sodas and funny bread that was greasy and relatively unappetizing. We passed through a small town and the foreign affairs person pointed out his father's home. We went on a half-hour more and arrived in *Xinyang*. We came off to be greeted by more crowds and waiting taxis.

We arrived at the school to find only mounting disappointment. We were ushered down a dark and damp hallway at the basement of a hotel, to find our new "apartment" in the back basement, semi-subterranean. The bathroom was stopped completely from a plugged drain, and the floor was flooded with filthy water. The entire rooms were filthy. Furniture consisted of odd cast-offs by the hotel. It was not the worst of it though. That night the Foreign Affairs person had arranged a special dinner at the campus restaurant.

He had told the chef to serve us fried chicken and French fries (alas, Chinese style) because we were Americans. We were hot, tired, dirty, and wanted to rest and clean up, and all he seemed to really care about was parading his new 'prize' around the campus for people to see.

In hindsight I guess we disappointed him at least as much as he proved disappointing to us. Not only were we not as he expected, but we were perhaps more than he was counting on. The meal we ate was horrible.

We waited in a small room at a vinyl couch. The glass top coffee table was so filthy with grease and grime it looked as if no one had bother to wipe it off for months, even years. We were to eat at a large round table by the door. There along the wall ran a rat, one of the Foreign Affair's 'squirrels.' A young waitress who was wearing a Chinese evening gown, or Cheong Sam served us tea. When we went to sip the tea we found what we took to be pubic hairs in the teacups. We politely set the cups back down without drinking.

Soon (a half-hour later) the food was brought in on large plates. We sat down to a meal of chicken heads chopped up in sliced potatoes and a kind of river fish that was not very tasty. He had a couple of bottles of the local beer. It was called "*Ji Gong Sh*an" beer (or *Ji Gong* Mountain). It was probably the worst tasting beer I ever had, and I don't think in the year there I could ever finish an entire bottle of the stuff. It has a slightly sweet flavor, as if it had been fermented with some kind of fruit, and it always had an off-taste (I never finished an entire liter bottle for what remained floating around at the bottom.)

But Ji-Gong Shan was good for getting a large party going at little expense. It was sold in sets of ten bottles bound together at the stems with plastic raffia so that the bottles formed a bundle. This bundle of ten one liter bottles cost the equivalent of about U.S. $1.60 and it became quite apparent to me in the course of the year that alcoholism, even among students in broad daylight, was not an uncommon problem in central China. I drank a couple of glasses of the warm beer with my host, and he wanted to get more, but Rosie insisted on our precipitous return to our new apartment. I was in agreement with her.

We lost our appetites when we saw the chopped up chicken heads starring at us, with exposed brains and gobblers and beaks and all. I offered for the foreign affairs person to take the plate home to his own family to eat, since he said that it was his son's favorite meal, and since they must have been hungry from the long train trip like we were, but he refused. I managed a bit of the fish but it did not have either texture or flavor but had a peculiar smell that was almost like mud or algae.

I was almost a little insulted by everything, as if this was an elaborate but crude joke being played on us by our hosts, and it proved not far from the truth. I looked the foreign affairs person in the face and told him in no uncertain terms that even in Malaysia we would not feed such food to dogs. We must have really disturbed and disappointed our Foreign Affairs person because we proved not to be the gullible Americans he expected us to be. From that time on my distrust in him and in the other authorities only grew worse. Not only were they insincere, but they were incredibly poor and inveterate liars.

We returned to the apartment with a confused state of shock mixed with both hunger and exhaustion. The place was a total mess, and we had not the will to unpack any of our bags. The only thing we wanted was to flee as soon as possible out the front gate and back to the train station to reverse the long and laborious journey we had just completed. We felt stuck in the middle of a world completely distant and cut-off from everything we had known. We were beyond a mere case of culture shock--this was cross-cultural disaster.

By Two A.M. that next morning, sleepless and still in a dazed state, I had reached a conclusion that these people were either totally inept or without moral fiber. I could not accept this judgment anthropologically, and I decided that maybe they lacked any sense of class and refinement at all, which I also found to be anthropologically incredible. I could not but help wonder if this was not the cumulative result of the work of communist liberation, the true state of 49 years of communist repression and totalitarianism.

I realized in a state of horror what I had gotten us all into, and I felt miserable. Rosie was insistent that we leave as soon as possible, and I was in agreement with her, except that I didn't think we could get very far by ourselves before the authorities would detain us, and escort us back to our abode. Were we therefore in a prison basically against our wills? In a sense it was true and that was part of the issue on a fundamental level. An existential sense of a fundamental loss of control plagued us the entire year, and crept up on us increasingly to undermine our psychic dispositions in ever more perfidious ways during the course of our sojourn.

Such was our first and most lasting impression of our China sojourn. We felt very vulnerable stuck in the middle of a completely alien world. We were fundamentally at the mercy of a single individual, our dear Mr. Z., who was himself quite insincere about anything and proved in time to be quite nefarious in his dealings with everything.

He showed himself eventually to be an out and out liar, and in the course of the year not only perversely stood in the way of any research I tried to get done, but was reading our personal mail, particularly the letters sent from my mom, and he was regularly spying on us from the room above.

How much of this activity had been an authorized part of his job, and how much was merely a function of his sociopathic predisposition will never be clearly delineated. He had cultivated an unusual skill in speaking English, and this was his ticket to a good position next to the President of the campus.

He had above average intelligence, and his eyes would shift and flit in a peculiar nervous habit whenever he appeared to be thinking about something else privately. But this did not offset his basic spinelessness of character. He was the main English translator for the entire city and surrounding area that probably encompassed a total of half a million people.

We arrived about four days before the beginning of the semester. I spent the first two days and nights cleaning the apartment as best I could. My wife had gone through a period of psychological denial and refusal, insisting at every turn on our immediate departure. I scrubbed all the walls and all the floors, and tried to arrange the odd pieces of furniture in a way that would be suitable to us.

The first six weeks were perhaps the most difficult. It took about a month to get used to things enough to even find food for us to eat. After about the first week, when Mr. Z had managed most of his paperwork, there was little else he had to do with us that was not somehow a "control" function.

In a sense I knew we were pretty much on our own. Some more aggressive students did mediate for us that month. Our diet fell to pieces, and by the end of September we had hardly eaten more than noodles and crackers, and were starved for protein to the point of having early symptoms of protein-calorie malnutrition.

Our breakthrough came when the Fall National holiday sent our normal "mediators" away on Beijing holidays, and a new group of milder students came and told us where to get food behind the campus. My wife went with a couple of the female students, and from then on for about a month or two we began buying real food there, enough to keep us from feeling hungry.

At the same time, by then, my family's 'care' packages began arriving with enough dietary supplements to off set our chronic hunger.

It did not take very long to realize that we were in our hotel room invaded by numerous rats and the first three months of our time there was marked by regular attempts to kill them without mercy. They had gnawed holes through the door jams at the bottom and created a pathway that led probably through the entire hotel and out beyond. I lifted cement and sand from the many construction areas around the campus and I closed in as many of the holes as I could find.

Fortunately, I had my mom mail us some rat poison, so after the first month I baited them in the kitchen area, and in the room next to ours, as well as outside and in our own rooms. In such a manner, after a couple of weeks, I managed to keep most of the rats at bay within our own area. They seemed to be a bit territorial, and I knew that in time they would come invading from the area from behind the hotel and the forest that was just on the other side of the wall that held back the earth in our compound area.

About two months into the affair, I found the package of rat poison in the adjoining bedroom that we normally kept closed and vacant to be totally chewed up and eaten. I referred in my classes to the rat family who lived next door, and I invited them to dinner. Occasionally we would find a dead rat smelling underneath a piece of furniture or in the morning having tried to get out the door we sealed to find fresh air. During the first month there, I kept hearing noises in the bathroom area above the old tub.

Everything in the bathroom was jerry-rigged and there were numerous spaces for things to hide and crawl in. One night I heard a sound of splashing from the bathroom in the wee hours of the morning. I got up to discover a mature rat splashing in the toilet bowl, trying to get out but unable to get a grip on the porcelain. I don't know if he had fallen accidentally in from above, or tried swimming up from underneath. I grabbed my baseball bat I had brought with me and I tried smashing him, which I eventually accomplished but not before having cracked a hole in the porcelain of the bowl.

It was not only the rats, but numerous centipedes that liked the constant moisture in the drains. Some grew to eight inches in length and looked very tough and intelligent from a standpoint of natural selection. I counted about forty centipedes that I killed or captured within the premises of our dwelling in the course of the year.

Such was our introduction to China. I was almost immediately engaged in teaching, and the first couple of months were spent really trying to get my feet on the ground in this regard. I was overloaded with classes, virtually teaching all four grades in English, and the senior grade in two classes. I can say I really learned my English in that semester, but it left little time over for anything else. I fell pretty sick just before Christmas time, and had to lay up in the darkness of the bedroom for a couple of days.

The first semester was difficult, but the second semester, which resumed at the end of February after a month-long and much needed Spring break, went much more smoothly. I had really gotten my act together and I insisted on cutting back the number of class-hours, essentially eliminating two of the least productive and most antagonistic grades in order to concentrate on the two grades that seemed to need and appreciate my help the most.

Things went better in the second semester than the first, and proceeded quite smoothly up until news the middle of the second semester when the American bombing of the Chinese embassy in Yugoslavia touched off a near violent student action on the campus, most of which seemed directed at us.

The wintertime was the most difficult for us because of the cold and damp of our dungeon. So much moisture came through the walls that where the light did not penetrate, there was a constant film of moisture and a strange algae growing on the walls, under all the furniture and all the other unseen nooks and crannies. It was cold and there was no heating. The walls were basically brick without any insulation. The ground surrounding us except for the front came up above head-level.

We had one small electric space heater that would produce enough heat to warm about a three foot radius from its front, and if we were not at class bundled in four or five layers of clothes, we were huddled in front of this small heater wrapped in all our blankets and quilts. We stayed this way through the Christmas season and into February, when at the end the days began lengthening again and the shadows emerging stronger on the tiles through the bars of the windows.

It was not entirely bitter that first semester. We found considerable consolation in the kindness of a few of our students who had large hearts. We took their friendship quite seriously. We had no connection with any faculty members of the campus. The most they seemed to want to do was get me out and get me so drunk I would make a fool of myself. I was warned about this beforehand, so I avoided such a situation as best I could. I did not mind, as I liked the younger students a great deal. We put on a nice Halloween party, and then a Christmas party, that was quite successful for many of my students.

Things worked much better for us during the first half of the second semester. I had formulated a teaching regimen that minimized the labor input and maximized the gain from the students, and the students seemed to be enjoying their classes more. I adopted a radical approach that deemphasized the examinations, for which I discovered a pattern of chronic cheating even involving key department and school leaders, and an approach was very daring and unconventional from the Chinese perspective.

I was taking my students out regularly to do activities outdoors once it warmed up, encouraging them to use their English loudly and in public situations. We maintained the normal schedule, but got so much more accomplished at the same time. Within a couple of weeks of the semester, we had also organized a student library that started in one class and soon came to incorporate almost all of the students of the English program as it fulfilled a strong need of the students for extra books within an open framework. We met with some resistance from the authorities, and I found out through connections that Mr. Z, the Foreign Affairs person was trying to destroy the library in almost anyway he could.

He would block letters the library sent to the President of the campus, throwing them in the trashcan, and he recommended to the President that the library be destroyed and the books confiscated. This was only the beginning of a sordid and lurid story that involved manipulation, illicit sexual misconduct, lying, spying and cheating. It was all too much to bear, even with a grain of salt or a glass of beer.

But everything about the second semester, whether positive or increasingly negative, paled in significance to the bombing episode. We heard news about it first from one of my students in the morning. The Americans had bombed the Chinese embassy in Sarajevo. Soon Mr. Z showed up and told us that we had better sit tight and not go out much, and explained what he knew of the unfolding story.

Auto-Anthropology

By evening a number of my students showed up to be with us. Groups had been forming all day long under our apartment below the wall, and slogans and hate posters had been pasted on the walls directly below our apartment along the main thoroughfare of the campus. My students didn't want to leave, and it grew very restless outside after dark.

We heard stones often pelting the walls outside. A couple of windows could be heard breaking above us. We slept very little that night and several students slept in our main hall and in the room next door. The next day, and the next couple of days, we couldn't go out. A student demonstration and march was held that led down the thoroughfare of our apartment in the afternoon. The students had been organized and mobilized by party leaders from above.

Their mobilization was remarkable, and it was clear that the communist party leaders, ever secretive, were behind it all. Police in riot gear showed up in some vans and cordoned off the hotel in the forest and in the parking lot on both sides of our apartment, and school officials were all over the place.

It was at that point that my spirit broke. I sat in our kitchen area where I was trying to grade my mid-term examinations above the den of the shouting students. I decided it just wasn't worth being there any longer and wanted to return as soon as possible to our own country.

Later that week I communicated to Mr. Z my desire to terminate the contract. I was not too surprised when in fact he seemed almost happy and relieved to let me go, and I found out afterward that he hoped to gain some cash out of the default on the contract for himself.

But the students and the President of the college all encouraged me to continue, though I saw that the context for doing the active teaching I had been pursuing before the bombing was all washed away. It was hard to teach before forty students at a time, when you knew on some level most of them hated you or despised you for being an American. It made the remainder of the semester difficult.

We were in fact confined to our apartment area for a couple of weeks and were told not to venture beyond the school gate. I could not go out on campus by myself without groups of students catcalling and even aggressively confronting me. It was bad enough from the beginning--a sign of more than 90 percent closure of the people to the outside world. But it was even worse after the bombing, as a lot of poor and frustrated students didn't need many excuses to find vent for their anger and pent-up hostility.

A week later I did go out, and the posters were still on the walls, and I stopped to read them on the way to class, and one had a picture of Clinton with a Hitler mustache painted on, and another exclaimed in red letters "blood for blood." Unlike the library posters we had put up in the same location earlier that semester, these were not torn down the first hour of their appearance, but remained untouched on the walls long enough for the rain to eventually wash them away.

We returned in July, the day after the finals were finished. The finals went quickly and relatively smoothly. A little cheating was unavoidable in China, but they were as fair as I could manage them under the circumstances. By the end of the year in China, we had grown adapted to the local context. Food was no longer a big problem—in fact we grew fond of some of the local diet and rarely ate what was sent to us from Overseas anymore.

Mahala had developed a coterie of Chinese girls and was talking fairly fluently in her own Chinese style. She even looked quite like a young Chinese girl. In the end, the Foreign Affairs person tried to send us back unescorted, knowing we would have difficulty. But the secretary to the President, whom I had befriended and trusted, accompanied us with his girl friend, saying our final farewells to a handful of my closest students at the train station. We stayed two or three days in Shanghai before departing in late July.

We returned a year ago from the time of this writing. Our return from China, unwittingly marked probably the worse period of our married life—nothing seemed as before, nothing, especially ourselves, didn't fit in and we felt estranged and unfamiliar in an odd way.

When I got back, we stayed about a week with my Grandma before we got on the road to go back east to look for a place to live. We drove back as far as St. Joseph, Missouri, and then backtracked and drove through most of Wyoming. We landed in Lander in Riverton County, Wyoming.

Auto-Anthropology

It was a nice little town and we decided to give life a go there, but finding
a place to rent proved difficult. We had most of our things in storage still
in Rock Springs.

After we managed to secure a place, we returned to Rock Springs,
renting a large Ryder Rental Van. We loaded it all up and then drove
back over South Pass to Lander, only to discover when we got there that
the people who were supposed to meet us there to rent the place never
showed up. We waited several hours and tried making phone calls, but
to know avail. Loaded down with a huge truck, we didn't know what else
to do but to get back on the road and drive back down to Rock Springs.

We explained it to the rental guy who let us keep the truck loaded a few
days longer until we could work something out. Rosie's friend from
where she had previously worked found us a small but nice apartment
downtown, and we decided to take this. We stayed there all of two or
three weeks.

I found out over the Internet that my previous employer at the restaurant
there had filed copyright of the Robidoux book with his own name as the
author, and this destroyed me. It undermined my desire to be there any
longer, and, so giving up on most of what we owned, passing it to the
Mormon "Bishops Closet" we left Wyoming one final time with only our
books and old research papers. We returned to Southern California
where we are still currently residing.

While in China the previous year during December I had a bit of a mid-
life mini-crisis, and I had decided that I wanted to go into my own
business. In our life circumstances that seemed like the best thing we
could do for ourselves. I had been planning this since then and now was
anxious to try to put my plans in motion. I am still at it even now.

Here we are now. It is late October. We have been back at my mom's
house since last October. I have been continuously working on my
business, mostly over the Internet. I reached a crisis period in late
January of 2000, full of uncertainty about our future and realizing that
Southern California was a dead end for us. At that time I put out about
thirteen applications to community colleges throughout California, as

well as one application to a graduate program at Humboldt in Northern California.

I received rejections eventually from most of these schools. I did get admitted to the Humboldt program, and to me, Humboldt didn't sound like an unreasonable deal, as it was more or less aligned with my own professional and private interests, at least on paper. Of course, it was hard to be certain of anything under our circumstances. As summer approached, all I got were rejections from my job applications. I was most angered by the local community college. I got back a little green post card telling me I was not selected for an interview. I was so angry by it that I tore it up.

Afterwards, I thought better of it and taped it back together again. Now I call it my "green card" and keep it as a reminder of the contradictions of our current system. If I felt under qualified for these jobs, or if I felt like the people being hired to them were more qualified, then I would not mind the near blanket and absolute rejection.

But to know that I spent so many years of my life gaining the qualifications, and that those being interviewed were probably far less qualified, but probably mainly selected for their ethnicity, I found disturbing. As my wife says to me now, these are jobs that we should be getting, and that others probably far less deserving are taking from us.

My wife and I went up to Humboldt in mid-April to look around there during my daughter's Spring break. It was a pleasant trip. We left about 3:00 A.M. on Sunday morning and drove up through the central valley and veered over the coastal mountains near Lake County just north of Sacramento. It started to rain as we got into the mountains, and it rained the entire next day while we were up there, and the entire week, in fact. We drove through the mountains and then up Highway 101 through "redwood alley." It was beautiful in spite of the rain.

We got into Humboldt at just about 4:00 P.M. Sunday afternoon. We ate in a Chinese Restaurant just on the Highway in downtown Eureka to get our bearings. The Chinese food proved to be some of the worst we had ever eaten--not remotely like anything my wife ever cooked. We then drove up to the small town of Arcata to be next to the campus. We

Auto-Anthropology

checked into a small hotel off the main highway, and settled in for the evening while it rained.

The next morning, we checked out of the room fairly early, ate some donuts in a small coffee shop downtown Arcata, run by a Thai woman, and then we made our way to the campus to walk around a bit. I found a small map of the campus and then we walked to the environmental sciences department where I was supposed to be a student.

I found nobody around but one woman who seemed quite self-conscious of her own underdog status as a junior lecturer in the program. I left a note for my primary mentor in his mailbox and then we looked at the bookstore and the main center of the campus. I was astounded by the huge trees growing on the campus, and found it to be the most impressive thing about it. Especially near the playing track there was a huge Eucalyptus tree that was in girth as round as any of the redwoods nearby.

Not knowing what else to do with ourselves, and missing our daughter after only one day, we decided to leave early and head back down to Southern California. In the parking lot we met a woman who wanted to take our parking space, as there were not enough for all the students, and we pulled our van out and got into a conversation with her. She was a middle-aged returning mother who was moving back onto apartments on campus. She told us it took her six weeks to get an apartment there the first year.

We drove back south down the highway in silence for a while, the rain coming and going intermittently. We stopped to take a break in a redwood grove about an hour down the highway. It was pretty, near the Eel River. Rosie and I were talking about the school. She was disappointed by it all, as I was also. It seemed too much like going backward in our life. She was crying in her unhappiness. We walked by the river as I tried in my own cold manner to console her about our sad state of affairs. I understood that she was very unhappy about a prospective move to Humboldt, and about my becoming a student again in such a program.

We talked as we drove back south, and in an hour or so she seemed to be feeling much better. We drove down 101 through Napa Valley and then into San Francisco area, across the Golden Gate Bridge, and we got temporarily turned around downtown, which seemed busy and chaotic. We finally got back onto the 101 South, and ended up stuck in traffic through Silicon Valley. We couldn't believe how much San Francisco had grown and become impacted even in the last decade since we were there during my daughter's first year.

We had intermittent rain and clouds and sun the entire trip back down, and we got into L.A. at about 1200 P.M. at night. Later that week we decided to take our daughter and my mom down to San Diego to Sea World. It was still a little rainy, though we managed a good morning at the amusement park until the rains came down harder in the mid-afternoon. The park was interesting, but a bit disappointing compared to the expectations we had of it based on the commercials advertised on television.

On a whim, after we left the park, we decided to look for my father's gravesite at Rosecrans National Cemetery. It turned out that we were not very far from it, and my mom had thought enough to bring her papers that had the number of the grave. We got into the cemetery just about 15 minutes before it was closing. It was still raining intermittently. We drove around looking for the grave, but couldn't find the matching numbers or even the alphabetically arranged areas. On a whim we drove down to a second, third and fourth entrance to the cemetery, which stretched along the main road that ran through the Naval base there up to the Point Loma National Park at the end of the finger of land that jutted out into the sea.

On a hunch I pulled into the last entrance that was a small circular drive in the middle, and without even looking at the numbers on the graves I knew the location from more than thirty years before. When we drove near the place that the funeral had been, I strangely recognized the hillside, the road, and even the trees, which had grown quite larger by then. We found his grave not far off the road. My mom immediately broke down crying.

Rosie commented on the wonderful *Feng Shui* of the place. It overlooked the bay that was mainly dominated by the Navy installations directly below us and on the other side. I recognized the San Diego airport and a part of the Marine Corps Boot Camp nearby. Both Mom and I had tears in our eyes from some deep source within that we had kept locked up probably for the entire thirty-five years. It started raining again and after a few minutes during which we took a few photos, we got in the car and drove up to Point Loma at the end.

The facilities at Point Loma were all closed, but we found some restrooms and in the rain I walked my daughter to the lighthouse that overlooked the vast Pacific Ocean. It had all brought back haunting memories from an earlier and almost forgotten period of our lives. I do not know if ghosts dwelled at that cemetery ground and beyond at the lighthouse, but it would probably be a good place to hold a seance.

We returned to Arcata for a couple of days to renew our search, but it was not long before we realized we were making absolutely no progress and spending more than a hundred dollars a day. So we decided to abandon the Humboldt idea.

On the way back down we stopped at a small roadside state park with a redwood grove and ended up camping there for a day near the Eel River. It was the same place my wife and I had stopped at on the previous sojourn to Eureka. This time it was sunny out. The river was only half the size it was in April.

Mahala went swimming and in the evening I took her out swimming again and we tried to catch the trout under the water using my daughter's goggles. We could see the fish almost within arm's reach, and we spent a good hour or two in shear delight in the shadows of the evening. Needless to say, on our return journey the next day the most my daughter and I caught was the flu, and we did not get back to Southern California too soon to feel the full brunt of the symptoms over the next few days.

In a week we had taken the back bedroom and converted it into a small office. I am sitting there now, writing this. It has been about six weeks, and we have slowly managed to get the business off the ground. I applied for car registration and have been walking through the steps in declaring myself a legitimate businessperson. Things have improved a bit for us in this time, even though we have no money and are in some debt. Not two weeks after I made my final decision just to remain where we were at, I received a phone call from an apartment manager up at Arcata asking me if I was still interested in an apartment, but I told her she was about a month too late.

So this is where I am at now in this unfinished story. I am sitting in front of my computer, writing this story as a conclusion to another chapter in our life, and perhaps as a prelude to what may lie ahead of us.

Sometimes I would give anything to have a sense of what lies around the next bend on our road. I know that I am anything but conventional or even convention-bound.

I have learned that nothing in life is without its contradictions. I must struggle everyday and with too many sleepless nights with the complete lack of status or support within our system. I have become a total pariah in our society. I mean this in an absolute sense of almost complete social isolation and exclusion.

In regard to my anthropology, I've come to terms with it in my own life. I continue to take my own professional identity as an Anthropologist quite seriously, even though nobody else but my wife does also, and even she has her critical doubts that are tied to our chronic underemployment

My opinion of American anthropology has changed considerably over the years, and, simply put, I can no longer afford to look to them or count on them professionally for my sense of identity or self-worth in the world. I have learned to begin defining myself as an anthropologist professionally and independently of any academic context, and fundamentally, I feel better about this than to continue to wait to receive more "thin slips" in the mail.

I have come to the conclusion that Anthropology and anthropologists are mostly class-tied and professionally self-serving, preoccupied with their own ego-status identity in the world, much more than they probably were in a by-gone era of Margaret Mead or even Napoleon Chagnon. Unfortunately, the political atmosphere surrounding the articulation of Anthropology in academic departments across the country leaves a lot leftover to be desired.

I do not take the professional ostracism and discrimination very seriously any more. I simply can't afford to. I consider through experience

Auto-Anthropology

American society, and the vast majority of participants within it, to be too caught up in the class system to see themselves objectively within it. But in this most Americans are not so different from any other human beings on earth. The small world contexts I found articulated in every anthropology department I was ever associated with, were not so different from the small world contexts of any other social situation I was involved in over the years, whether in the U.S., or Malaysia or China. On a basic anthropological level, people behave in such settings in a very predictable and characteristic manner.

It all mostly seems grandly hypocritical to me now, but I have not abandoned my faith in myself nor in my anthropology in the world. Most illusions about being an anthropologist in the world are destroyed now. We live now in a strange, anti-climactic kind of limbo. Anthropology for me exists in the world primarily, intrinsic and extrinsic to it, and is no longer context-bound within narrow academic parameters determined by an even narrower political culture.

Even if I had managed to land that golden opportunity of a real instructor job in Academia, I doubt I could ever now reconcile myself anymore to such a narrow vision of Anthropology or of the world squeezed through its fractured lens. And yet, in the final analysis, I cannot lay the blame fully at the doorsteps of the Anthropologists. They are guilty perhaps of some hypocrisy and double standards, but they are mostly the products of the society that made them, nothing more and nothing less. And, in the end, I must include myself as an unfinished anthropologist as well.

Part Three

I made a decision to remain in Southern California in August of 2000 and for the first month and a half focused upon trying to organize my business scheme without any capital to invest with. By October, I came to focus in my room converted into an office upon writing a book entitled Natural Systems (it was general system theory,) and this book progressed rapidly through the next eight weeks, in which almost all of my time was devoted to the project. It represented for me a real breakthrough in my thinking about natural systems, and provided me with a context for learning rapidly in a number of areas of the sciences.

I had finished the manuscript about a week before Christmas of that year. At the time, I had received a call to an interview for a part-time position at a community college in Compton, California, and went to the interview of the same day that I was printing out the first copies of my newest manuscript. The interview did not go well, and by the end of it I realized that they did not want me, and probably had not intended to hire me from the start. They never called me or got in touch with me after the interview.

In the next few weeks after Christmas, until February, I wrote another book entitled Cosmology and Reality, which was an extension of ideas in physical systems theory, developed the months before relating to the dynamic state universe. I made ten copies of this book, but stopped halfway through binding them.

At that stage, I had grown fairly discouraged, and it was in May that I turned my sights once again to searching for a job through the Internet. For the next three months I applied to many different kinds of jobs, many relating to the government in different areas. I did not apply to too many schools, but targeted either government or private sector jobs.

I did get a call for several interviews, as well as for another interview with a community college in Los Angeles that was similar to the program in Compton. In all the interviews I came to the conclusion that they probably did not intend to hire me, or if they had so intended, had

Auto-Anthropology

probably changed their minds, in part and in hindsight I believe because I represented a threat to the interviewers.

By July, I was little further ahead in my job search, though it appeared to me that there were "nibbles" from the State of Alaska that intrigued me. In part discouragement that seems to come strongest at that time of year, I set my sights once again on the possibility of returning to a school and applied to the University of Alaska, Fairbanks.

At the same time, a school system in *Ponapei,* Micronesia, contacted me to hire me for a position. I finally passed on going to *Ponapei* as I was concerned about the educational situation for my daughter. I chose instead to return to school at the University of Alaska, Fairbanks, in order at least to obtain a teaching credential. We were immediately given an apartment on campus through residence life, which proposition influenced my decision even though my wife was not happy with the prospect of relocating again.

Bidding our farewells was far more difficult this time around, unlike anytime previously. Mostly I lost my little dog, Socks, who had become my best friend and only companion over the previous two years. My daughter had to say good-bye to a whole network of her friends.

By the first of August we were on the road to Alaska, driving in our little mini-van up through the states of Northern California, Eastern Oregon and then Washington State, entering Canada and passing through British Columbia and then the Yukon Territory along the Al-Can highway. It was much longer than I realized it would be, and turned into a 7-day road-trip during which I drove for more than 12 hours per day. The Canadian northern frontier was huge. Besides the natural beauty of Canada, my only other impression was of long tracts of washed out dirt roads and being shortchanged for my US dollars at all the petroleum stations, to the point of dropping at least $35 US more than I should have by the time we crossed back across the boarder into Alaska.

We arrived at the Alaskan boarder in the late afternoon of the sixth day on the road, and we proceeded a couple of more hours to Tok junction, which was my first impression of Alaska besides an interesting discussion with a filling station owner at the border. My immediate impression of Alaska was the tremendous cost of everything, the food, the room, etc., compared to anything we had previously spent upon the trip. The next morning we got up early enough to make the remaining four-hour trip to Fairbanks, arriving there in the early afternoon. We ended up stuck in a hotel the first couple of days as we got in on a Saturday, and had to wait through Sunday until Monday to see about our campus housing.

Coming into a new city that is to become one's future home is always a daunting and somewhat confusing task. One learns a little bit at a time as one constructs a map based upon one's experience. Fortunately, Fairbanks was built more or less like a giant square in which the main highways or boulevards were the perimeter, and everything else branched from these. Therefore, as long as one stayed along the main highways, one could not easily become lost.

My first impression of Fairbanks was the high cost of everything, the lack of luxury of many accommodations, and the continuous daylight of the late summer. I was not disappointed when we got to check into our apartment immediately on Monday morning, as the apartments, though small and also very expensive, were in a nice forest setting at the edge of a larger trail system that led behind the campus. I had missed so much being able to walk amongst the trees, and I found the boreal forest at that time of year, with its many kinds of mushrooms and toad stools, its lichens, and deep, plush carpets of moss, quite inviting to explore and walk through.

I found a part time job within two weeks with the campus mail services, which made me feel good, and by the end of the month we commenced our courses. I had taken a field ecology course in the biology department, a mandatory chemistry course, and a Native Alaskan class in Anthropology that was preparatory to becoming a teacher in meeting state requirements. The ecology class I found the most interesting, as it involved field-labs that took us out with different activities around the Fairbanks area.

I remember that Sept. 11th, 2001 was my first day with the class, and the World Trade Center had just been bombed that same morning. The students were all in a kind of daze, as was the T.A., and as we walked through the Boreal gardens and forest area of the school Arboretum, taking notes on all the plants and trees, we were all distracted and thinking about other things. I remember thinking to myself how good it was to be sharing this kind of experience with American students for a change rather than being caught in a foreign setting with people whom I could not relate to or understand in such times.

I became busy with schoolwork and my mail job, which involved me carrying the afternoon mail between the campus extensions and on-campus between the main administrative offices. This involved handling the monies transferred between these offices at the end of the day. I did not mind the job, as it gave us extra income and it was good to get some physical exercise which I sorely needed, but a few of the other student employees were a little less than professional and immature in their conduct and aggravated me somewhat.

In November I came down with a severe respiratory infection and a flu that made me bed ridden for at least a week. This was around Thanksgiving time, and I believe our stream-ecology course where I accidentally got wet on my shirt sleeves up to my shoulder, precipitated this illness. It was at a time when I had started another book, entitled Meta-systems, which was combining things I was currently learning, especially in the ecology course, with my previous work in Natural systems. I came out of the semester with straight A's and a finished manuscript that was somewhat haphazardly constructed.

Christmas in Fairbanks was a dark and somewhat depressing affair. We did not have much money to buy gifts for my daughter, and we had very few things in our apartment. I did buy a nice tree and stand to celebrate, against the protestations of my wife.

School resumed in mid-February, and I had by then just quite my Post Office position because it would have interfered with my coursework, the hours of which I increased. I took a microbiology and cellular biology course in Biology, the second half of the mandatory Chemistry requirement, and a course in Archaeological theory and method, which I found most interesting. I had arranged to take the Praxis exams to meet the state requirements for entering the credential program, and did this in early February.

I was very disappointed with my Biology courses, as one was instructed by a young student who did not yet have her Master's degree, and she proved the poorest teacher I ever had, unwilling to explain anything or to try to contextualize the thick technology knowledge that comes with a detailed understanding of cell biology. The microbiology course was also very disappointing as the teacher was fairly authoritarian and overly strict with everybody. I found myself working very hard for both courses, but my grades dropping in spite of what I was learning.

Our cellular biology instructor failed nearly 75% of the class on the first exam, myself included, and on that day I dropped her class and also made a commitment to get myself admitted into the credential program by summer time. I had interviews with the people of the program, and they disappointed me greatly when they told me that I must devote all of my time and energy to their program, even in lieu of employment or other involvements. Coming home that evening, I immediately sent off an application to APU University and, later that week, to Cal State Fullerton, with the idea of abandoning Alaska as a fair proposition for us.

Our Native American neighbors in our apartment block had exacerbated my disappointment. They returned from their summer camp sojourn at the beginning of the Fall Semester, almost to the day, and the apartment went from pleasant to extremely noisy on that day. They made noise at all times of the day and night, and the unwed woman had three small kids which she hardly bathed or watched, and they banged on the walls and jumped from the furniture often until 2 or 3 in the morning.

By Halloween I filed an official complaint with the Residence Life people, but they refused my request to relocate to a new apartment. I told them that the likely outcome was not good, but they flatly ignored my interests. By New Years, I once again filed a complaint with the Manageress of the apartments, but she did little, and believed the family next door who made up lies.

After that, she did not answer any of my phone calls complaining about the neighbors. After a drinking session by my neighbors in about April that went until 5:30 A.M, and that was the evening before a big examination, I once again wrote a letter and this time bypassed all the people and went straight to the top. Nothing constructive was accomplished, but after complaining one more time, the Residence Life manager called me and offered me a new apartment at the end of the year.

Auto-Anthropology

By then it was too late as I had already set my sights on returning to
Southern California to complete my credential with APU University. I
reasoned that, in spite of the high tuition, the total cost would be almost
cut in half.

Regardless of the noise and the unnecessary hassles in my coursework, I
managed to finish a second manuscript relating to Archaeological
systems theory, entitled <u>Digging the Past,</u> a week before the finals. I had
also landed a job with the Community Service Officer program on
campus, which I worked for about a week before we made our final
decision to relocate to Southern California. I had booked passage on the
Alaskan inland ferry that went from Haines, Alaska, to Bellingham,
Washington in four days time.

We left Alaska about a week after finals and a few days before my
daughter's school ended. There was no one there to see us off in our
departure, and the day we left Fairbanks was about like the day we
arrived. We could have been in Fairbanks for fifty years and still have
been as anonymous as the day we arrived there. We made haste to
Haines before the departure date of the ferry.

We enjoyed the twelve-hour drive, and found Haines expensive but
beautiful compared to dirty Fairbanks. We were in Haines a day-and-a-
half before departing on the ferry back to the lower Forty-eight. The
ferry trip was luxurious compared to what we had experienced in all our
previous sojourns, and we enjoyed the four days on the boat in a manner
we had not previously known.

We arrived back in Whittier about a week after our departure from
Alaska, in late May. I had several weeks before starting my first summer
semester with APU, and we stayed busy doing different things since then.
I do not this time regret coming back to Southern California. The social
atmosphere here has changed since 9/11. There are more signs of
American patriotism and no Mexican flags being flown at public schools,
and people seemed a little more tolerant and friendlier than ever before.
My daughter immediately reestablished her network of friends, and my
wife is much happier here than she ever was in Alaska.

Since having returned, for the last three months, I have remained quite
busy. We got ourselves a new dog, a female mix named Zoie, who was

quite lovable though not very beautiful by dog-human standards. I have managed in the last few months to reconstruct the system that I had let go of the year before and couldn't get going in Alaska. The components of my multi-faceted system are coming together quite well for a change, though we are in greater debt now, more than we have ever previously been.

In hindsight, our venture to Alaska was a mistake mostly, though the coursework was good for me and I have managed to be able to advance my theoretical work considerably.

My anthropology I carry forward in relation to my meta-systems science and natural systems theory, though I no longer see any academic relationship to it. I have dropped almost all of my previous academic mentors as basically unreliable and unrealistic in their orientation. I quit trying to apply to academic positions with my degree, and am thoroughly disgusted with the double standards and hypocrisy in professional Anthropology that is evinced at almost every level. It is no longer a dying field, but it is essentially a dead and moribund discipline, supplanted as it has been by more politically correct 'ethnic studies' and its scholars replaced by more correct 'others.'

Though I am a professional persona non-grata, I still believe in the functionality and theoretical relevance of anthropological knowledge especially in its applicability to real problem sets in the larger, non-academic world.

I cannot afford to regret the losses of opportunity and null development that we might have achieved in a more open and more equal world. I learned in Alaska and subsequently that I was not even given a chance to achieve anything significant professionally in Anthropology--these screens of opportunity were systematically sold off to foreign and minority scholars in the interests of elites bent on globalization. Too many years have now passed to be concerned about the politics and prejudices that have so stifled and determined our fate but about which we have had no control whatsoever.

Though the future remains increasingly uncertain for all people, I continue with a basic sense of faith and hope that we can yet create a better world for everyone. Though I fight everyday as a total social leper against insuperable odds, I realize that my best fight and my best days are yet in our future.

As I continue this work, I realize that life, as long as we live it, remains an unfinished book. The next chapters are yet to be written, and as long as there is a new chapter to write, there is always the hope for a happy ending rather than yet another tragedy in the making.

I had joined a teaching certificate program at APU College, a small Christian (Methodist) College in Southern California. Classes were at night, and student teaching was arranged for our placement during the weekday. I was placed in a first-grade class at one school, and then the following Spring in a 6th grade 'honors' class in a middle school. I devoted myself that school year to finishing 36 semester credit hours (for which I earned a 4.0), including student loan debt close to $20,000 U.S., including about half in books and other incidental fees/expenses. For about two years after, I applied to job-openings at schools throughout California with a multi-subject (K-12) credential, to little avail. I did land a part time subbing position at a local school district.

This last part of my story is really a very short story of the rest of my life as it had been centered on Southern California. In brief, my Mom died in the spring of 2005, unexpectedly but not-too surprisingly, of an iatrogenic bleeding of a main artery after a normally simple and popular procedure.

Taking care of the physical estate was almost as painful as figuring out what to do with her ashes, but her death ended any further connection I might otherwise have entertained with sunny Southern California. With very little leftover, we ended up putting my Mom's house up for sale and I eventually accepted a teaching job in Southeastern Arizona.

We found ourselves in the state next door, Southeast Arizona, where we have lived since and where we began a new chapter of our lives. My anthropology played unexpectedly into this new life, for both poorer and richer. It proved a threat to many who often sought to stand in my way to gaining a better living for my family, but it also proved an unexpected boon to helping me build that life in totally unanticipated ways.

I did not travel as I had done before with my family to conduct anthropological fieldwork, per se, even though in subsequent years I have traveled for different reasons related to my work.

My anthropology grew with me in my later years—I dedicated myself to my family and home, and to more writing on General Systems, on various forms of Anthropology, and in anthropologically driven fiction.

This has taken me to the trajectory and position I am now at. I had to wait in essence four decades for new technology to catch up with my writing and to make my self-publishing a truly viable plausibility, unlike twenty years before.

Indeed, though all things have their time, and the books now being published are twenty to forty years past their prime, their publication wouldn't before have been either possible or affordable before now.

In my professional estimation, this opens new doors to areas of exploitation and development, which from an academic administrative point of view may be called "fringe" nevertheless permitting greater access and voice in a global marketplace.

Greater detail of this engagement must come in a subsequent chapter installment, perhaps a new or revised book, beyond the scope or intent of this current story line.

REWITNESSING ANTHROPOLOGY ANOTHER TIME

Notes and Queries of a Post-Anthropological Travelogue

Self-Reconstruction and Other Un-Destructions

Someone fairly smart in the late Nineteenth Century said something like "God is Dead" and this was supposed to be a kind of last, final statement ushering in a bold new age of Science, Secularism and Grand Existential Suffering. Strange it is to find, in the early Twentieth Century, the God seems very much alive and thriving in expensive North American Suburbs and Middle Eastern Sky-rise Cities. And this God is surely an angry and vengeful God, unforgiving and perhaps blind to many contradictions of its own state.

I sit here now, on the verge of yet another life change, a new chapter, closing out an old chapter. I wish to bring my story up to date from where I last left off from our rebound from the cold wilds of Alaska. I dearly miss the Great Alaskan Wilderness—the moose, the fox, the ptarmigan, the ravens, the squirrels, the mushrooms and toadstools that carpeted the mossy green floors of the Boreal forest. I miss all the many cedars and birch, the alders and pines. I even almost miss the slippery snow and the sniffling, frozen whisker cold of the Alaska winter.

Everyday almost I trudged a mile or so back and forth between the biology or chemistry classrooms and our small apartment, taking the back woods trails, no matter the cold or wind conditions. I treasured those moments most.

And this story is a continuation of the previous story, but there have been basic changes, and that strange middle age thing of returning to some early childhood state and walking back out again, step-by-step, has come to a close (almost, but not quite completely.) There is no longer any going back, or any sense of returning, or even any desire to go back again. We move forward, slowly, blindly, inexorably, to our destinies. I sit at the same computer, in front of the same monitor, that I composed my last installment, Re-Witnessing Anthropology, some five or six years ago. Much has happened in the interim.

I've come full circle yet another time it seems, and now, a panorama of my past life stretches in my mind's eye into the past--the many days and nights gone forever but not completely lost. This has been an evolving document, begun 16 years ago, about something that began a half century ago, back to my earliest memories. Of course, the document has evolved because I've evolved--rich or poor, I've not ever been in a rut too long, and I've always developed in new ways.

I have come to accept in life a grand sense of, for want of a better word, Serendipity, with a capital "S." It is not fate, it is not blind luck or justice, it is a sense of things working the way they do for reasons, even if we cannot fully comprehend those reasons. Trying to make things work sometimes runs awry, and often even Amok, in the structure of the medium range.

I have experienced enough of it in my time to at least take me from healthy skepticism to a bit of awe-struck dumb-foundedness. I don't really know how to explain it except to say there is structure and order even in extremely complex and seemingly chaotic things like the unfolding of our own lives and our life-worlds on a grand global stage. Of course, there is a thing of making wrong turns, or of making turns that are neither right or wrong--of choosing roads less or better traveled, etc.

Whatever it may be, and perhaps just my own subjective sense of "SOMETHING," it at least has taken the edge off the stress of the uncertainty of all the outcomes and moves one must make in life--a sense of stress that at times can seem overwhelming.

I wish to begin, not where I last left off, which was our rebound from Alaska, at least not directly. I wish to start with a story of a memory about my mother, rather than my father, this time around. She was after all a much larger part of my life than my dear old dad had ever really been. I

Auto-Anthropology

loved my father no less than my mother, but my mother was the rock of my life no one else had ever been. Whatever I've been or become in my life, for better or worse, richer or poorer, and it seems mostly the latter, it was unequivocally the result of my mom's unconditional love and her unfailing support for her prodigal son.

I wish thus to begin this third installment of my self-reflexive diatribe at what has proven to me to be the most important point in my entire life. It came neither at the beginning nor the end, chronologically, of this latest installment, rather right in the middle, almost.

Her health had been gradually waning over the past few years. Each year that we returned from our prodigal sojourns, she seemed smaller, more frail, and she complained more of her aches and pains. She was gradually less able to do things for herself--even simple things like open cans or bottles of food. She was increasingly reluctant to drive her car out.

The last few months, especially in the first three months of 2005, I was taking her several times a week to make her appointments with the medical system. She was a member of an HMO, and she always needed to go to one place or another across town to have blood-work done. She was also taking medications that were extremely expensive, close to five thousand dollars for a year's prescription. I couldn't understand why the medical people needed to take blood so frequently from her, and being as extremely and sometimes disconcertingly private a person as she was, she never ever told us why or all that she knew.

She grew harder and harder to live with. She would have more frequent bouts of anger which was due I believe in large measure to her own frustration at her enfeebled condition as well as her chronic pain. She was less and less herself, and had fewer lucid moments in which she could engage in a meaningful and reasonable conversation.

She had gone to lunch with a coterie of her old Cronies from her school district. One of the sons of her friends had had a procedure done, an "angioplasty" in which his main aorta was "rotor routered" out. My mother thought that such a procedure would help her feel better, to regain some of her vigor and vitality. I did not want her to have the procedure, as I didn't like the way the current medical establishment was treating (or mistreating?) her by giving her a constant runaround and replacing doctors every few months. I thought the procedure ill advised for her age and her known condition as her whole arm would bruise up black and blue from a simple bump.

I made the mistake of voicing my opinion to her one time, about a week before the procedure, when she was showing me the medical hype and brochures about the procedure, as well as the release from liability and consent forms that were part of the sign up process. Her anger to me shut me up, and I said nothing for the remainder of the week. Then she criticized me for showing a lack of interest in her health affairs, and I said nothing, as I could not win that kind of argument. I did not have a good feeling about the procedure.

I took my Mom to her appointment on Monday morning, fairly early, at the outpatient clinic in the parking lot of the old Presbyterian hospital, the main hospital of Whittier. We waited with her in the main lounge-office, until a nurse came and got her into a wheel chair and took her away. There was nothing else for my wife and I to do but to return home and wait for her and the outcome. We went to pick her up in the main hospital lobby, at about five in the evening. She was wheeled out, still in a wheel chair, by another nurse, and seemed in good spirits. I figured she had probably been given a fairly heavy dose of painkiller medicine. I thought it strange she would be released so soon after her procedure and asked her how she felt.

We got her into the car and drove her back, and helped her back out of the car, up the steps and into bed. Later that evening she came to watch TV in the living room and sat in a chair. It was one of the most lucid conversations I had had with her in a couple of years, and we talked about my brother. I was surprised that my Mom had few illusions about my brother, apparently less than myself, confused as I've always seemed to be by some notion of filial or brotherly love.

She was tired and went to bed early. The next morning, she couldn't get out of bed. My wife and I went to a local food-market that she liked, that had a lot of imported delicacies and nuts, and we bought a number of things on a shopping list she had. She asked me if she could take a shower in my bedroom bathroom, which I found unusual, as she never showered before, always bathed. She said the shower might make her

Auto-Anthropology

feel better. We went to the market, and returned, to find her back in bed and complaining of having to urinate but not being able to. It was by then about noon, and she said her kidneys hurt her a great deal. She tried to get up but couldn't and would lay back down. I took her temperature, which was low, and falling, and then took her blood pressure, which was erratic and hard to get at all.

I tried calling the doctor's office that had performed the procedure to ask for advice, and he was out and the secretary said he would return the call. I waited about an hour, taking her temperature and finding it falling very low. I became concerned and called emergency services, and the dispatcher told me to put her feet up and cover her with a blanket as she was in a state of shock. The emergency medical people arrived--first a fire-truck with a crew, and then an ambulance crew, about fifteen minutes later.

The fire-truck crew didn't want to take her out--refused in fact, and I got into an argument with the crew chief, as my mom was obviously down for the count, in a severe state of shock. Then he told me how expensive removing her would be, and said that perhaps I should take her out myself and drive her. Once the paramedics arrived, they immediately took her out of the house, and back down to Presbyterian hospital where she was admitted to the emergency ward and underwent a second operation.

I called my sister at her work, and she met me with her boyfriend at the hospital that evening. We waited there in the emergency lounge for most of the evening, until about 11:00 in the evening when we got to see mom on a hospital gurney, between stations. She was half-awake. She talked to Kathy, and then to me a bit. She said that I never would kiss her as a child.

She asked what had happened and we explained to her that she had had an emergency procedure and everything would be all right. She fell back to sleep and was taken to ICU. We went home and slept. In the middle of the morning, about 3:00 AM the next day, the phone rang and the emergency technician on the other end told me that my mom had taken a turn for the worse and that we should come down immediately.

My brother had arrived back at the house with his family that morning. We went back down to the ICU to find my mom hooked up on all the gizmos and gadgets, her heart beating on the monitor, being provided oxygen, and a small bag for urine. We stayed with her for two days, hoping for signs of recognition, alertness, beyond her finger moving once in a while or her heart rate changing on the monitor. The end of the first day I went home and slept. We were all taken into a room with a doctor and a grief counselor, and advised of the outcome and her condition.

My brother was angry and blaming the doctor and the hospital. The evening of the third day, on one doctor's advice, who told us she had had leukemia from her white-blood cell count, we took her off life support. My sister, my wife and I stayed in the room as the technician removed the gizmos and gadgets, one at a time.

She slowly expired, after about an hour. Her breathing was shallower and shallower. She never regained consciousness. Finally her heart rate became increasingly erratic, and slower, and then finally flat-lined altogether, gradually. We said our good-byes to her, and left the room as her body was taken to the county coroner's office for an autopsy into her exact cause of death.

We returned home, to an empty, silent house. My brother had left and gone back to his home up north. My sister had returned to her own home in West Covina.

The next morning we began in her room, and slowly putting things away. We were careful to separate out what things we could find for the four children, creating a trunk of things for each person. My sister came by later in the day and we talked about memorial arrangements—it was a weekend, and we tracked down a memorial place on Whittier Blvd that seemed reasonable. We went together to talk to the people at this place, and made arrangements for her service. On the way home, my sister talked to me about her recent divorce and her therapy and our childhood and things she had never spoken to me about before. I saw a side of her I'd not seen before.

My mom's sisters flew out that weekend for the service. I had called them all from a phone in the hospital to tell them that Mom had died.

Auto-Anthropology

We had a dinner that night. I barbequed chicken on the deck and everyone ate and talked. I didn't feel like talking much at all.

We held the memorial service late on Monday Morning. I was surprised by the number of people from Mom's old district who showed up. My sister's ex showed. My dad's family came. My brother met me in the parking lot, while we were setting up. He asked me about a geisha doll that my daughter had, one that my sister had given to Mahala the Thanksgiving before. I told my brother I had it. He wanted me to drive home to get it for him, which I did. I drove back to my mom's house, and fetched the Geisha doll out of the closet and put it in a large shopping back with handles, covering it with tissue paper to protect it.

I gave the doll to my brother in the parking lot. There were three dolls-- of three sizes. My daughter had the largest. It had come in a wooden box with straw—my sister had gotten rid of the box, I suppose. My brother accused me of losing the box. I told him I didn't know what had happened to the box. He took the doll. He left right after the memorial service and went back to his own hometown. He didn't go to the wake after the service, which was at my mom's best friend's house.

We showed up late after the service, because of the doll incident and having to take all the flowers and plants given at the service, back to the house. I missed my cousins and uncle, who were leaving just as I got there. I met them briefly in the front yard. It was the last time I had seen them. The memorial went well. I was there a couple of hours, but didn't really talk much to anyone.

We got back to the house late in the afternoon. There were about fourteen large plant and flower arrangements that we had to set off the front porch and put back on the deck. My mom's sisters all left that afternoon back to the airport. The next day we began slowly dismantling the household, one small piece and part at a time.

Dealing with my mom's death, in hindsight, was like being in a deep dark well, emotionally, looking up at the light of an opening high above, and there seeing other people's faces. There was a sense of disconnectedness. I would wake up in the middle of the night, and seemingly cry for no reason. I was more aloof from everything than emotional--emotionally dead, I think.

It took us about six weeks to clear up my mom's household. My brother came down twice hauling a huge car transport trailer, which he managed to load each time with my Mom's nicest furniture. He had no interest in anything that didn't have some monetary value or that was intrinsically expensive. He wanted to take my mom's car, but I insisted that we needed it.

It was the only thing I insisted upon, really. My sister took only a few things, but those things were always those few things of my mom's that were exceptionally nice, including my mom's few journals, photos and writings. She came once, with her boy friend's car, which we filled with lamps and clocks, and small tables until we could fit no more. No one seemed much interested in a lot of things my mom had collected over the years, pots, baskets, tins, frogs, and clocks—many of these things found their way into a donation to local thrift shops.

My mom's best friend took the baskets off our hands, a not inconsiderable collection. My mom had probably a hundred pounds worth of old greeting cards--the oldest going back to the 1950's--many I remembered giving her as a child. These no one wanted, and were eventually tossed into a rental dumpster, along with many National Geographic magazines, Scientific Americans, old furniture that had been broken and stored in the garage, as well as many of my own hard-copy manuscripts and doctoral research papers that I had stored in a shelter in the backyard.

We threw away my dad's remaining old stuff as well, old golf clubs, fishing poles, etc. We ended up dumping the rental dumpster three times before we were done. It was not that my mom hoarded or was a pack rat. If anything she was exceptionally organized and clean. We ended up giving most of her wardrobe to thrift shops. Her nicer clothes she had saved from the 1940s. Pots and pans, kitchen-ware that no one wanted, we tried to sell at a yard sale but ended given up to thrift shops as well.

My Mom died in the last week of April. By the first week of June, my mom's house was put up for sale by my brother and sister, who were named co-executors of the estate in my mom's trust. None of us had looked at her trust before, and we didn't realize both my brother and sister were executors. We all took it for granted that it was my oldest

Auto-Anthropology

sister's responsibility. Once my brother realized he was co-executor, he hired a lawyer and the trouble started.

They all showed up unexpected on a Saturday and brought a local realtor in to put the house up. They didn't ask me, and my sister had agreed earlier to go slowly. The house sold on the second day after it was put on the market, and even though my brother promised us a forty-five day escrow, they closed in 15 days. We had still not entirely cleaned the house out by the time we had to leave, and we were still getting rid of things that last day.

One of the last things we had gotten rid of were all the plants given at my mom's memorial, which we had repotted in the interim. I didn't want my brother to get these, as I felt he didn't deserve them, so I gave them all, over forty nice plants, to my two neighbors who had helped and known my mom all those years.

I end this over-wrought story for a new page, a new chapter, and a new book on the rest of our lives. We drove off early in the morning with our pouting teenage daughter in the back of the car and our dog. It was my final day, near the first of July, to be in Southern California, and we found ourselves moving at the other end of the long drive to a nice house rental in a small city on the other side of Arizona. We did not know what to expect of our future, but as we finally parted California, we knew at least that our past was forever sundered.

Witnessing Afterward
A Senior Auto-Anthropologist in Retrospect and Prospect

My witnessing anthropology, both as a living text and as a lived autobiography, essentially ended upon our final departure from California for greener pastures in the deserts of Southeast Arizona. It marks the end of my "Witnessing Anthropology" and the beginning of a new phase of my life reconnecting my time in the USMC with our current lives in Arizona.

Since then, I have not been "witnessing" anthropology so much as I've begun witnessing the larger world more or less through an anthropological lens—if not as an Anthropologist in any academic sense, then fully and completely as an anthropologist in the alternative, applied and basic senses as it relates to real world research and design development.

I have been an "anthropologist" now for over forty years, though I have never been a professor or academically employed on the basis of my anthropology. While I do miss not fulfilling my potential, I do not otherwise regret much the unusual course of my life.

The last 17 years have been more or less the same, and they would require their own addendum, that would not be overly wrought. Instead I have chosen to conclude this work with the idea of our having become in a sense "reborn" in our last relocation to Arizona.

I do regret greatly that my life and my life's work could not have been better aligned with one another. The main consequence is always having felt both out of place in much social company especially, and always being marginal to what others in the world have deemed important.

I never felt a need to be famous or feel important, but I have felt a very strong need to do work that I felt and thought to be meaningful and in some way truly significant in the world. That was why I couldn't be just a dishwasher that I was in high school, or a tanker in the Marines. I would

<u>Auto-Anthropology</u>

not have been satisfied only studying the Vietnamese, or for that matter, the Peranakan, or just, later on, the Robidoux family of the Fur Trade.

At some point I had to engage further, in various aspects of Systems theory, and to extend my anthropological research engagement beyond the academic and the basic to include areas of actual application of important anthropological principles including basic research, but also reaching well beyond such work to applied frameworks and systems in addressing real world problem sets in real time settings and situations.

In my senior years I look back in retrospect and realize how I've been a jack of many trades—an artist, an accomplished wood-worker with my own style and techniques, a writer of many different kinds of texts. I've been a family man. These things, since I was a young child, have been what were always most important to me.

The Professional Pariah
Ethnography of the Anthropological Self
1996

Hugh M. Lewis

<u>Auto-Anthropology</u>

Black dog
So handsome and strong
Your entire life
Spent on the end of a short chain
In the hot humid sun
In the pouring tropical rain
Kept by a heartless, cruel master
Sores festering your limbs
Ticks crawling over your body like acne
I buy you off the chain
With a pound of sugar
And a lot of love
I give you a few weeks of relentless freedom
To run unendingly about
Madly around the compound
I clean off your ticks
And fatten you up with scraps
I give you a few brief weeks of patient
Careful attention
But you prove too hard to handle
Difficult and uncontrollable
Too much for me to deal with all the time
So I deliver you to the dog shooter
Who must put you down forever?
And as I put you into that small kennel cage
Alongside all the other yelping, crying animals
Your eyes knowingly look into mine
A look of sensitive intelligence
Of ultimate abandonment and betrayal
Penetrating deeply into my soul
The only person in the world you trusted
Who allowed you off that cruel chain?
With the total devotion only a dog knows
Now I have forsaken you
And somehow you know
In some uncanny way

That your time had come
I walk slowly away
Not looking back
As I hear you howling miserably in the distance
I listen to your howling
All nightlong
Calling for me to come back to get you
On the way home the next day
Walking by that dreaded, terrible place
I sense something strange in the air
There is only a silence hanging heavy
The shooter looks annoyed with me
As he shows me the carcass in the truck
The bloody head wrapped in newspaper
I stroke its stiff flank with my hand
One last time
Before I finally turn away
Unable to keep back the tears
The storm then came in mid-day
The rain and thunder was heavy that day

For my family

And the unfortunate Black Dog

Introduction
Autobiography as "Self" Ethnography

A great deal of lip service has been given over the last decade (1980s-90s) toward a more "reflexive" Anthropology, and, implicitly at least, the deliberate inclusion of the sense of self in the construction of ethnographic descriptions.

To say that ethnography is a matter of construction as much as it is a matter of science is to point up the "facticity" of the realities that somehow manage to account for the background contexts in which the ethnography as a written document is situated in the personal life of the ethnographer. The apparent fact of the act of fabrication of the story is then exposed for what it is in truth rather than what it is supposed to be.

Important in this call for greater reflexivity of our ethnographic accounting is to somehow provenience the "Other" in some sense of real place and time—in intersubjective relation with ourselves—in a shared world that is contemporaneous and contiguous to our own, and not merely a facet of our construction. The reflexive problem that autobiography highlights is not one of the professional "Other" but rather of its antithesis—the professional sense of anthropological "Self."

In this case it is the identification and contextualization of the anthropological self that relates to others as largely a result of the cross-cultural experience.

That the professional "Self" is somehow critically tied to our conceptualization of the "Other" should go without saying—except to reiterate again that if the "self" is seen as somehow problematic, so must the "other" as well be seen as also fundamentally problematic relative to the self.

Professionalization of the self, a process that is articulated primarily in Anthropology departments, involves the identification and subjective internalization of certain implicit knowledge structures and core values of what it is to be and become an anthropologist.

Part of this professionalization process seems to inevitably entail some form of internal symbolic and behavioral dichotomization of the self

Auto-Anthropology

between ideal and real, or foreground and background, across many situations in which the ego-ideal over-rides ego-reality and subjugates the superego. Then the "other" who exists in the imagination of the self is but a projective reflection of a narcissistic alter ego.

It is a dichotomization that involves to some extent separation between personal and private as well as professional and potentially public domains of one's own life. There is quite a bit of variability in how professional anthropologists finally achieve this compartmentalization of their lives--some apparently do a better job of it than others and for many it seems to have been a downright frustrating process.

When we are forced to put our best foot forward in professional arenas, we are simultaneously compelled to hide our worst points from view. Unfortunately this repression of a part of ourselves comes to influence our projective construction of the other and of how we professionally externalize and define ourselves in relation to each other. To say "compelled" is to point up the subconscious and strikingly compulsive nature of the entire process.

We find ourselves doing it whether we realize it or not, much less control it well or not. If the definition of our professional self in the critical arenas of the department become a somewhat neurotic style, then at least a part of this neurosis embodied in our self-denial and internalization of Anthropologos becomes projectively transferred upon our constructions of the "other."

This can become a quite frightening phenomenon when its potential extent is considered, especially when we consider the extent to which arbitrary prejudice and judgment is being passed upon others in lieu of actually getting to know the other better.

Autobiographical accounts are an overlooked style of ethnographic description, even though many descriptive reports are actually framed in a first-person voice, and even though a great deal of what passes for objective, impersonal description may actually be based upon first-hand subjective experiences of the participant-observer. Such autobiographical inclusion of the anthropological ego, sense of anthropological self, lends itself readily to existentially transcendental and phenomenological approaches to methodology.

The explicit use of autobiographical accounting as a meaningful form of ethnographic information can move beyond the anecdotal narrative of personal experiences to provide a systematic document of psychological attitudes, changes of attitudes and feelings, of subjective experiences in interaction or withdrawal from the field situation, so that a reader might more objectively than the author separate the real from the contrived.

The aim of such ethnographic autobiography is to attempt to centrally provenience the anthropological self and the vital context of the self in its relation with the other—to bring the sense of self and the factors that influence the construction and identification of the anthropological self both in the field and outside of it (back in the department.)

Of course, Great Persons write great autobiographies, and so, very minor, anonymous anthropologists must ultimately write very minor, anonymous autobiographies. But there is an overlooked ethnographic virtue in such humbleness, that one's own personal accounts, disinvested of any of the illusions and allusions that greatness is heir to, may somehow lie closer to the common voice of humanity, and more authentically resonate the forgotten experiences of so many lesser biographies.

Looking critically at one's own past experiences, and then writing about them in a narrative voice and in the first person, is sometimes to open a Pandora's box that is usually kept safely locked away and hidden from view.

It is a challenge and one must not forget ever to be critically careful, not allowing the narrative to become a vanity mirror. If I am so hesitant to fit others into impersonal, mostly anonymous frameworks, then we should be willing ourselves to suffer those tasks and their framing through analysis and interpretation.

There are many facts that I would have rather not mentioned, some now embarrassing and ridiculous that makes a good yarn, others too close to home and too revealing. It is sometimes the height of unwisdom to reveal too much about one's self and one's human foibles when one's central concern is to try to leave a good impression upon the world about who you are supposed to be, professionally at least.

But somehow I felt that if I were going to put down on paper and publish the life stories of other people, most of whom gave them to me very generously and honestly, then I must also demand of myself the same requirement.

If I am to give countless rounds of tasks to an endless stream of informants, then at some point I must feel an obligation to give myself

Auto-Anthropology

those very same tasks, even if I had performed them vicariously countless times over while giving them to different informants.

Besides, there are many valuable and interesting experiences in the course of fieldwork that cannot be best described except in the first person, that, if they were omitted, would entail the loss of many valuable, insightful and interesting anecdotes. It would be a disservice to the spirit of the entire study not to try to put these experiences down in some detail and thus to omit them as if they never happened.

I have chosen to include a document in the first person as a nonfiction narrative of my own experiences abroad in Malaysia, especially while conducting fieldwork, mostly because I have a firm faith in the value and importance of human subjectivity and subjectivity of attitude in the world—in its fundamental honesty and value in bringing meaning to the world.

I take as a fundamental symptom and failing of an impersonal "System" that grows beyond human proportions that it inevitably squashes human subjectivity and subjective attitudes into little square holes and stamps them with the label "irrelevant," "to be ignored," or "insignificant," or even sometimes as "dangerous." Almost as bad is render an entire person, their life, their family, as but objects or attachments to some grand "structure" or "system" or even "culture."

To me the epitome of the fascist is that person who has so repressed and denied human subjectivities and rendered the self so selfless and impersonal in service to some ideal that is larger than life (in the modern world usually involving either some kind of "statism" or statist loyalty to the machinery of the state, or else to some guru of a cult or other counter-cultural movement, that the person is not only more than willing to sacrifice his/her own hide to the cause, but also the hides of anyone and everyone else who may be deemed as interfering with that cause.

Thus, as strange as it may sound to some, I take it as a fundamental duty, both anthropologically as well as professionally and personally as a human being, to at some point at least reemphasize at some point or to some degree, the irreducible importance of the subjective point of view— not just my own, but of anyone and everyone that I come into significant contact with.

One of the saddest and most important lessons to have been learned from years of exclusion from within different anthropology programs is the importance of human subjectivity in the full accounting of facts, and of the danger of the denial of such subjectivity in the social construction of objective realities of other people.

But writing of one's own life-events has another important dimension and function, and that is of making objective and rendering critical what otherwise remains only subjective and uncritical. In effect it forces a kind of integration that both allows one to work out a lot that might be bubbling around back in the old head, and to reconsider and rethink those past experiences and rearrange them in an order that best fits the current or anticipated demands of one's life.

Of course, subjectivity should not be confused with the lack of a certain critical objectivity, as it most often seems to be the case. Adopting a subjective point of view is not a substitute for attempting an objective description or analysis of the subject at hand.

But subjective and objective points of view can coexist in the same complementary realm without conflict or contradiction, and there may even be considerable overlap that can be productive and "dialectically creative." Furthermore, subjective experience can be approached "emically" in a manner that does justice to the humanness of the experience and that yet remains at the same time true to objective form.

Anyone who shallowly criticizes or lightly dismisses the field of cultural anthropology does not know or appreciate the tremendous amount of work and energy involved in its production. The personal sacrifices have been incredible in the pursuit of a degree that somehow always seems to slip from grasp, or the promise of a full professional career that always falls further on the horizon of a receding economy with all its socio-political double-standards.

Long without medical insurance, we venture into unknown, strange, alienating and potentially hostile environments at some risk to ourselves, and often our families, supported only by a shoestring "budget" and without any of the conveniences or creature comforts of modern life. We deal with hunger, insects, disease, animosity, prejudice, and anonymity. We suffer often the lack of dignity at the hands of arrogant and ignorant "others."

We give up the hope of having a home, of a regular paycheck, of a good retirement or even just a substantial nest egg, of material belongings, of even professional respect or acknowledgement, for the pursuit of professional knowledge and entitlement in a world that too often can be downright cruel and unfriendly.

Auto-Anthropology

We sacrifice many personal friendships and any social identity for the sake of this mad pursuit. Sometimes we even sacrifice family and ourselves in the process. At that point we reach some kind of limit line— "thus far, no further" (my limit line was somehow strangely over-reached in Mainland China.)

A professional pariah is what might be considered a fifth generation cultural anthropologist in an academic world now dominated by linguists, political scientists, ethno-biologists and computer wizards all of whom claim to be cultural anthropologists but who seem never to have had the time to read Levi-Strauss or Clifford Geertz or to conduct genuine cross-cultural fieldwork.

Culture is no longer a force to be reckoned with, but something to be explained in terms of some other more important scientific process. Even more important perhaps, culture becomes either a materialized commodity, an ethnic identity in a social market place, or a political lobby to protect or promote one's interests.

A professional pariah is a person who has learned their professional skills largely by default—by the hard knocks school of trial, tribulation and sometimes error, without a great deal of funding support and almost no professional recognition or acknowledgement within the field. It highlights the inescapably liminal dilemmas of a new generation of cultural anthropologist lacking any real context of social identity or support in a larger world.

In deed, it is a generation of anthropologist in a new global world order largely without colonial connection or post-colonial revolutions. Bereft of supportive contexts, they often plant their flags abroad on whatever ground that may afford them a standing.

Being a pariah means to become excluded from normal participation in social life in almost every sense but in the most minimal contexts. It is to be indirectly ostracized from such participation, and to suffer the psychological consequences of such ostracism.

In a professional world, it means a basic lack of respect or interest in one's work, the exclusion from vital dialogue, as well as from information sources and critical professional resources.

The process of exclusion is almost total in a social sense, and is a social reality that is of undeniable statistical significance. The observation that such behavior is class-tied has been made, and it is not necessary to belabor this point except to reiterate the importance that larger external structural connections play in influencing such behavior.

Such connections are largely defined along lines of class—class interests, styles, prerogatives and background.

Achieving, negotiating and maintaining one's identity and position in a competitive status hierarchy within the department setting often becomes of paramount importance, even more than the project of doing good ethnographic work itself, and even if successful work remains implicit to the background of social identity within the field.

With increasing years in departments, the lack of any strong, necessary correlation between skill, capability and talent and professional position as an anthropologist becomes much clearer, as does the continuous, across the board application of extreme double standards in the treatment of persons within the profession according to the relative estimation of their status within the field by departmental standing and standards.

This account covers only those periods of my involvement with Anthropology subsequent to my discharge from the military—roughly from 1980 until 1995—before, after, and during which we were actually residing in Malaysia, or interim periods between our times of residence in Malaysia.

During these periods, no great events tragically affected our lives—our daughter was never kidnapped and my wife never won a lottery. Mostly it was a long, hot, tedious and boring wait at bus-stops, or long rides on overcrowded, dirty buses, or long walks in the hot sun to accomplish some silly, daily bothersome task. Occasionally it was interesting, and only rarely any great fun.

I had to become selective in what to include and exclude from this document, simply for the sake of brevity and legibility. There were some points that I glossed over or excluded altogether because either I felt them to be too private and thus no one else's business, or else because they seemed irrelevant to the main thematic direction of the storyline.

Thus, in the chapters dealing with the interregnum periods especially, and in the foregrounding and back grounding of the story, many details were left out that may or may not have some indirect bearing to the story as it appears.

Auto-Anthropology

This is especially true for the long second interregnum period between August of 1987 and July of 1993—almost six years to be exact—during which we went through a whole series of critical periods that had a profound shaping influence on the course of our subsequent lives.

This interim period was marked initially by underemployment; a decision to go back to graduate school; the decision to leave the first graduate program for the sake of finding a better one; the birth of our baby girl who more than any other single thing has served to reshape our lives and lifestyles; eventually finding a more suitable program after several dead ends; and finally successfully completing this program and returning to Malaysia.

It is a dry, banal and somewhat sordid story—one similar to what has probably been repeatedly played out in literally hundreds of anthropology programs across the United States.

The most important lesson I've learned in my years in Anthropology Departments has been to never pass judgment on people whom we really don't know—something anthropologists seem do all of the time. But, after all, anthropologists under the skin are only human too, even if they live sometimes in Hobbit land.

First

The old cow's day old carcass lies stiff in the earth
Bloated and rotting
The lions, the hyenas, the rats, the vultures, the ants and maggots
All get a share
The photographer and filmmaker got their share too
It was a fine and fitting kill
An agonizing and obviously painful death
Choked by the lion's powerful jaws
One can even smell
The nauseating red flesh through the Television screen
Nature's laws fulfilled once again
On prime time
A primal scene
Recounted again and again
In a never ending series of stalks, and leaps
And failures and successes
The great cycle of life comes again to another completion
As a commercial comes on
And I go to make some popcorn

Old mother is now dead
She died naturally
Silently and slowly
Each takes its share
The Hawk sib, the Wolf sib, the Snake sib
And even other tribes
All carry off parts and pieces of her body
In separate directions of the compass
To make sacrifices and offerings
To feast and celebrate
There is so much of her to remove
Else they would all have forgotten where they got it
And still so much more remains
That the carcass is left to rot and stagnate
And flies are allowed to fester on it

Auto-Anthropology

And then seeds will germinate and weeds will grow on it
And in its forgotten place,
Perhaps a tall tree will grow.

Before

I first came to Malaysia in January of 1987. I had been planning the trip a few months in advance, since I had graduated with my Master's degree in cultural anthropology the previous August and the subject of my thesis had been the Vietnamese boat people among who I had done ethnographic fieldwork the previous year.

This thesis led to a greater interest in Southeast Asian studies as a personal and professional goal. Of course at the time I had no real clue as to how to go about achieving that goal, and no one was around to give me any good advice on the matter.

I finished my M.A. degree just under the deadline, and getting the thesis into a reasonable shape using an old typewriter had just about left me with all my hair pulled out. I fell into a kind of limbo those few fall months after completing the thesis without a sense of where to go from there. I tried applying for work to a few places, but found my Master's degree didn't really qualify me for much of anything in our great society.

I was working part-time for a handy-man, one Mr. Crow, an ex-WWII veteran from whom I learned quite a few tricks of the trade about how to hang doors and balance garage doors and get automatic garage door openers to work and install water heaters and rain gutters and fix door-bells, etc. I learned mostly that none of it was very difficult to learn and that he earned about 50 dollars an hour for barely 15 or 20 minutes of real work. He paid me five dollars an hour out of his pocket, in which he always carried at least a thousand in cash.

During this time, I tried getting back into my art that I had gotten away from during the fieldwork, and I began painting more pictures and tried to finish that monstrous wooden statue I had begun all the way back in 1984 and which still sat in my Mom's garage.

At the same time I began giving a young Indian woman whom I had met the last semester at school some art lessons about twice a week. She had divorced her arrogant MBA husband the year before and worked as an editor of the local newspaper. I enjoyed her company and we occasionally went out together to a movie or to other events.

Auto-Anthropology

During this time also I got into reading everything I could about Vincent Van Gogh, about whom there is a lot to read. He became a spare research topic of mine. I had always felt a special affinity with the man, especially after waiting 10 hours in line in the hot sun in downtown L.A. just to see his paintings when I was a young boy.

I had looked in all the books I could find in local libraries on the topic of Southeast Asia, which were mostly outdated travel guides and old government published social geography surveys. Among the many countries then available for extensive travel, I decided that Malaysia would be a good place to start, partly because English was still a common language and partly because they allowed a three-month social visit pass without the hassle of getting the passport chopped. I had formed a vague plan in my mind about meeting up with someone somewhere in some college or university and that I would thus somehow fall into Southeast Asian Studies.

Besides, after five and a half years of fairly intensive education, I had enough of books for a while and I wanted to see some of the world first-hand. I had decided to myself that there was no adequate substitute for first-hand experience, and besides, all the real scholars were also old Salts of the Seven Seas.

Most of the people whom I knew at that time were either foreign or else were people who had traveled the world at some time in their lives. I felt so homespun. I had been living with my mother at her home for the last seven years, mostly to save the little money I had leftover from my Marine days and my $325 a month G.I. bill checks, and I didn't realize during that time how much of a rut I had gotten into.

Among the books I had read about Malaysia was one written by a kind of British explorer and naturalist who had spent most of his life living in and exploring the jungles of Malaysia. His descriptions of the tigers and elephants and the hippopotami and the smaller animals, of his explorations and feats and exploits during the Emergency, created a romantic illusion about what Malaysia must have been like that was at least 50 years out of date. Another book about the British Anthropologist, Pat No one, of the 1920s and 30s, written by his brother, spurred on this illusion of going to the jungle to become some kind of explorer.

I also became somewhat obsessive over snakes, and I began reading everything I could find, particularly on venomous snakes, and particularly those found in Southeast Asia. I remembered that the summer before I went up to the Sierra Mountains on a weeklong backpacking/fishing trip. I remember while laying alone in my sleeping bag at night I developed almost a paranoid phobia of a large tree that I could watch swaying against the stars and clouds falling over on top of me in the night, or the large boulder that was just above me on the hillside, suddenly giving way and squashing me forever beneath it, and also of some nasty viper deciding to make my sleeping bag a cozy den for the night.

All in all, the four-month period between finishing my M.A. and leaving on my flight to Malaysia was a curious time for me. Autumns were always my worst time of the year, during which the worst things that have ever happened to me always happened. My father died on December 1ˢᵗ, when I was a seven-year-old boy, and I went into boot camp in the Marine Corps in November.

That season was spent mostly alone—visiting libraries or doing my painting or woodwork. Since I had decided to myself early on that I wanted to travel and to somehow "live" abroad, I didn't take much too seriously at the time.

As I look back on my life, this period really wasn't a bad time, though it also wasn't a good time—it was the first of those "in-between" times, between finishing one period of my life, and waiting indefinitely to begin the next, without really knowing very well what that next period would bring. Since that time there have been several such periods in my life, and each time they had become more and more difficult to deal with.

Thus most of the things which I carried as part of my luggage on that first trip consisted of a handmade hammock I had bought from a Vietnamese woman, a camouflaged plastic tarp, a mosquito net, several bottles of water purification tablets, canteens and canteen cups on a webbed belt, and an oversized first-aid kit that took up almost half the space of my bag, my old Marine Corps issue combat boots, and my Olympus 35 mm SLR camera with telephoto zoom lens and filters.

I had precious little room or strength to carry anything else, except a handful of toilet articles and a couple of changes of clothes, consisting of a couple of pairs of light-material pants, a few button down short-sleeve shirts, and a few pairs of socks, as well as an extra pair of shoes.

Auto-Anthropology

Besides this I had brought as well a handful of heavy anthropology books and a Malaysian-English dictionary. I thus had three bags plus a small luggage dolly that proved to be one more thing to have to carry.

It took me a couple of weeks before the departure to get everything ready and to run around buying all the "right" things that I "needed" just in case I found myself alone in the middle of the jungles of Malaysia. Leaving that first time was a big occasion for my small family.

My brother had me over to dinner and to see a movie--<u>Star Trek III</u>-- the night before I was to leave, and the day before had gone out without telling me and bought me a nice cloth Samsonite suitcase that cost over $200 U.S. dollars.

I felt as if I were leaving forever and would come back a changed person, if I came back at all. That morning I drove with my Mom down to the Disneyland hotel where I was to catch my bus to the airport for my noontime flight out of LA to KL.

My mother cried, of course, and I remember that bus ride down to the airport to be particularly crowded and unpleasant with impersonal, overly quiet people. The bus got off the freeway at some point and drove halfway to the airport by side streets. It was certainly no shortcut.

Anyway, the entire airport had been radically transformed since I had last been there before the 1984 Olympics and it was not what I expected. I somehow found myself on level 2 of a split-level airport when I should have been on level 1, of an airport that I had always known to have only one level.

I got down at the first stop as the buses and vans entered the airport, and I ended up walking the entire length of the concourse with my three bags loaded and strapped with bungee cords upon the top-heavy dolly. Two or three times the top leather bag with my books and the second small duffle bag with all my camping equipment and boots would work itself loose and begin to fall off the big red Samsonite bag with my clothes, trinkets and first-aid kit, as I hit the cracks in the sidewalks. Thus I learned to slow down and ease my load over each of the cracks in the sidewalk.

Pause

We wait for the smokey Hin Bus
To come rattling down the road
At our usual stop
Up by the Chinese Cemetery
On the hillside where the Feng-shui is said to be best
For one's parents and the rest of one's ancestors
Overlooking the Ocean a quarter mile below
Usually we sit alone for however long it takes
The bus running off and on schedule
Our only company the gravestones
Across the narrow road
There we bide our time
Waiting to find out
What we came for

First Trip: January to March, 1987

I had gotten to the airport a couple of hours before the flight and I checked my luggage directly in as I came into the Departure floor of the Tom Bradley International Terminal. Fortunately, the MAS ticketing counters were the first ones by the front door, so I didn't have to reel my luggage very far inside the terminal building. They took my tickets and put luggage tags on my two larger bags, the other one I carried on board with me.

I went through the metal detector and airport security without any difficulty. Waits at pre-departure gates are always tedious. One watches the planes taking off and landing in the distance, and once in a while a large one taxies by, a couple nosing right up to the window. Then all kinds of men in different uniforms come out to perform their jobs on the large flying beasts.

I watched them load the MAS flight. They loaded a red sports car and a lot of baggage. I wondered if my bags were somewhere at the bottom of it all. I couldn't but help thinking how they could put so much in a plane, plus all the passengers and the plane could still be expected to take off at the end of the runway, and then fly at high altitudes halfway around the world.

I looked at the wings and wondered how they could be built strong enough to withstand so much stress from the flight. At some interminable point a barely audible voice could be heard over the loudspeaker system announcing the loading of my flight number to Narita Airport, Tokyo, and to Kuala Lumpur, Malaysia.

I found my assigned seat and sat down and waited the half-hour or so for everyone to settle on board and for the plane to begin taxiing down the runway, make a turn, wait for a couple of minutes, and then suddenly take off into the air.

The first taking off and landing, when the forces of acceleration and deceleration are most noticeable, are the moments of greatest consternation of the entire flight. Human beings were not naturally meant to fly, and the feeling of taking off under so much force from the jet engines comes in the gut that's fundamentally hard to get used to.

I took right to reading that first flight. It was one of those Anthro-300 type texts, "The Clash of Cultures" that a friend of mine, the head of the anthropology department at my old alma mater, had given me as a gift.

I read most of it the first few hours of the flight, and ignored almost everything going on around me on board the plane, including the stewardesses serving the meals and the coffee and drinks. Mid-way through the book I grew tired of it, and then turned to learning Malay words from the vocabulary list I had made up from the dictionary I had.

I think I was relieving the anxiety of the flight as well as of a trip alone to an unknown part of the world. I noticed that the "The Tres Hombres" with Chevy Chase was being shown as an in-flight movie, and how strange it was to watch a movie without hearing any sound, trying to figure out what was happening by the gestures and actions of the actors.

At some point I returned to the book I had put down and finished it. I looked at my watch and I still had about 4 or 5 hours to go before we landed at Narita. I thus had one overweight extra textbook already read that I didn't need to carry around with me for the remainder of my journey, and yet it was one I wanted to hold on to because it was a gift from a "VIF" (or "Very Important Friend.")

I put down the book I had been reading in the dark because everyone else seemed asleep and the entire plane had been darkened and all the window blinds pulled down. I was afraid to tackle the other book I had brought for the journey, the large, logical, fine print "Historian's Fallacies" because it was too large and too small of print to try to tackle sitting there in the darkness of the plane. Besides, I figured I'd better save something for the rest of the journey.

I sat there, half asleep and half awake, trying to look comfortable and happy for the oriental looking stewardess so that she would not feel too bothered by me, for the remainder of the trip. By the time the plane was banking in to land at Narita I remembered feeling very relieved that we would have a chance to get off the plane and onto solid ground again for a little while.

The plane landed, and after another interminable wait of taxiing and standing in the aisle we at last were allowed to walk out and through a long man-made flexible tunnel, pushed along at a rapid pace by all those passengers from behind.

Auto-Anthropology

The Japanese girls were waiting at the end of this tube, with a perpetual smile frozen on white faces and their hands motioning like motorized mannequins pointing out a special at the grocery store. Behind the girls were standing some very stern looking Japanese men, about a head taller than the women, dressed in blue suits and looking somehow very important.

We found ourselves within a large circular departure lounge with only limited access down the hallway to some overpriced souvenir shops and a soda-snack shop and the toilets, for which almost all the men and women headed at the same time. I remembered to put my toothpaste and toothbrush and comb in my pocket, for my main objective in getting to the bathroom was to clean up a little and brush my teeth to get the after-taste of the last ten hours out of my mouth.

I washed my face and stubbly whiskers with some water from the faucet that kept turning off by itself, only to discover that there were no napkins or hand-towels in the room, only the hot-air blow driers for the hands that miraculously turned on by themselves as soon as you put your hands under them and turned off again as soon as you removed them.

Since I always felt pretty ridiculous standing there trying to dry both my face and my hands at the same time, I decided that I would look in the toilet stalls for tissue. There I saw a dispenser for the longest roll of toilet paper one could imagine—a roll that when completely unrolled must be a few thousand miles long.

What havoc a small child or a kitten would play in such a stall with such a long roll of paper. I wiped my face dry with some of this toilet paper only to find that now there were white pieces of paper left on the whiskers of my face. Managing to brush these off, while a couple of Japanese were studying me curiously, I felt good enough now to go out and join the unfriendly crowd waiting on the backless black vinyl benches outside.

I have come to the conclusion that there is no comfortable place to sit and no way to completely avoid feeling at least a little awkward in such situations. No matter which place you find to sit and which direction you look in, there is always someone facing you on the opposite side so that you get to look at each other and study one another and even sometimes smile at one another, without ever exchanging a single word, especially if the other person is a Japanese or Malaysian or some other foreign nationality.

And then there are always the one or two loud voices you always can hear above the din of all the rest. The young woman going to conduct research on such and such a topic; the business man exchanging local knowledge of good hotels and exotic places to visit that one had never even heard of before.

At some point, after several hours of going nowhere and doing nothing but looking at the many planes outside, they announced the boarding of our MAS plane and everyone again crowded around to be first to go through the small man-made tube. I went back through a new set of stewards and stewardesses standing by the entrances of the plane, smiling and saying "welcome" and "watch your step," etc.

As tired as most of us who had made the first leg of the flight were, we were immediately treated to a third coarse of our menu and then to another in-flight film--about a couple of intelligent young upper middle class boys who play hooky from school and take one of their father's expensive sports cars for a romp. More modern American culture, a la Ferris Bueller, being exported to the rest of the world.

The last leg of the journey seemed interminable and everyone seemed both exhausted and on edge. A British man, dressed in a funny camouflaged uniform and with a strange short hair-cut, would not sit down and just paced back and forth and stood near the door of the airplane. I kept wondering whether he might suddenly push the door open and jump out, as it looked almost as if one of the bags he had with him was a parachute.

I realized we were about to land in Kuala Lumpur, Malaysia at about midnight when the air hostesses brought around little entry cards that we had to fill out that had the "Death for drug trafficker" warning.

I peered through the window of the plane as it slowly banked on its long descent. I could see only small crumbs of lights in the middle of an ocean of darkness, and thought to myself that I was indeed about to land in the middle of the jungle.

I felt as if we had reached the point of no return, sort of like the bus pulling into boot camp in the middle of the night with Drill Instructors waiting outside. There was no turning back now, no matter what I was in for on the other side. It was an ominous sign, "Death for drug traffickers." It as a message that was reemphasized by a big billboard that was plainly visible as we taxied down the runway.

Auto-Anthropology

So we landed and waited and finally walked down off the plane onto the tarmac in the old style that one always saw in the movies. My very first impression of Malaysia, besides the strange music being piped over the airplane and the incomprehensible speech of the pilot and the curious smiles of the strange, dark-eyed air hostesses, was the insufferable heat and humidity that hung like a fine mist in the midnight air over the runway and felt as if one was descending into a boiling pot.

We were led into a terminal building and I followed the crowd down a flight of stairs and along a long corridor. Why there are always corridors that were so long at airports I will never know—until we were led through the immigration counters where they checked out passports.

It was a moment of truth. I was already dripping in unrelieved perspiration. The person quickly looked at my passport, and without saying anything gave it the rubber stamp and handed it back to me. I didn't know what he had stamped in it at the time but I was grateful that he just returned it to me.

Then we waited for our bags to come out of the luggage room on the conveyor belt. I was surprised to find my small plastic duffle bag that I had bought just for the trip had popped open at the zipper to reveal all my jungle equipment that lay inside. I gathered all my bags over my shoulders and my book bag and luggage cart in my hands has I then made my way to the customs counter.

I wondered what their reaction would be when they discovered my first aid kit and my camping equipment, but I was surprised and wore a grateful smile when the woman just waved me through. I came through some glass doors to the hot night air outside through a group of swarming men. I was assaulted by a group of men offering to give me a ride. I didn't really have a plan and didn't know where I was. I didn't even know that there was a hotel just across the road.

Finally a nice looking Malay man wearing some kind of nametag came forward and asked me where I was going. I told him I didn't know but figured I should try to find a hotel in KL, which I somehow imagined I had landed in the center of downtown. He told me that it was a twenty-minute ride by taxi to get to hotels in KL and that it would be hard to find a room because it was the beginning of Chinese New Year.

I agreed to let him drive me into KL and he went to three or four different hotels until he found one that was used a lot by the police with a spare room. I paid him 50 dollars for his troubles and he helped me up to my room with my bags. He told me that he would call on me the next morning.

It was a clean but old looking room. It had a deep red carpet and a bed with a night table and the walls were veneered with a wood that I liked because I was part carpenter and appreciated anything done in wood. I looked out through the window and could see the lights of the city spreading out below—of course I couldn't know what it looked like in the darkness. It was just so many red and blue and white stars twinkling through the dark windowpane.

I had fallen asleep around 2:00 AM only to be awakened by the Muslim criers a few hours later whom I could hear all over the city. It was a strange sound I had never heard before and realized even more than the giant Dadah billboard that I had landed in a Muslim world. I couldn't sleep anymore and so got out of bed and drew the blinds to behold a morning panorama of tall buildings and jungle and hills at the distant edge of a pretty large city.

Someone had slipped a New Straits Times under my door and I decided I had better look through it partly out of courtesy of having been given the gift and partly out of curiosity of what an English language paper contained. My eyes caught a short article that described the case of a young man being whipped under Muslim law for having been found at a dark bus stop with a young lady. This article reinforced my vision of a thoroughly Islamic social order, in which I had somehow managed to end up in the middle of.

It was not too long before I heard a knock at my door and the Taxi-driver had returned with his two small children, who were at first very timid to come into the room and to look at me. He had one small boy and a small girl, both with curly black hair.

He offered to take me out to see the city, and we went to A & W to have a small breakfast. He drove me around downtown that he said was mostly Chinese. I will never forget that my first impression of KL and of Malaysia, besides the "Death for Drug Trafficker" sign at the airport and the criers in the morning, was of Ronald MacDonald sitting up in the back seat of an open convertible VW bug like it was a parade with a loud speaker blaring, waving to all the little Asian kids who eagerly lined the sidewalks of the downtown street to see him.

I thought it a strange twist of fate that I had come expecting to combat leeches and tigers and pythons in the midst of dark jungle only to be

Auto-Anthropology

greeted with a very familiar clown figure of my own childhood. It was then that I most realized that I was not getting what I had expected or planned to get.

We talked awhile and he wanted to take me to the national zoo. He said it was OK, that he had the time. It was understood in our discussion in his car the night before that if I paid him a small sum of money he would act as a tour guide for me and show me some of the sights about the city. I asked him how much he wanted for this service and he told me it was up to me, counting on my own American generosity and naiveté. Since my days overseas in the service I've always been fundamentally suspicious of such fast arrangements. I said that I would think about it.

So there we were the next morning, sitting in an A& W, eating the food I had paid for everyone, and looking at Ronald MacDonald drive down the road outside.

We drove out to the zoo on a windy road that led away from the city along what I took to be the edge of the great jungle. He pointed out a few squatter huts that he said the government tolerated because the people were leaving the kampongs in the interior and had no place to stay in the city. He himself had left his Kampong not too long before to seek more gainful employment in the city, and the airport had allowed him a kind of quasi-official status to serve as taxi.

We got out to the airport to find a couple of young men acting as parking attendant. We walked into the zoo and I again paid for everyone's admission. The zoo I found to be interesting, though quite old and some of the buildings in dire need of renovation. My friend the taxi-driver cum tour-guide enjoyed mostly the big fish in the large aquariums as he pointed out all the different kinds that could be found in the rivers.

I remember the black and white Tapir, and, though I had seen it in photos, wondered what a strange combination of colors could bless such an odd-shaped creature. I wondered what it would be like if people were half black and half white.

We spent most of the day at the zoo, and ate a lunch on a large green area. The only untoward experience was when a group of 8 or 10 young Chinese men, faddishly dressed, began laughing at us and two of them began acting as if they were mounting each other in front of us. My friend became angry with them but paid them no further notice.

That evening my friend took me back to his home—it was a flat several stories above the ground. His wife had made a fish curry and seemed nice. She wasn't wearing a veil and I thought that Muslim women must be more relaxed in the domestic privacy of their own homes. She had a nice cupboard with glass doors filled with nice plates and dishes and small ornaments. We sat down to eat and it was the first time I realized that Malays eat with their fingers without the assistance of a knife or fork or spoon.

I had never known that before and was always taught that it was the epitome of ill manners and dirty, as well to eat with your hands. Also it was the first time I had ever eaten a curry mixed with rice. At first, I almost felt like vomiting, though I tried to hide my discomfiture from my exceedingly polite host.

But at some point I gradually had gotten used to the idea of eating with my hands--they were already covered with rice and curry--that I decided to try to finish it all on my own. I think though that in the course of my meal I must have somehow disgusted my host and his wife, who couldn't refrain from laughing at me at one point.

The little girl at some point had taken to me during the day and managed to sit on my lap as I sat on the floor eating the food. I didn't mind it but felt a little nervous because I thought that all Muslim women were supposed to be shy and retiring in the company of men.

We talked and he told me about his family and how hard it was to make a living in **KL**. He had some sparklers and his children had fun playing with them out on the balcony. I told him about myself and my interest in getting in touch with the University system there, in order to teach or do research in Anthropology. He seemed quite impressed and told me he would try to help me out, as he knew some people in the University system.

He then settled in to watching a movie on television. It showed Americans in Saigon during the Vietnam War and struck me as quite graphic. It was not an American movie and I had never seen it before. I was growing tired, as my friend seemed totally engrossed in the movie. Finally I asked him if he could take me back to my hotel room, even though the movie was only half finished. He agreed but seemed reluctant to leave the TV.

On the way back he asked me about the Vietnam War and why the Americans left Vietnam and why the morale was so low. I tried to explain it as best that I understood it, based upon my own experiences in the post-Vietnam era Marine Corps and my ethnographic work among the Vietnamese Refugees.

The next morning was Saturday and he came a little later, about 10 or 11 in the morning. I heard the sound of his children's voices as they came running up the hallway and knocked upon my door. His wife had accompanied them this morning and she was dressed in a pretty red and pink flower patterned one-piece outfit with a veil over her head. They all appeared genuinely happy to see me, and he wanted to take me to the national museum.

It was a sunny morning as we drove out to the museum near a large green area on a hillside. On the way he again asked me about why the Americans couldn't win the Vietnam War, and I again tried to explain to him how I understood it—the army had become demoralized and there was no frontlines and the war had become increasingly unpopular at home. Many soldiers had tried to do a good job but were often arbitrarily constrained from fighting effectively.

The children all came into my room and looked around in the room as if they had never seen a hotel before. We went back out and I held the children's hands as we went down the corridor and took the elevator out to the street below.

It was a nice sunny morning and we drove out to the museum. When we tried to find a parking spot at the busy parking lot that a Chinese man came in a pretty nice car and tried taking the same spot as my friend. They got angry at each other and exchanged a few words.

We spent several hours inside the museum. I found it quite interesting and my first introduction to the culture of Malaysia—the Kris and the Nonya wedding chamber and the Malay kampong house. That afternoon we stopped at a shopping center somewhere downtown. He parked inside a multi-tiered parking garage and we had a dinner at a MacDonald's.

The next morning he and his family, with his wife, drove me down early to the train station. At some point he had decided that I should go to Penang to visit for a while. I had no idea of what or where Penang was, but he assured me that it was a nice place to visit and that I would enjoy myself there. I bought a Rail-pass that gave me unlimited rail-travel within a two-week period. I thought it was a bargain, although that was the last time I was to ride on the train for several months.

Since I had so many bags I decided the night before to repack everything and leave some things behind with my friend. Thus I left my nice pair of leather shoes, my leather book bag, a couple of heavy books and my luggage dolly in the trunk of his car, so that I had only two overweight bags to carry on board the train. He promised to keep them safe for me until I returned and gave me his address, phone-number and name on a slip of paper.

As the train lurched forward on the platform I remember waving to my Malay friend, his wife and their kids, wondering if I would ever see them again, and not really knowing whether we were traveling north, or south or east or west. I had luckily gotten the air-con coach and there were not many people riding in the car that day.

An older Sikh man with a white turban and long white beard came up and sat across from me on the train. I had a seat number and remained in my assigned seat, even though there were a lot of empty seats and people came and went from one seat to another. I began talking to this man. He told me that he was just retired, and that he was the ex-police inspector of the KL police force. He showed me his home that was along the railroad track as we passed by. I told him that I was in anthropology and had come to pursue my studies.

He told me his daughter was studying in Australia, which fact he seemed quite proud of. At some point he asked for my address and I wrote it down for him. Because it was a P.O. box I wrote the "#" sign before the number and he was quite interested in what this sign stood for, as he had never seen it used this way before.

I told him it meant "number." I told him I was headed to Penang, though I didn't know what Penang was. He said it was a nice city, and highly recommended that I stay at the YMCA—it was in a quiet place and was clean and safe and not too expensive. He said he knew the manager there and that I should give him his name. He asked me all about the U.S.

He started talking about women. He said that he had traveled to Europe but found that the European women were all spoiled and conceited, and that no Asian man could afford them. At the time I was quite inclined to agree with him. Then he told me that I should go to Thailand because the girls there are the best and know how to treat a man right. At that point I felt a little embarrassed by what I interpreted to be his blatant male chauvinism, and wondered what he really thought of his daughter in Australia when he had such attitudes about women in general.

He told me that Penang was a Chinese city and that he knew everything about the Chinese gangs. He then warned me to be careful and not to do any drugs. He asked me if I did drugs and I told him no. He gave me his address and told me to look him up when I came back down to KL. He got off at Ipoh, which he called the cleanest city in Malaysia.

The remainder of the journey I watched the jungle and the train turning along the tracks, the sound of the rails as the wheels rode along, entering tunnels in hillsides and the deep jungle growth outside. I saw mile after mile of plantations, and large holes in the ground that had once been tin mines, and clothes hanging outside of wooden homes and terrace houses and children waving at the train as it passed and workmen doing construction along the edge of the rail line and a wide lake that we seemed to ride out on the middle of on a low, straight bridge. I kept watching into the jungle growth to see if I could spot any wildlife.

I saw a few buffalo but that was about it. The train would pull into a small station and the voice on the loudspeaker system would announce the stop in Malay. I was afraid to leave the train because I didn't know how long the train would stay at each stop, but shortly it would move off again, staying just long enough to unload and load new passengers.

The train arrived at Butterworth that I thought was Penang, in the evening after dark. I came down off the train carrying the two bags under my shoulders just as I remembered humping my sea bag and equipment in the Marine Corps. A young dark Indian man offered to carry my bags for me but I told him no, because I didn't trust him and thought he would steal my bags. He looked a little offended at me and I just walked off along the length of the platform.

When I got off I didn't know where to go or what to do, so I just followed the crowd as it walked up off the train platform along a raised wooden concourse and came down on the other side where a bunch of buses were waiting. I was sweating profusely again, and I stopped a young Malay man and asked where the YMCA was.

He looked a little bemused and told me I must go back along the platform and take a ferry. So I picked up my bags and walked back along the wooden concourse to where there was a turn and another concourse that lead onto a large ferry that was waiting to launch and was filling up with people.

I got on it at the last moment as the gates raised behind me. The ferry was crowded with people and I put my bag down by the rail and sat on it, trying to internally control my sweating and feeling quite grateful that the wind helped cool me down after the ferry launched.

I saw only lights all around and the foam of the water being cut by the ferry below. The motion of the ferry could be felt below, and it had been a long time since I had been on boat like that. A couple of Malay women were staring at me as I sat there on my bag, not knowing where I was or that I had to take a ferry to "Penang" because it was actually an island and not just another city.

When the ferry bumped into the other side and the gate opened and the walkway dropped I followed the crowd off the boat and along another long wooden covered concourse to where it let out among some shops and a lot of taxis and men trying to get me to ride in their trishaw.

Finally I reached the end of the line and didn't know which way to go. A young Indian man offered to take me in his trishaw and I asked him if he knew where the YMCA was and if he could get me there and how much it would cost.

I remember riding at night through that strange city. I felt like I had landed on Mars and was completely disoriented as we rode down one street and up another. I had lost complete track of any direction and sat feeling more helpless than I ever felt in my life before. The lights and the strange architecture of the buildings were all completely new to me.

He charged me seven dollars and I paid him ten, when he let me off at a small hotel called the "New Asia" in the middle of town. I asked if this was the YMCA and he told me no but this was a safe hotel at a good price. I later found out that the hotel people paid him a commission to bring customers off the jetty to their hotel.

He helped carry my bags up the narrow flight of stairs and an old Chinese man in a tank top T-shirt greeted me. I paid about 17 dollars for a room and noticed they had beer in a refrigerator for sale. The Indian took my bags to my room, which was the next floor up. I found the room sparse and in a curious design which seemed thoroughly Chinese.

The beds were low and had a thin mattress on hard planks, and the chairs sat back low to the ground almost like black Adirondack patio chairs with short legs. The ceiling fan twirled round and round and the spare light bulb cast shadows on the walls. I put my bags down and sat there, and then went back down to get a quart of beer and a glass full of ice. I learned to drink beer with ice with the Vietnamese.

The beer had a thick flavor but was quite good as I hadn't had one for several days and I was hotter than hell. The beer helped calm me down a little and I imagined all sorts of things about being in a genuine-Far Eastern city in which everyone was a member of a secret society.

Stepping out onto the balcony and watching the street below reinforced my view of the city, as it was close to midnight on the 9th day of the Chinese New Year (a fact I only learned afterward) and they had all sat out large red tables with roast pig and fruit and cakes and palm fronds adorned the entrances of their shops and huge piles of paper money were set in the streets.

I noticed as I had come up the second flight of stairs to my room a large strand of firecrackers hanging from a rafter from the ceiling. I took them to be decorations, as they were almost as large as red sticks of dynamite.

After twelve I discovered that they were indeed real as they exploded with a loud "BANG, BANG, BANG" that I thought could wake the dead, as they indeed woke me up. I went out onto the balcony and believed I had indeed landed on the moon, as everywhere large piles of curiously folded paper were burning up in large bonfires in the middle of the streets and everywhere was the sound and smell of firecrackers in a ceaseless, cacophonous repetition.

I laid on the hot bed, watching the ceiling fan, wondering if this happened every night and how long it would go on for until it ended. I was too tired and hot and confused to feel annoyed.

The next morning I woke up early because of the heat. It was hot and sunny outside. I walked outside and found myself in the midst of a morning Chinese market where people were buying and selling elbow to elbow while motorcycles came and went. I tried smiling and saying hello to some Chinese, but they just gave me a stern face as if I didn't exist and I decided that the Chinese in their little shop houses must be among the most unfriendly and impersonal people on earth, whose only purpose on earth must have been to make money.

When I came back I decided I'd go see some of the local sites and the young Chinese man at the desk showed me a map with some of the things to see and do. I decided I'd go to see the *Khoo Kong Si* building and traced out how to get there from the hotel. He seemed quite friendly.

As I walked down the road a young Malay man started following me and then came up beside me and asked me if I wanted some drugs. I told him no and tried to move off but he stalked behind me. I turned around and told him to stop following me, and just then I saw him give another young Malay some money while the other one gave him a small little piece of round substance which he then showed me and told me it was heroin. His eyes were glazed over and he seemed to walk as if he were on clouds. I walked away leaving him across the street.

I somehow managed to find the *Khoo Kong Si*. Just outside the square on the street a young Australian man was being peddled by in a trishaw, looking every bit the white Raja with his bags under his arms. I was standing there holding my Olympus camera with the Mickey Mouse strap I had gotten at Disney Land a couple of years before working with Vietnamese children. He pointed to me and stopped the trishaw in the street and came running up to me and just took the camera out of my hands as I stood there.

I was surprised and didn't know what to think as he started asking me where I got the camera and accusing me of stealing his at the airport in Sydney, Australia. I told him I'd never been to Australia and I suppose he realized that it wasn't his camera after all, and he handed it back to me without an apology or anything, got back in his trishaw and rode off down the road. I just stood there wondering about what had just happened and how rude and nervy the guy was.

I took pictures of the *Khoo Kong Si* building and its intricate, ornate carving and furniture and wall paintings. I had never seen anything quite like it before, it being a far cry from Grumman's Chinese Theatre on Hollywood Blvd. I felt like I had just descended into the heart of 16th Century Ming China.

On the way back I got lost, and was feeling hot. I stopped by a small booth selling flowers and pictures of Hindu child deities. The young Indian man behind the counter started talking to me. Soon he was asking me if I liked to have sex with men and he wanted to come and visit me in the hotel. He said he had made it with many Europeans and he liked to play the role of the woman. I wouldn't tell him which hotel I was in and told him I wasn't interested. As I was moving off he told me to come and visit his house behind the snake temple, which was just a short walk down the road.

Since I was feeling hot and lost a sense of what direction I was in, as I was standing beside a large yellow mosque, an Indian trishaw came by and I decided to pay him five dollars to take me back to the New Asia hotel, at which door he shortly dropped me off.

The strange events and interactions in the morning left me with a sense of alienation and a fear to travel too far from the hotel for fear of getting lost again or into some kind of situation I couldn't get out of.

That evening I came down to eat a bowl of Laksa from a hawker lady just outside the entrance of the hotel, and a Chinese man from across the road who was drinking some coffee came over and started talking to me. He told me about Penang and about the Chinese and how the Malays owned all the land on the Mainland.

He told me that he would come the next day and take me out to see the sites, if I wanted, and that he worked in a shoe factory just across the road. He told me about the thieves market that went on there every morning at dawn and how sometimes snake charmers would come and perform.

That evening I invited the Indian trishaw driver up to drink a beer with me who had brought me to the hotel the first night, as he was outside the hotel resting in his trishaw. I bought him a stout and we sat outside at a round table in an open court by the hotel lobby.

He told me he was married and they were trying to build a house with bricks. He told me how he punished his children when they were naughty by making them hold their arms out while holding something— he would punish them like that when they did poorly in school or did not understand their studies. He told me he earned about 18 Malaysian Ringgit (RM, or dollars) a day as a Trishaw, and that he worked more than 12 hours peddling each day.

The next morning I got up early and went out to see thieves market. I saw a few odd-looking men sitting along the opposite curb with blankets spread out and a few odds and ends on them. There were not many people out and I was afraid that one of them might try to steal my own camera. I walked down the road and came to a gate that looked like another Kong Si house in a square beyond.

Three Chinese men were sitting around a small table near the front of the gate under a tree, playing draughts. As I asked if it were all right if I took a picture of the building they said "OK" and one of them then got up, bid farewell to his friends and followed me out onto the street as I walked. He asked me where I was from and where I was going. At first I didn't want to be bothered with this man, as he was thin and wiry and left me with an uneasy feeling.

He told me he was a construction worker and had a couple of days off and had nothing to do and would show me around the town if I only gave him a few dollars and paid for his food. I told him I wasn't sure of it but I decided I'd let him lead me around for a day, as I wanted to see some of the city. So we went to see the Burmese Sleeping Buddha the first day, having taken a bus from the main depot at the shopping center.

That evening he came back with me to my hotel. He had told me that he now lived with his mother in Tanjung Bungah, and that he was married but now divorced and that he had to give money to his wife to support his daughters. He then asked me if I had five dollars to spare and I gave it to him and told me to wait out on the street while he went up to a old Chinese shop house, where he wanted to give his wife some money for food.

He came back down and we ate some rice with curry for only 40 cents per plate in an outdoor hawker complex under a wooden roof. It was a part of town that was full of older buildings and the people looked poor.

That night I followed him to watch a live opera perform at night. He walked fast and didn't wait to cross streets. I learned how to walk fast and jay walk across busy roads without getting hit, though in hindsight it seemed dangerous and a crazy thing to do.

We stood and watched the opera for over an hour. Old men and a few children were sitting in chairs as the actors performed. The women were dressed in the gaudy, glittery traditional costumes, with white made up faces and red mascara. It all seemed a very strange and fascinating thing to watch, as live musicians played just behind the stage.

He brought me back to the hotel and asked me if I could put him up for the night since it was too late to catch a bus out to *Tanjung Bungah* for the night. Since there was an extra bed in the room I agreed, although I was wary of my travelers checks and cash which I kept in a secret pocket on my leg just below my knee at all times. The old watchmen at the lobby who let us in didn't want to let him up to the room and they got into an argument but the young man came up anyway.

When I came back from taking a shower I had found him going through one of my bags, trying to find things to take out of it. I didn't mind too much as he had seen earlier that I had brought extra cigarettes in the bag as 'gifts' even though I didn't smoke, and he wanted some of them. So I gave him a bunch of cigarettes and a small bag of other assorted "gifts" I had brought with me--small travel sized bottles of Tylenol tablets, combs, disposable razors, etc.

He was pleased that I gave him these things and he laid down on the other bed and went to sleep. The next morning we went to the Kek Lok Si temple and he showed me around. I met a young Malaysian Chinese couple who asked me to take their picture for them, as they saw I had a nice camera and was taking photos. He told me that he had been to school in Texas and had majored in art. He then looked at my self-appointed tour-guide and told me to be careful because some people were not to be trusted.

That afternoon my tour guide decided that he wanted to take me fishing from a fishing village, and told me to check out of the hotel I was in. Since he seemed fairly trustworthy and his story was not as yet inconsistent, we took a bus to his Mom's home in *Tanjung Bungah* where I left my bags.

I took a bath there, not realizing that the large basin of water was for dunking water in a small plastic scooper and pouring over one's body. I ended up getting into the basin as if it were a bathtub, not knowing how else to bathe myself. When I got out my friend realized what I had done and scolded me for wasting all the water. I felt very sorry and embarrassed for what I had done and never repeated the same mistake.

We took another bus out to some fishing boats at the 'end of the world." He knew some of the fishermen there and spoke Tamil to them and said he liked to go out fishing with them sometimes. We paid a boat driver about 15 dollars to take us around a point and drop us off on a beach where there was nobody.

The boat let us off about twenty feet from the edge of the beach in water that was waist deep. I felt bad that I was going to get my travelers checks wet in my secret pocket on my leg, but I had wrapped them up securely in plastic and so didn't worry about them much, and was later able to slip off the pocket without being noticed and make sure that they were still dry.

My tour-guide spent the evening digging for little "*siput*" shells that he collected. I was amazed by his boundless energy in the heat that easily fatigued me. We built a small campfire on the beach and had bought some sodas and some canned sardines with us. We ate and drank this and soon laid on the large square of plastic I had and slept until morning.

The next morning we caught a large long centipede in the trees and he found a plastic he put it in. He wanted to take it back to make medicine with to eat it. We made our way back along a trail that wound around the coast and over a couple of ridges and streams and around a couple of big boulders. We came across an area that was restricted where experimental work was being done, and a young Malay man waved us on.

When we got back to his mom's house, she exchanged a few words with my tour-guide and I found that my bag had been gone through while I was away. They began accusing me of being a drug pusher and I picked up my bags and walked down the road. My tour-guide followed me down and was behaving very rudely too me, scolding me. I went down the road through a Kampong and came out to a bus stop at the bottom of the hill.

He was standing near me, pestering me, and followed me on as I got onto the bus. I sat in the back of the bus with my bags as the young man stood by the rear door and kept looking at me. I felt embarrassed and didn't know what to do, but I quickly formulated a plan.

When he followed me off the bus downtown I immediately hailed a yellow taxi and told the taxi to take me to the police station, and then I told the young man to get into the car with me, as I thought he should explain himself and why he was bothering me to the police. But as soon as I said this and turned around he had disappeared into the crowds, and I have never seen him since.

The entire incident left me feeling very nervous. I got off outside of the gate of the Police headquarters and told the guard at the gate that I wanted to report the incident. I waited in the guard booth a few minutes, until a young plain cloths Chinese detective came out and told me that I should be careful with people here and to check into a better hotel that was just down the road.

Auto-Anthropology

I went to this hotel, which was more modern and more expensive than the first. It had nicer accommodations and a television and a phone and a nice large bathtub with hot water.

I washed my clothes and was afraid to go out. By that time I had been in Penang for less than five days and I was already feeling totally alienated and disoriented. I realized I was not really cut out for long distance travel, and everybody I had met so far seemed ingenuine and who only wanted my money. I made a long distance call to my mom and told her that things didn't seem to be working out for me very well and that I was going to return home the next day.

I soaked all my dirty clothes in the tub with my Wool-Lite travel pack and then hung them up to dry on my elastic clothesline I had brought with me. I watched television and then laid down and slept a while.

That evening I came down to the lobby and ate a meal at the fancy Indian restaurant that was in the basement of the hotel. It was only the second time I had had Indian food, the first being with my Indian friend who once had me to a nice Indian dinner in the states. I had a hot mutton curry with dosa. I sat there alone, eating my food with a beer.

A large table just next to me was set around for a large party and soon a whole group of young Australian men who looked as if they were young military officers came in and started eating and drinking and boisterously laughing. I watched them while I ate my meal, remembering back to my days in the Marine Corps and the young officers I knew then.

A couple of them stopped and turned and looked at me, and one of them said something to the other, then they laughed, and turned and ignored me. I got up and left, thinking that the Australians must be the rudest people on earth since I had met the one who grabbed my camera several days before and these young arrogant blokes.

I decided I would stay one more day, as I would catch a train the following morning back down to KL to arrange my flight home. I went to see a movie that afternoon at a theater close by the Hotel. The movie was about a ship captain in old China who had married a beautiful Chinese woman but who was excluded from the rest of the white community, even though he was a founder and leader of the community. It was a strange theme for me in that dirty and dark theater in a strange Chinese city in a strange country.

After the movie I went back and noticed that there was a sushi bar nearby the restaurant, and I decided I would eat sushi for a change. My friend and his Japanese wife had introduced me to sushi a few years previously, before it had become a yuppie thing to do, and I remembered having sushi while I was stationed in Okinawa about a decade before.

When I went in I didn't realize how expensive it would be, almost over $70 dollars for just one person. I ate a few pieces of fish and rice and had a couple of beers.

A couple of young American women were there and I talked with them a little while. They had just come from Burma and were taking their summer vacation traveling around Southeast Asia. They were schoolteachers who worked in Alaska. I felt they were a breath of fresh air as they were the first genuinely friendly people I talked with since being there in Penang.

I remember that I felt like they were old salts as seasoned travelers compared to myself who couldn't even last an entire week in a foreign country without falling to pieces. After eating and paying my enormous bill (what the heck, I was leaving the next day without spending anything anyway) I returned to my room.

On my way back to the hotel I noticed a hotel lounge was open and I decided I'd stop there to have another beer before going back up to my room. I went in and found that it was a Japanese Karaoke bar. I sat at the bar and ordered a draft mug from a young Chinese bartender who spoke pretty good English and seemed pretty friendly. A couple of Chinese women were in the bar, not too pretty but it was hard to tell in the dark.

I noticed that they would not come over to sit by me, but stayed sitting in the low cushioned square chairs talking with themselves, until a few Japanese customers came in. These girls immediately went for the Japanese customers, who started drinking and singing into a microphone so that they could hear their own voices being played back to music. I thought it was all pretty absurd as I watched the haughty Japanese and the girls who hung closely on to them. I joked with the bartender about it and we laughed. The bartender then poured me another beer on the house.

I told him that I didn't like it here much and that I was leaving to go back in the morning. We talked for quite a while about this and that, and I had quite a few beers before I left and went back to my room.

Auto-Anthropology

The next morning the bartender came in his little white car and he brought his Chinese girlfriend with him, whom he introduced to me as his sister. He offered to take me around the city to show me the sites but I was dead set on getting back to the ferry terminus to get the train leaving that morning back to KL.

He kept insisting and then I finally gave in and said that I would let him take me to the ferry, and only the ferry, if he let me pay him a little. He agreed and I got reluctantly into his car. We drove around for more than a half hour, and then he took me to his home out in *Tanjung Bunga*.

I was more than a little pissed at his deceit, but he was friendly and apologetic enough and I went into his house and met his mother and his father. It was a nice, sizeable, comfortable two-story house. He offered to let me stay there as long as I wanted without any charge.

I changed my mind at the last minute, seeing how I wasn't going to get to the Ferry that morning, and told him I would stay there for just a couple of days. That afternoon they drove me around the island and we stopped and ate makan at a few food stalls along the way.

He was heavily into his religion and for a couple of days I followed him and his girlfriend about to the different temples where they would make offerings and prey. I met the whole family and they all seemed quite friendly and pleased to have me there. One day turned into two, and two turned into three, and three into four, and with each passing day it seemed like a more and more difficult chore to get down to the ferry to leave.

It turned out that his "sister" was pregnant, and one morning I followed them down to the maternity ward at the General hospital. Her boyfriend walked me through the hospital as if we were visiting doctors or something, and one Malay man came up and asked me in English if I were there to see a European man who had been hit by a car a few days before and was in pretty bad condition.

It seemed as though nobody knew who he was and they didn't quite know what to do with him or about him. I told him I didn't know the man and didn't want to get involved.

Because I was getting to see many different small temples and followed my "friend" around with his network of other temple-followers, I felt as if I were indeed getting something interesting happening finally, and that I may actually have broken through the barrier before which everything is just a matter of money and that's all. So I stayed there, and with each passing day became more and more comfortable.

I began noticing some inconsistencies in my friend's story. I was always careful to carry my traveler's checks and money on my person and never to leave anything of any value in my bags. In hindsight this was wise because I afterward found out that my friend and his "sister" whom he stayed with in the same room and made pregnant had most likely gone through my bags, and on more than one occasion.

He kept talking about getting enough money up to start a hawker business and then to make a down payment on their own flat, even though I plainly saw a nice, empty stainless steel hawker stall sitting empty outside their front-door. I surmised that he was leading up to asking me to loan him a few hundred dollars, but he never got around to coming out with it.

It was actually his own father who warned me away from him. One day I paid the old man who spoke very good English in the proper manner a couple of hundred for a month's rent there. He told me his son was no good and feared he was involved with gangs to whom he owed money for gambling debts.

Then I met Rosie, a young Chinese woman who was renting a room from this family. At first my "friend" and his "sister" told me that Rosie was nothing but a "fat ugly pig" and not to bother to talk to her. I didn't understand why they said that and thought it was a mean thing to say.

One day I stayed home and Rosie was there and we played games with the youngest daughter. I got to know Rosie and found she was a friendly person who spoke good English. Her mother and daughter had died and she was all-alone there.

Once I started to talk with Rosie, my relationship with my bartender friend suddenly changed and they put on a totally cold face and ignored me. I moved my bags from their room where I had been sleeping on the floor, and was going to catch a taxi to leave when Rosie told me to stay and leave my bags with her in the room she rented where there was an empty extra bed. She had a small black and white television set which she watched in her room so that she didn't have to be downstairs with the others.

She told me that our "friend" had on more than one occasion broken into her wardrobe and stolen her money, and that he and his girl friend were really not to be trusted. Rosie seemed to be a nice person and I felt sorry for her, as she was alone.

She cried when she told me that the family would threaten her and had tried to beat her up one time, and that they always wanted to take her money for themselves. I started to wait for Rosie during the day and take her out at night, down to town to see a movie or go to dinner or go window-shopping or to the Pasar Malam that came into town about once a week.

In the mornings I would follow the old mother down to the morning market where she would shop and sit and have coffee with her old women cronies.

She was a "Goish" person of Portuguese descent, and her old cronies all looked the same in this way—mixed Asian and European ancestry. They would sit around the table and poke each other in the side and cry out "*puki shibai*" and other foul words. They referred to me as the "thorn among the roses" because not only was I the only man to sit around a table with a bunch of old women, but I was the only young white man to do it.

It was the first time I had witnessed Latah, though I had remembered reading about it in one or two of my anthropology classes, and it seemed almost a cruel kind of joke to play on an unsuspecting victim, who would be almost inevitably embarrassed in the company of others.

During the day I would go with the older sister of the family who was married and had a young girl. We would go and wait to feed the daughter lunch at her school and go down to eat in coffee shops and then pick the daughter up at her school. In the afternoon we would sit and have beer with ice at a coffee shop near the house before she went to her work as a barmaid at a nightclub. I was always amazed at her capacity to put away beer and never noticed its affects on her. Her husband was a locally popular singer who worked in *Langkawi* at an expensive resort hotel.

I had met an older woman who somehow was related to someone in the family. She was old and half blind from cataracts and lived alone in an old house and had nobody to take care of her. We visited her on several occasions, and at some point I would buy her groceries—some canned goods and canned drink and things like that—because she had complained about not having enough food.

One evening Rosie and I had taken her food like that we had bought in a nearby sundry shop, and we missed the buses getting back because it was pretty late. I didn't know where I was and Rosie led me down the hill to try to catch a bus on the main road.

We both felt a little frightened being out like that late at night, and I thought we should go one way down the road and Rosie thought we should go the other way. I tried using a public phone to call a taxi to take us home but none of the phones worked. Finally a bus came along and we got on it. I was a little mad at Rosie and thought she was a little dingy about some things.

It went on like this for a couple of more weeks, and I had been in Penang for almost a month until I decided that I wasn't getting much more accomplished besides spending money and I decided to leave. I was put in touch with a travel agent, a young Chinese woman who was very nice to me and really worked to get me a flight out.

The mother of the house took me down to a special shop to buy gifts for my family. I bought quite a few presents for everyone—tea sets, vases, pots and pans, batik cloth, etc., and spent quite a lot of money on these gifts and then on the airfreight to ship them back home.

I had gotten to know Rosie and liked her quite a lot. I felt sorry for her because I had seen how the family she stayed with could abuse her and how the mother had made her cry in a coffee shop on more than one occasion, and thought to myself how cruel this illiterate woman was.

The first time it happened I had stepped out to get something and when I returned to the table I saw Rosie crying and get up and leave the shop. I followed her outside and found her sitting on the curb by the roadside crying her eyes out. The mother and daughter were quiet and dismissed it as if nothing had happened.

Rosie was of a gentle disposition and she was generous and pleasant to be around. I couldn't understand why they all treated her so poorly except that they felt like she was vulnerable without any family and thus somehow dependent upon them, even though she helped to support them with her money.

The morning of my flight we got up before sunrise and drove in the little white car to the airport. I had got a connecting flight from Penang to KL to Tokyo and then on to LA We got into the airport and I carried the vases I had bought as presents in my bags, having given away all my little trinket gifts and gotten rid of my old shoes and made room for all my things in a single bag.

Before I left I went down to *Komtar* and bought Rosie a little gold pendant with the letter "R" with roses on it, and an electric table fan so that she wouldn't have to use a hand fan to keep herself cool in the evenings. I surprised her with it and she didn't know what to say.

When I went to get on the plane there were tears in my eyes and tears in Rosie's eyes, and I felt almost as if she should be coming with me, as if there was something unspoken there between us which neither of us were saying. I got onto the plane thinking that I would never come back there, and that I was leaving behind at least one or two true friends in all of Penang.

The return trip was in a sense anti-climactic. Almost like the plane trip out, except everything was in reverse. I remember the plane riding from Penang to KL and seeing the morning twilight landscape below that looked almost surreal, like a lunar landscape or the surface of some unknown planet--and of how in the distance thunderheads could be seen with lightening flashing within them.

I met my Malay taxi-driver friend at the airport. He had since gotten a job within the airport itself and he was wearing a nice blue coat with black pants. He asked me why I hadn't come back and told me that he still had my things with him at his house. I was in a hurry to get on board my plane that was leaving within the hour and he escorted me to the departure gate via a shortcut.

I told him as we walked down the long corridors together that I had met and stayed with a Chinese family while in Penang and that I was now returning to the U.S. without a sense of ever returning. I told him to keep the things I had left with him, thinking he might get some use of the shoes, leather bag and folding airport dolly, if not the books and other photocopied materials. He told me that he was expecting me to come back to KL, that he wanted to take me out to the Kampong where his wife's family stayed to meet people there, and that he knew some people in the University he was going to put me in touch with.

We said goodbye to one another and soon I was back on board another airplane bound for Tokyo and then to LA. I never saw my Malay taxi-friend again and don't know what became of him. In Tokyo we got down in the same lounge as before and I went through the same routine with the tooth brushing and the face washing and the toilet paper. It was a long, and forgettable plane flight. One of the same movies that were shown before were being played again, and it was interesting to watch it with the sound this time to see what different impression I would have than the first time without the sound.

Looking back on that first trip now, I often wonder what would have happened if I had done things differently at different times--if I had really not taken that particular taxi to KL that night, or if I had really gotten back on the ferry that morning and returned to KL, or if on returning to KL I had stayed with my Malay friend and followed him into the Kampong like he wanted me to.

Though I did not then realize it at the time in going abroad, I discovered that what I was really seeking was a genuine relationship with someone, some "other" from the third world, one that was not predicated on money or the asymmetries of the first and third world.

This was totally congruent with almost all my anthropological training and with my previous fieldwork among Vietnamese refugees, work that left me burned out because of such asymmetries that I felt I could not overcome. I had many barriers and hurdles to pass through to get to that "other's side" where money was no longer the primary or underlying issue.

The road abroad twists and turns in unexpected directions, and there are choices to be made at almost every turn. Why we make some kinds of choices and not others I do not know.

At the time I only realized I was leaving behind in Penang a rose among all the thorns.

Second

Like a new mother who in pain screams,
Like a new born child crying
Who in purity beams
Like seagulls far inland flying
Like a trickling stream
And the roaring waterfall
Like the currents that ebb and flow
The tides that rise and fall
And the waves that endlessly roll
Like a stone smoothed all round
And the wood that drifts ashore
Like the invisible wind that whistles and howls,
And the dust that imperceptibly settles
Like that tiny toiling ants that abound
Like the heat of the sun
And darkness of the night
Like the ugly cawing crows
That flock and take flight

First Interregnum

It was not long after I was back that I decided I wanted to return and get Rosie. I realized that I really liked her company, felt sorry for her all alone there, and I missed her a great deal. I decided I better write to her and ask her in a letter to marry me, before we lost track of one another. It was a foolish and impulsive thing to do, but I'd long felt alone in life and was growing tired of being alone. I talked until the early hours in the morning with my mom about it (partly because I couldn't sleep from the jet-lag). I'd spent very little of the money I'd saved from the first trip and had more than enough to buy another round-trip ticket.

My mother gave me support in this endeavor as she had always supported my decisions, even when they proved to be wrong ones, and she promised to help pay for Rosie's return ticket. I wanted it to be kept secret and for no one else to know the real reason for my return.

After a day or two my brother's girlfriend drove me back down to the airport to get the crate I had shipped by airfreight back to the U.S. I had bought a load of gifts for everyone of my family and most of my friends-- a couple sarongs, tea-sets, tin and aluminum cooking vessels, straw and cloth mats, handkerchiefs and a few pieces of clothing. I had bought my mom an entire dinner set of blue and white dishes, only to find most of the large dinner plates hopelessly cracked at the bottom of the box.

I arranged the return flight the following week, but the earliest I could leave was about four or five weeks later, in the early part of May. Thus I had about a month or so to spend and didn't know what to do with myself. I wanted as little involvement in daily life there as I could, because it seemed to somehow interfere with my main goal of getting back to Malaysia.

So for almost an entire month I stayed at my Mom's home, and hardly left the house at all except to water the plants sometimes. I stayed in my room and finished a collection of poetry I'd started writing back in 1983 but had run into a writer's block on it and couldn't finish it until then.

I had since collected a number of odd poems I'd written now and then, and so I added these together and wrote several more to make a finished set of about a hundred. I put this collection together in a different style than any of my previous poems, playing with the words on the page and with the punctuation so that it was hard to tell where one poem began and another left off except for the spacing between the lines.

I also wrote to Rosie several times, telling her more about myself and my feelings and my plans, etc. They were the only "love letters" I ever wrote, either before or since. I also read more about Van Gogh and venomous snakes.

Toward the end of this period I took a short trip up to Northern California to visit my friend Jim and his Japanese wife, Yukiko. He had been attending UC Davis, just west of Sacramento, for a few years as a fully funded PhD student in Anthropology.

We left at about 2 AM in the morning. I drove my Indian friend up to visit her friends along the coast in Santa Cruz, and earlier left my sister off in Chowchilla with my Grandmother. From there I headed north in my old 1972 green Plymouth Valiant along the coast, through San Francisco and across the Golden Gate Bridge and then cut across to the coast to make my way up the windy and resplendent coast along Coast Highway One.

It was the most beautiful drive and most spectacular scenery I had ever seen, before or since. Then there were not many cars along the way, and the sky was clear, and the pine-trees came right up to the edge of the cliffs. The rocky coastline wound directly below and the rough blue gray windy seas broke in huge waves far off shore.

I had been driving almost the entire day, and had not eaten anything, and as dusk was falling I became anxious to find a place to bed down for the night. I stopped at a few state beaches but found them all booked up. I drove on to a point just beyond a river inlet and then turned inland on a small highway.

I came into a dark redwood forest just as darkness fell and soon came upon a roadside campground that had empty lots squeezed in between all the trees. I pulled in, paid my six dollars in a little envelope, and threw my sleeping bag on the picnic table and then made a small fire and cooked a pack of noodles and a can of tuna I had brought with me in my Willy Peter bag, and then I went to sleep. I had been driving for almost 22 hours straight.

I got up early before sunrise the next morning just as it was beginning to rain and I threw my gear into the trunk of my green valiant and headed on the down the road. I felt better after the sleep and emerged from the forest and the coastal range just as the sun was breaking on the horizon.

That morning I drove through all the pretty vineyards of the Sonoma valley, at some point turned inland again along a small two lane road that wound around a dam with a lake and then along a river where a lot of people were camping. I came down onto the flat farmland of the central valley and at 65 mph headed for UC Davis that was just about 15 minutes down the road.

I followed my friend's directions where to park and how to find his apartment on the campus. They had a spare bedroom with a spare bunk bed just like the one's I used to sleep on in the squad bays in the USMC. I got there early and went with my friend out to the garden he was tending nearby and helped him pull weeds.

Later that evening I went with him and his Japanese wife down to some cherry trees on campus where we sat and drank wine and beer and celebrated the Cherry Blossom festival. The campus was deserted on an extended weekend break and we had the place all to ourselves. We played with a Frisbee and I met a few of his friends.

That evening we all went back to his apartment where we drank more beer and strummed out old Beatle's ditties on his guitar. His Taiwanese friends, a quiet couple, were reticent about drinking much at first but they began getting into it more when everyone was pressuring them to drink more.

Everyone woke up the next morning feeling a little hung over and stretched out, but we roused ourselves and drove out with the Taiwanese couple and a few other people to a friend's ranch nestled in the foothills where we fished at a small private reservoir-pond nestled in the hills. An orange orchard faced the pond on the northern hillside and I remember thinking how childish all these graduate students were acting when they began talking about their professors as if they were their parents and then they began throwing the oranges from the trees down to the Taiwanese people below who were the only one's to catch any fish.

We returned to have a more subdued evening, where we went out and ate an Italian dinner at a restaurant on campus, and the next day I went on my own down to Sacramento to visit the old-town area they had and then to hike along the American River where the trail extended for almost 15 miles. I walked about six miles down the trail and then turned around and walked back.

Auto-Anthropology

It wound among the trees and fields, in and out along the river's edge, and it was a pleasant hike all by myself. At the end of the trail where I turned around I noticed that three boys were playing with a snake that they killed and left headless on the trail. It was a long and old garter snake, and was harmful to no one but the field mice.

That evening I said my farewell to my friend while his wife was still at work, and left to make the long ten-hour trip back to LA. I reached LA about 6 AM in the morning, after a few cups of coffee and few tanks of gas, with the engine of my car overheating.

A few days later I was back on the plane again, headed back to Malaysia. This time I didn't bring all the extras, not even my camera, as I was disappointed with the fuzziness of the photos from the first trip and decided not to take any more pictures. I had just one red Samsonite bag with my clothes and a few presents—mostly a box of See's chocolates. I was headed back to Malaysia again, so soon since I left it, with just one bag and one purpose in mind.

Third

Rain is falling
Falling, falling
Spirits are crying
Crying, crying
Cats and dogs are calling
Calling, calling
Thunder is booming
Booming, booming
Lightening is striking
Striking, striking
Gods are fighting
Fighting, fighting
Ancestors are mourning
Mourning, mourning
People are dying
Dying, dying
Children are laughing
Laughing, laughing
Palms are growing
Growing, growing
Worms are crawling
Crawling, crawling
Clocks are turning
Turning, turning
Earth is rejoicing
Rejoicing, rejoicing

Second Trip: May to August, 1987

The flight back again went almost exactly as it did on the previous trip. I even think that a movie was the same as before. I had brought along a novel to read this time--Paul Theroux's "Mosquito Coast," and a couple of other non-fictional books that occupied me for the first couple of days of the journey.

We landed at Narita and again went through the same routine as before. We landed in KL again around midnight and again I filled out the cards that warned death to drug traffickers and I again saw the huge anti-*Dadah* billboard greeting the plane. We stepped down onto the tarmac to become once again drenched in warm sweat.

This time I was perspiring so much that the first thing I did when I cleared customs was to avoid all the taxi people and go directly to the domestic flights departure lounge and to go into the bathroom and change my shirt that was sopping wet. I stayed within the waiting lounge the rest of the night until the morning time, at which I caught the 7:00 AM flight from KL to Penang.

Nobody was in the waiting lounge that early morning except one or two young Malay men who were cleaning and waxing the floors, and a old Chinese fellow who came in and sat with me and told me in broken English about how terrible the 1969 riots were and how the Malays all had machine guns and there was nothing the Chinese, who only had sticks and *parangs,* could do.

I tried to call Rosie by phone. A voice on the other end picked up the line and I asked for Rosie to let her know I had arrived and was coming and they said just a minute. I waited about 15 minutes, putting more money into the phone, as no one then picked up the other line, until finally I gave up.

I caught the morning flight to Penang along with some young looking Chinese businessmen who all had their morning papers and drank their orange juice. We lifted up above thick cumulous clouds and went out over the sea and along the edge of the coastline far down below. No sooner had we leveled off from our gradual ascent then we got the message to fasten seat belts and we began a long descent.

We landed at Penang and again I had to go through a custom's check. This time, I was pulled aside by a man with a scanner and he had me lift up my pants leg and asked me what I had in my ankle pocket. He pulled out the tightly wrapped plastic bag that held my traveler's check and he asked me what this was. I was feeling nervous and embarrassed as I told him that it was my money. Then he gave it back to me and let me go.

I went outside and tried calling again. This time Rosie picked up the phone and I told her I had landed in Penang and was coming down by bus. She said she had taken two days off from work and would meet me at twelve noon at the center of *Komtar* where the plants grew. So I caught the bus from the airport down to *Komtar* with the Indian bus conductor hanging on the door half outside the bus. It was a nice morning as we rode into town. The bus was not very crowded and the breeze that blew through the windows was cooling.

I waited at *Komtar* for about a half-hour, thinking they would not get there. Finally I saw two people whom I hardly recognized and smiling and waving at me and Rosie, shorter than I remembered her to be, wearing shorts and t-shirt, came running up to me and hugged me, bumping the top of her head against the bottom of my chin, making me bite my tongue.

I was a little embarrassed and in more than a little pain by our Brecks "the closer they get the better they look" reunion. I bought some KFC chicken and we went down and got into Joy's car and she drove us to a hotel down in *Tanjung Bungah* that I had seen before along the coast.

We checked in there, not knowing that it was actually a whorehouse. The matron behind the desk laughed when we told her we wanted a room for a couple of nights, and the other girls were looking a little jealously at Rosie. We went up to the room and found that it wasn't too bad. It had a couple of beds, air-conditioning and a walk-in shower with a shower curtain. Rosie wanted to stay with me longer but finally went back to her place for the evening. I stayed in the room and read the rest of a couple of my books. The next morning Joy bought Rosie back again to visit along with some *roti chanai* that she knew I liked.

She asked me about a loan. Before I left L.A. she knew I was coming back and had her daughter write a letter to me to borrow **RM $800** from me. She promised to pay me back within the month, and so I loaned it to her out of my traveler's checks. After that I didn't see her much, and that was the beginning of the end of our relationship with that family.

Auto-Anthropology

We surmised that she had gambling debts on the side that she needed to pay off.

From then on Rosie stayed with me. We stayed in that hotel one more night. That evening we went out and bought some makan and I came back and went down to the hotel bar to buy some beer.

Inside the bar the lights were all red and there were two or three overweight Chinese women sitting there. When I walked in they all looked at me as if they wanted to pounce on me. I bought a beer from the bar and as I was leaving one of them asked me in broken English if I wanted to sit down. I said no thank you and walked out.

I noticed during the day and night young Malay and Chinese men coming and going from the rooms, and decided we had better find another place to stay. So we went next door to an older Chinese style ma and pop hotel that only cost RM $15 per night and that had a bed that took up almost the entire room and a toilet raised up on concrete steps several feet above the ground.

My wife had taken off from work, and, with the assistance of her friends from work, arranged the marriage. We had to fill out and have notarized forms and show evidence of our birth certificates. Rosie went back to work the following day while we were still at the hotel. I would go downtown to look around at all the cheap tools at "Cheapside" and then to wait for her at lunch.

The day before getting married, about a week after my arrival, I walked out along the sea wall along the Esplanade, feeling the cold-feet jitters that all young men must the day before their wedding day. A young Malay man came up on his motorcycle.

He was from a Kampong from the Butterworth side and just came over to visit for a while. I told him I was getting married the next day and wasn't sure about everything yet. He offered to take me around on his motorcycle and then to come and visit his kampong where things were relaxed. I told him no thank you and then I moved off.

The next morning we went to the magistrate's office where we had an appointment to be married by a civil magistrate. I remember a Malay couple before us and an Indian couple after us, and everyone sitting unceremoniously and uncomfortably on the hard wooden benches in the windowless Portico with the overhead ceiling fan whirling round and round.

Our friend's husband, who was to be our "best man" to witness the ceremony couldn't wait and was feeling hungry and walked out and down the side alley to find some noodles at a nearby hawker. His wife ran out after him and scolded him and called him back inside.

The magistrate was a tall, thin, stern looking middle-aged Chinese woman wearing glasses who did not smile and read over all the documents to see they were in proper form and then had us sign the marriage certificates.

I paid the RM $105 dollar fee and she unceremoniously, in a matter-of-fact style, announced us officially married. I inquired whether this document was legally binding in the States and she declared that it was legally binding everywhere.

Our honeymoon was spent in a small ten dollar a day room without air-conditioning on the third floor of Lee Kong Si building on Burma Road next to the Buddhist Chinese Association. I moved into the room because it was cheap and I was already beginning to collect a set of heavy C-clamps and vices that I was finding such a bargain down at Cheap-side.

The very day we moved our things into the Lee Kong Si, I took a taxi with Rosie down to her old place where she had all her things. The family wasn't talking with us and the old woman had circulated rumors about town that I was a confidence trickster, an abalone diver from California, and a spy.

We told the taxi to wait outside the house and we walked right in, as it was unlocked. The old man pretended to be asleep and not to notice us as he sat in his usual chair in the living room, although we made no secret or silence about being there.

We went straight upstairs to her room, and she gathered all her things, which amounted to a few clothes on hangers, a radio with a small box of cassette tapes, the fan I had given her the previous time out, and a few toilet articles, into my old Marine Corps net laundry bag and we went back down.

We put these things into the trunk of the taxi, and left, never to see any of the people again except for Joy who came to visit us a couple of months later to pay us back RM $300 of the RM $800 she had loaned us because she got scared after the brakes in her car went out when she was going down a hill. The taxi driver figured out what was happening and he was nice to help me unload the things at the Kong Si.

Auto-Anthropology

We spent the next week or so at this Kong Si, with all our worldly possessions stuffed under the single double bed, listening to all the Lee clan members playing badminton in the indoor court that occupied the entire second floor directly below our glassless round window.

Every evening we watched grand wedding dinners held on the ground floor hall that was opened to rental for such occasions, and these celebrations served to highlight the contrast between our own humble wedding day and that of other peoples from Penang.

My principle concern at that time was to save as much money as possible (aside from spending it all on the C and F clamps and tools)

A friend of Rosie's put us in touch with a dependable real estate broker who took us around to see several old homes to rent out in the *Tanjung Tokong* area, and we decided on an older three bedroom house with compound and outside outhouse and semi-furnished for RM $350 a month.

So we ended up moving the next Sunday into our new house. A bunch of Rosie's friends came along in the car to help clean the place up and give us a small house warming, so to speak.

I even had a dog already as I took a black dog that the proprietor of the *Kong Si* had kept all its life on a short chain outside, come sun or rain, sleeping in its own shit and already having worn a bald spot in the lawn where it laid all the time. I gave the old man a *kati* of sugar for the dog and he was happy with the offering.

I had taken to feeding the dog and giving it water at night and even took it inside the main hall when it started to rain cats and dogs the night before Wesak day. There it managed to poop all over the clean polished floor of the hall, much to the chagrin of the proprietor and much to my own private joy. I tried getting it in the crowded car once I let it off the chain, and had a hard time of it, while it sat at my feet and panted in my face the whole way to our new home.

We stopped down the hill at the *Fettes Park* market and bought all the buckets and brushes and mops and brooms we would need to clean the place. We had some coffee and makan and then went up to start in on our "new" old home. It was quite dirty and cockroaches were all about. Our friends washed down the red tiled floors and mopped and dusted the place.

During the next week we still had much work to do to get the place squared away. I would go down each morning to get things for the place and to buy more tools while Rosie went to work. On the following weekend we went down and bought curtains and linen for our bedroom. We had a simple set up. One of our friends took me by lumber yard run by Indians where I was shown the different qualities of wood and I ordered quite a few long sixteen foot lengths of *Minyak* and *Meranti*.

It was delivered that afternoon and the lorry backed right up to our front door and the old Indian guy shoved the wood off the lorry to the very front door, blocking the entrance and at some point hitting my big toe, crushing its end and making the toe nail eventually fall off. I was glad to have the rude Indian leave and I loaded all the lumber into the front hall. I was going to make saw horse benches and saw horses and tables on which I would set up a small woodshop.

In the afternoon I would come back to town and work around the house, cutting down weeds and over grown plants in the yard, trying to repair the gate in the back, and mend the chain-link fence that was torn in a few places to keep the uncontrollable black dog from getting loose.

The dog was uncontrollable and was nipping and biting at my heels. I could run around the compound of the house 10 times leading it with a sock in its mouth and it would follow me that way the entire time. Fortunately the RSPCA was just a few houses down from us and I got some inexpensive tick medicine and we gave it a bath to get rid of the ticks it had.

We couldn't let it inside the house because it would tear everything up and jump up and bite at our hands. It got so that I had to get a small rattan cane to whip it to make it behave, although the cane didn't seem to phase the dog much at all. Finally I couldn't deal with the dog anymore and decided it would be better to take it down and have it put down at the RSPCA.

I put a rope around its collar and pulled it down the street. I will never forget the look it gave me when we put it in the cage and it seemed to realize something. It looked at me as if I had forsaken its trust. That entire night I heard it howling and crying in its cage.

Coming back from town carrying a set of four 360inch F-clamps I had bought, I happened by the RSPCA to see the doors of its van open. Something made me stop and go inside to see how my dog was doing. Its body was lying stiff in the back of the van, its bloody head wrapped in newspaper. The Indian man who had shot it looked at me in silent askance, and I stroked its flank and thought that it was a handsome dog.

The Indian told me it was a nice looking dog and I agreed and left without explaining the situation to him. By the time I had reached the compound of my own house tears were in my eyes. By the time I got inside a huge thunderhead had loomed up and lightening struck close by and it rained real hard, as if somehow the gods of heaven had witnessed what had just happened and were angry about it.

I felt bad that day and that evening, after Rosie got home from work, I felt like getting out for a while. We decided to go down to see a movie at the Rex Cinema along Burma Road. We walked out to wait for the bus stop just around the corner and down the hill from our house. I was carrying the metal pointed umbrella that her niece had given us.

While we were sitting there waiting I noticed a motorcycle pass by with two young Chinese on it. Soon they passed by looking at us going the other way, and then they came by a third time and turned their bike straight for us and tried to surprise us.

I figured they were going for Rosie's purse which she slung across here shoulder like a drum, and I pushed out the metal tip of the umbrella at them and caught the one on the back off guard, poking him in the elbow.

He let out a howl and started yelling at us and telling us that they were going to get us for assault and to give us money for the doctor. They tried to edge closer to Rosie and they were putting their hands on her when I inter-positioned myself between them and Rosie. Rosie was scared and wanted to concede to them their requests, while I had my adrenaline pumping and wouldn't let them touch my wife and began pushing them back.

They stood there arguing with us for several minutes. I had my right hand in my pocket, fingering my Swiss Army knife that I always carried with me. It wasn't a long blade, but it was a sharp one. They seemed to have formulated a plan between themselves, signaling each other with their eyes and hands, to lead us away from the bus stop and into the darkness of the park nearby where they wanted to conk us over the head with their motorcycle helmets.

People had walked by the bus stop but no one offered to give any assistance. People in the houses behind the bus stop were home, because music and television sets could be heard, but nobody came out to see what all the commotion was about or to call the police. At that time I felt more alone in Malaysia than ever before, and it has been a feeling under my skin that I have never really forgotten--in a pinch nobody can be counted on to help you.

I was just about to pull the knife out of my pocket as I was trying to convince Rosie to start walking back toward our house while I would hold them back to cover her escape. I was beginning to get really angry and impatient with them and I've been known to fly off the handle more than once when I get worked up. They were short and young and too well dressed with fashionable haircuts to be very tough—they were all bluff and bluster and unmercifully victimized only the weak.

Just then a police car drove miraculously by and I called the police car and hailed them and they stopped and began backing up. The two punks jumped right away on their motorcycle and sped off down the hill in the darkness. The police car gave them hot pursuit but they got away and the squad car came back and took us down to the police station in *Pulau Tikos* to file a report.

We told the officer in charge what had happened and he told me I should have beaten up the two guys. I agreed with him and felt a little embarrassed for not having known exactly what to do at the time. Both of us were more than a little nervous as we walked down to a nearby coffee shop and drank some coffee to relax our nerves.

A friend of Rosie's recognized us there and we told him our story and he told us about similar things he had heard about and how dangerous it was after dark and he paid for our drinks. We caught a taxi back home and from then on never went out to wait at lonely bus stops after dark.

I didn't sleep the whole night and from then on made it a point to sleep with the Chinese chopping blade I had bought for Rosie beneath my mattress. We told our Indian friends across the street what had happened and they told us that a nun who worked at the cancer hospital just down our street was walking home one evening and the same pair came up to her and grabbed her necklace and cut her with a knife.

After that incident we settled down a bit and only went out during the day and on weekends. We looked into my immigration status now that I was married to a Malaysian citizen and an immigration officer told us that it was no different than if I were on a social visa. I would have to leave the country every so often to have my passport chopped again that is unless I wanted to post a bond of a couple thousand dollars in order to get a yearlong visa.

I decided that our options of residence on this side of the globe were reasonably closed-off, and so we decided to go down to the U.S. embassy in KL to see about immigration status for my wife, who was now legally married to a U.S. citizen.

I took it for granted that permanent residence was automatically forthcoming upon attendance to marriage to a citizen. At the embassy we found that it was a four month long waiting process, quite a lot of U.S. dollars, and conditional upon being able to provide evidence to the U.S. government that Rosie would not become a dependent upon them within the next three years—which meant coming up with a considerable sum of money. The solution to this obstacle was to have my family--my mother, brother and sister—all to sign affidavits of support for us.

It still required three to four interminable months of waiting to hear from them, and positive confidence that it would come to pass is never really established until there is written notification. X-rays from Rosie's physical also revealed spots on her lungs which meant that at some early age she had contracted tuberculosis, and Rosie cried the whole night over it until we made an appointment with the doctor who assured her that she had been fully cured and recovered and it presented no obstacle to immigration.

Thus we set about waiting out our time in order to return together to the U.S., not really being sure that this time would come to pass. Rosie continued working as a clerk in a successful Lawyer's firm, while I worked everyday with my wood and hand tools and clamps I had bought and made a few pieces of furniture. I made a heavy cobbler's bench, a computer table for one of Rosie's friends, a large cutting board table. I learned the hard way how to use hand tools and how to do fine screw work using a Chinese hand-drill. After working everyday in the main hall of our home I would sweep up the sawdust that accumulated in the house and then mop down all the floors of the house.

In the afternoon the *roti*-man (the bread man on a small motorcycle) would come by on his motorcycle and I liked to buy nuts, taro chips and *krepok* and bread from him.

We rented a small refrigerator and about once a week we would go down to the supermarkets and bring back sodas, dried noodles, fresh bread, etc. On weekends we would also go down to the morning markets and buy back fresh eggs, chicken, vegetables and fish.

Every morning we would awaken to find a wide trail of ants marching through the entire house. Every day I would spray the entire trail down with *Ridsect* and sweep them up, only to have them back again by the next day.

We had a fully-grown *chi chak* living in the overflow drain of our kitchen sink and a large long centipede in our outhouse sink. At night when we would walk out to the outhouse that was lit with candlelight the large cockroaches would fly at us and attack us. I would spray these down with *Ridsect* and they would fly a little bit and then do a sudden nose-dive and beginning twitching on the ground.

It continued this way until my visa got close to expiring and we still hadn't heard any news from the U.S. embassy. So we planned a trip to Singapore by bus in order to renew my Visa. We took a bus from downtown Penang late at night and it arrived at Singapore mid-morning the next day. We stayed in Singapore over the weekend, going to the zoo by bus and then shopping at night, and then we took the train back early the next morning. While in Singapore I bought an electric lamp as a present to our friends but the Malaysian government charged me fifty percent of its cost as a tax for bringing it into the country.

I was very disheartened that they had chopped my passport for only one month and I would have to leave yet again to have it renewed once more within the month. We couldn't keep going on this way because traveling got expensive and I wanted to make our limited money last as long as possible until we got word from the American embassy.

On our return trip on the train we saw a reddish haired young man with a small sandy-brown haired boy. Something about Americans I can always spot, and I knew they were American when I heard him tell his son to sit down.

What I had grown to miss most was fresh cow's milk, for which *tau chooi* (white bean curd milk) provided an inadequate substitute. *Chitchatting* with other Americans, and someone different to be especially nice too. They were sitting a couple of seats in front of us, and as the train pulled out of the station early that morning, there were not many people in the car.

Auto-Anthropology

It was not long before I was making funny faces with the boy and we began talking to each other. He was headed up to Thailand but was stopping over in Penang to square away his passport at the Thai consulate and to check into some flower-patterned shoes for a friend.

By the time we got off the train that night in Penang, we were good friends. We hired a couple of trishaws and we went down *Chulia* Street and stopped and ate some makan outside. We ordered local specialties for them to try, and paid for their meals. Afterward we found them a room in the New Asia hotel that seemed to be within their price range, and we went back home. We offered them a place to stay at our home, which had two spare bedrooms complete with beds and dressers. They declined that night but we said we'd look them up anyway.

The next day we went down and bought a couple of extra pillows and a couple of cheap mattresses to put over the metal spring frames of the beds in that room. We tried to fix the room up as much as possible without spending too much.

The next day they wanted to be by themselves, and they walked over to *Komtar* and had some KFC. They said that they would go with us the following day and we took them to the *Kek Lok Si* temple.

On the way back it was raining and they agreed to come and stay with us the next day until they departed Penang. On the way back I stopped by the department store at Super-Burma to buy a few bags of extra groceries that I always carried back on the bus. It rained almost the entire day. They went by their hotel.

The next afternoon we came down to the hotel on Kimberly Street and got them and brought them back up to our place and let them settle into the room. That night we cooked an American-style breakfast with French toast, potato chips, and pork and beans, and we talked.

He was an ex-Marine like myself. He had served in Vietnam in 1967-1868 and had fought at *Khe Sanh* during the *Tet* offensive. He remembered landing in a cargo airplane somewhere, and getting off the airplane and onto a six-by truck, where they were taken to a place where they were given their M-16s and ammunition, and then they were taken directly to their assigned units on the front, without any orientation.

He remembered being the point man when they attacked up the backside of a hill on which there was an NVA encampment. He told me how he thought for sure he was a dead man when he heard just up ahead of him the clinking of mess tins and the chatter of guns being loaded, but when he walked into their compound area the NVA had vanished completely. He said his nerves were strung on end. He had been wounded twice. He took off his shirt and pants to show me the wounds.

The first time wounded, while they were searching a village another Marine with a grenade launcher shot him in the leg. Fortunately it was at too close a range for the grenade to arm itself and detonate, and it merely lodged into him. The second time he was shot in the arm and shoulder by someone he didn't even see. He remembered being medi-vaced to a bunker via a helicopter, and they ran into the bunker and had to stand there wounded for several hours while the medics attended to the more critically wounded. At last he was flown out to a hospital and was returned to the states, as his arm and shoulder were totally shriveled.

He spent his last six months or so in the Marine Corps in a field hospital. The Marine police in charge there kept trying to put him to work cleaning the place up, and they wouldn't give him an early discharge. They were about to desert from the hospital in which they were imprisoned, and a couple of his buddies actually did, when a Navy medical officer just walked by, saw him with his shriveled arm, and asked him if he wanted out. The officer signed the release papers right there and then and he was suddenly a free man again.

When he got out he went to a technical training school with his GI bill, and now he was a welder who worked at a shipyard in Oregon. He made enough money welding part of the year to afford being able to travel, mostly to Southeast Asia, the other part of the year. They lived in a small little cabin they leased on a large several-acre lot of woods. He had had a rough marriage and was now divorced, and he had custody of his son as his ex-wife was not dependable.

He had a girl friend in Thailand he was returning to see. He had spent the previous two years in Thailand voluntarily working on board a large freight ship they were trying to repair and refurbish. A scheming businessman organized it and the aim was to use the ship to ply the waters in the Gulf and the China Sea to pick up Vietnamese refugees fleeing the coast of Vietnam.

He didn't seem sure whether the girlfriend was still around or would get serious with him, but he seemed to like her a lot. He was also interested in going north to cross over into Cambodia and Laos, as he was sure that there were still American POW's being held captive by the communists.

Auto-Anthropology

He showed me the tattoo he had across his chest given to him by a Thai villager for protection against evil spirits and bullets and as a sign of courage--it was a large picture of Hanuman the monkey god.

I liked this man a lot and his son whom he showed great love and affection for.

The next morning was cool and overcast and we decided to go to see the monkey garden. We walked down to the bus stop at the bottom of the hill, past the playground where we stopped to let his son play on the equipment. His son slid down the wooden slide and hung from the monkey bars, on which he lifted himself and bumped his head pretty hard on the bar. He cried as his father comforted him.

We went to the monkey garden and bought some peanuts to feed to the monkeys. We walked about the park and fed the monkeys. The little boy was holding a bag of peanuts in his hand, and a large male monkey with gray-tipped hair just walked nonchalantly right up to the boy and grabbed the peanuts out of his hand and sat there opening the bag and eating the nuts.

The boy was taken aback and for a moment just showed a blank look of surprise. Then he let out a howl that the monkey had taken his nuts. Then the father walked up to the monkey and the monkey barred his teeth at him and he just as quickly grabbed the bag of peanuts back from the monkey. The monkey gave him chase while we laughed, until he suddenly stopped and turned on the monkey and barred his teeth at him, at which unexpected sight the monkey beat a quick retreat.

We talked like Americans do about the different movies we had seen and we walked up a small side trail that led into the forest of the hillside and to a small water catchment area in the jungle. There was a picnic table nearby and we sat there and the father hid the bag of peanuts in the boy's button down short-sleeved shirt.

Presently we were surrounded by a troop of smaller monkeys, and one of them crawled right up onto the table were the boy was sitting and began searching with its little hand the boy's shirt pocket and then reaching inside the boy's shirt around his collar to find the peanuts that were there.

The boy was frozen solid in fear as we all watched the monkey draw out the bag of nuts. Then it sat there as if it had conquered the boy who was about to cry for having lost his nuts again. Then his father quickly snatched the bag right out of the little monkey's hand as the monkey barred its teeth and moved aggressively towards him. We laughed and then walked down back down the trail, throwing a few peanuts to the monkeys.

We walked along the sidewalk until we came to a small bridge that crossed over a concrete rivulet that was about ten or twelve feet deep. The boy was playing on the rail and we remember the father telling his son to be careful and get away from the edge when the boy suddenly fell full body down onto the wet concrete at the bottom. I thought for sure that the boy had killed himself.

The father stood there, not sure what to do. The boy didn't even cry, but got up, a little bruised and scrapped and dazed from the fall. The father then got angry with him and told him to climb out by himself, and afterwards he went down and grabbed him by the arm and lifted him up again. The boy was a little worse for wear but otherwise seemed in good condition, much to everyone's surprise.

Afterward the father told us when we were alone that the boy had had severe medical problems when he was young, and showed us the plastic tube beneath the skin of his neck, implanted beneath his skin which ran from his skull down to the ground and for the purpose of drainage of fluid from the brain. The boy had coordination problems and now was beginning to have academic and social difficulties in school.

His father told us that was why he had brought him along to Southeast Asia. He had a fatherly wisdom that the experience would make him or break him, and he would learn a little more independence.

They stayed with us a couple of more days, and we went out to the movies and out to dinner with some Chinese business friends, and then we went downtown to the bus-station to see them off to Thailand. I will never forget the sight of him walking down the road, carrying his sea bag slung over his shoulder like a wiry former-Marine, his son in tow. I liked him for his honesty and simple integrity, in spite of the hard life he had led, and for the obvious love he had for his son.

We heard from them again when we got back to the states. The father contracted what appeared to be amoebic dysentery in Thailand shortly after their arrival there, and was laid up helpless with fever in bed for almost an entire week. He said he was proud of his son who actually seemed to manage better without his father, and who learned to go out and get things on his own dealing with the Thai people, and who took care of his father for this period of his sickness. They had to cut their trip short after that and he returned to Singapore where he got treated for his illness, having lost quite a bit of weight in the process.

He wrote us again about a year later, and as he was flying down to LA to catch a flight out on Korean Airlines. We went and met him at LAX and saw him off again on his connecting flight. His plane arrived about a half hour late, and we had to rush to get him over to the international departure terminal on time to make is flight out. We didn't have enough time to talk.

He told us that he was going to go north and pass into Cambodia to see for himself if there were any Americans held there. I gave him a pocket fisherman I had bought as present, and a couple of books on Southeast Asian culture that I thought he would enjoy reading.

We got a postcard of some elephants crossing a river from him again about six months later. He actually was still in Northern Thailand and said that the fish in the river were great. That was the last time we ever heard from them.

During this time, the owner of the House, an Indian Tamil who had a government position, wanted to sell the house and Rosie introduced him to some prospective buyers, a young Chinese banker and his wife, who wanted to buy the house and renovate it as an investment.

Normally, as mediators in the transaction of the sale, Rosie was supposed to have made some money, but nothing was forthcoming, except that the Banker and his wife did bring over some fancy odd gifts to give to us. They were useless types of things that people get as gifts and don't know what to do with but pass on to other people as gifts-- which was exactly what we did with the things.

The buyers came to inspect the house and I informed them of the termites that occupied the rafters. They called out an exterminator who injected some red powder into the walls to kill the 'white ants.'

I had finished up my woodworking and had a bunch of extra homemade furniture and tools and worktables and saw horses around the house. On weekends our friends would come over and we would have a coconut party. There were all kinds of fruit-trees in our compound, and I would tie a couple of narrow 16 foot boards with a sickle at the end and we would knock down the coconuts from the palms above and open the good ones to drink the water and eat the flesh.

We had befriended an Indian family across the street whose father worked at a resort hotel and whose grandfather had served as an NCO in the British army. I would let them come over to the house and pick the *burunga* pods off the back trees. While the house was awaiting the transfer of ownership, and while our departure was soon eminent, we were hesitant to start anything new.

With the leftover lumber and nails I built a couple of shipping crates and packed all our plastics and linen and all my tools in them. We had them shipped as "household goods" via our shipping agent friend for less than one hundred U.S. dollars. Rosie quit her job at this time and her boss and other girls at the office gave her a grand luncheon for a send off, to which I was not invited.

My visa was again about to expire and so we debated whether to go to Lake Toba in Indonesia by ferryboat or to go north to Thailand. We finally decided on Thailand as the cheaper and easier of the two alternatives and took a train north to *Hatyai* for a weekend.

We got off the train and were assaulted by taxi drivers who wanted to take us downtown for 10 or 15 dollars, and then we walked through the terminal and met a Chinese taxi-man outside who drove us downtown for only $1.50. We rode in the back of a mini-pickup truck with other Thai people, and were let off in front of a bunch of hotels. We picked one and found it was pretty nice and at a fair price. A lot of Thai girls were sitting around the lounge area outside.

I thought how pretty these girls were and how young, and how tragic their life situations must have been to be put on sexual display like that. We stayed in the room and went out shopping in the evening. We bought mostly gifts for people back in the states—clothes and some baby-warming gifts for my sister-in-law who was soon expecting. We went back to the hotel and I had bought a quart of an unusual kind of Danish European beer I had never had before.

We looked in some of the windows of the hotels and places and saw whole rows of young girls with short, sexy skirts, sitting alone waiting in the lounges.

We watched television that evening and then someone knocked on our door and I opened it and there was an older Thai woman asking me if I wanted a massage and that it would only cost 10 dollars per hour. Then I opened the door a little further and she saw my wife and was surprised. I told her no thanks and closed the door leaving her a little embarrassed and probably confused.

That night we got really hungry, and braved going out to find some *makan*. We found a side-alley where there were Chinese style hawkers and we ordered a couple of plates of what resembled mostly *char quay kak* with oysters or clams and bean sprouts. We went back and ate and went to bed.

The next morning we walked about the town and did some more window shopping, noticing that most of the smaller business people were actually Chinese with their little red altars in the back of the shops, even though they only spoke Thai.

We went to an open trade fair down by the train station that had some exotic furniture and clothes from the North of Thailand. We bought some neat looking clothes for fairly cheap there and admired some of the crafts and artwork on display. That evening we ate in a more modern, Western style restaurant and had some exotic espresso coffee that was percolated on the strangest glass-percolating machine I'd ever seen.

The next day we took the train back across the border, to have my Visa chopped again for another month. At the immigration office on the border some American and European tourists coming from the north of Thailand began acting really rude to the Malaysian Immigration authorities, for having to wait a few minutes to get their passports back.

One vocal American male who bragged about having worked in the refugee camps there refused to put his shirt on in order for the Malaysian officers to accept his passport. Finally he acquiesced but was very rude about it. Then we got our passports chopped and the officer was asking why I was coming back and had so many chops, and I explained to her that I was married to a Malaysian citizen, and she understood and was quite nice to us, perhaps because we were decently dressed and were polite to them as well.

On the train back we met what we took to be another American. We learned that he had just graduated from law school in Texas and had taken a short 60 days around the world excursion before going back to start his practice and get married. My wife, who had been a legal clerk in Penang, talked legal shop with him and they figured out some of the technical differences between the American and British systems.

He had already been to several cities in India and Nepal and Burma and Thailand, and had reservations for a hotel in the Cameroon highlands that night. We invited him to come across the ferry with us and see some of Penang that afternoon, and he said he would if he had the time. We told him about Penang and it seemed to interest him greatly. But soon he had fallen asleep and missed most of the scenery outside the train window.

We woke him up as we pulled into the Butterworth station, and we asked him to take the ferry over with us and have some makan on the other side. He agreed and we rode across on the boat. By the time we got to the other side he looked at his watch and realized he had only a half-hour to be back on the train. As we walked down off the ramp we met our Chinese business friend who was eating makan across the road.

We introduced our American acquaintance. Then he took our photograph and we took a photo with his nice new camera of him standing by the railing with the water behind and then he waved good-bye and fled back across on the ferry. We wondered if he ever made it to the Cameroon highlands that night and what he would remember most about his trip around the world.

But we did not miss him much because from about the day we got back we were back on a roll. Soon we got a letter from the U.S. Embassy in KL telling us to come down and pay our fees and pick up our documents and have Rosie collect her conditional residence card.

We were elated and we vacated our home and gave away the furniture to our friends and the work benches and spare cooking things and table fan to the Indian family across the road, and we took a bus back down to KL a couple of days later. This time we knew where we were going there and we checked into the same hotel as before, and the same day we went directly down to the embassy and the Chinese dragon-lady behind the window there who spoke with a falsetto Selangor-English accent treated us much more courteously than the first time as we paid our money and signed the paperwork and left again.

We took the train back the next morning and on it we met yet another young American man. He was a young student who had just finished his bachelor's in business at San Diego and his father had given him this trip with his girlfriend before he was expected to become a serious accountant in his firm. He was a tall, handsome, blonde, happy-go-lucky person with a friendly smile and of Czechoslovakian extraction.

Auto-Anthropology

We showed him around town and he checked into the same hotel with us--a nice hotel on *Leith* Street with high ceilings and marble tile floors and that had once been a brothel for the Japanese soldiers in WWII.

We tried arranging as early a flight as possible out of KL but the planes were all booked up with students and Japanese flying to the US. We used the same travel agent as before and we talked with her for several hours for a couple of days as she saw how desperate we were to get the same flight out. She could get us one seat, but two were difficult. We got to know her better then. She was a cute girl, and had a friendly personality. She had a clubfoot and was heavily into Christianity.

She made bead bracelets and necklaces on the side and we bought a couple from her for gifts, as they were nice and unusual. She was not happy staying with the family she was living with, as she always had to "refer to" their authority. She was soon migrating to Australia to start a new life for herself, all on her own.

I respected her for her courage in life and grew really fond of her. She finally arranged for us through her travel agent network two seats on a JAL flight a few days later for only a small amount of extra money. We went down to the JAL airlines office at *Komtar* and booked the seats and paid the balance in the tickets.

Thus, frantic one day to escape, on our way out the next. We had only a couple of days remaining. The first day was a Sunday and we hiked up the 1,200 steps to the temple of the Jade Emperor of Heaven in the back hills of Penang with our friends. We took our American friend around to see some of the sites of Penang--the sleeping Buddha and the Monkey Gardens.

The next night before we left we arranged a big steamboat dinner for all our friends and we paid the entire tab. We fed about 12 people for a total of around RM $150, including drinks and ice cream as a dessert. After that some of us went down to have a drink at the old and exclusive E & O lounge.

A middle aged white couple, the man dressed in a business suit, stared at us really mean-like as we danced on the floor and the band played the tune "Rose, Rose, I love you, with an aching heart. East is east and West is west and our ways will never part. Rose of Malaysia, I give my heart."

The next afternoon everyone followed us out to the airport to see us off. Everyone was crying because everyone thought they'd never see each other again. Soon we were landing at the KL airport and it was so busy and we got lost trying to find our transfer that we had to run and almost missed our flight out and made it just in time.

We got on a smoke filled Japanese Jumbo Jet full of Japanese businessmen smoking strong unfiltered cigarettes. At first we were assigned separate seats, but a very polite businessman, noticing that we wanted to be together, exchanged his seat for mine.

We landed at Narita and were bused to a special hotel for a 12-hour stop over. The hotel was posh and clean, and the room had all these fancy things in it—a small coffeemaker, combs, toothpaste and toothbrushes, etc. We tried to sleep for a few hours and put in a wake up call to catch the bus back to the airport. Back at the airport we had to go through customs and immigration, and I remember the immigration officer being very rude to Rosie and me.

We flew back to LA aboard a JAL 727. It was the most uncomfortable plane flight I'd ever taken in my life, including the time in the Marine Corps when the back ramp of our C47 suddenly fell open in flight after takeoff and our heads started exploding inside from the pressure difference. That JAL flight was bumpy and smoky, and the tall Japanese stewardess was impersonal and unfriendly.

As we banked over LA, we could see it was shrouded in a thick layer of gray smog, and we couldn't see the city until we came right up over the runway itself.

By the time we had landed at LAX and the plane was still taxiing down the runway every one on board frantically got up out of there seats and moved in the aisles toward the exit signs. The plane had not stopped yet and people were bursting at the seams to get out.

Again we walked down that long corridor while I fell sick. I was sick for several days after, with fever and cold sweats and nausea. I think I had food poisoning from eating some cold green noodles or cheese we were served in flight.

Rosie wore her kerbaya with its silver belt and sarong and fancy buttons. Customs gave us a harder time than before, and wondered why I had been in Malaysia so long. He held up our big bottle of baby lotion to the light and tried to see inside of it. Finally I explained that I was doing research and he then relaxed a little, and said, "Oh, I see" and let us through.

Auto-Anthropology

I remember helping an older Chinese couple who spoke no English move their large green duffle bags through the right customs line and then helping them to dial a phone to call people in LA to come and get them. We later met the old woman in downtown Chinatown in L.A. on a corner selling magazines for another woman.

My mother and sister then met us outside. They had bought red and pink heart shaped balloons and a box of candy for Rosie, and they drove us back home. The freeways seemed big and endless, and the cars countless, just as I always remembered LA to be like.

Fourth

We walk alone
Side by side
Down the crowded, chaotic street
The anonymous faces of abandoned people
Dirty hands reaching out for some shillings
The fast motorcycles and cars
We walk on
Past the temples and the coffee shops
Around the drains and the many obstacles
By ourselves
We walk
Without illusion
We suffer
Only the silence of the burning sun
Past the mourners dressed in black
Past the open doorway
And the old photo
And open coffin
We walk on past the roasted duck
Hanging on hooks
Past the hawker
Sharpening his chopper
Without words
We walk
Down the street

Second Interregnum

We returned to stay with my Mom, having no other immediate plans. I was soon engaged full time by my brother to help him set up a dental office not too far away. We worked for more than six months on it, and finished about the middle of January of the following year. After a few rough starts, we finally got going with it. I ended up doing most of the work, from electrical installation and plumbing to framing and plastering to dry walling and door hanging and carpentry and the final painting.

I even helped the carpet layer come in and lay plush wall- to- wall carpeting in all the offices and down the side hall. That Christmas I made my brother some nice hardwood diploma frames with oak and black walnut to hang in his office.

After that I set about looking for work once again. I sent off numerous applications to several different agencies in the Federal Government and in local government. I canvassed locally for lesser paying jobs. I found the amount of bureaucratic bullshit in hiring to be very unreasonable. I had qualifications higher than almost all of the people who did the interviews, and yet my schooling or degrees did not seem to mean anything to anyone. I did get a job hauling furniture and other junk off the back of a panel truck into the show room of a local thrift shop.

Though thrift shops are supposed to be non-profit, charitable institutions, the owner had a chain of five of them and from what I could tell was making very clean and large profits from items he was getting for nothing. They were more interested in the fact that I was an ex-marine than that I had a Master's degree in anthropology. They told me I was the last person of their applicant pool to be called, because everyone else had already quit.

They were surprised when I could fill out the job forms and income tax forms by myself without anyone's help. Needless to say I did not stay there very long as I was marking the prices on the stuff too low and everyone was buying the junk—they were surprised they had moved so much in one day. I quit the first day with cuts and sores on my hands and a sore back, without getting any pay. I quit and the next day the lady in charge desperately called me, telling they would pay me a whole $4.00 per hour. It was just not worth it to me.

I kept looking and slowly learned how to fill out the forms properly. The DEA was quite interested in hiring me, promising to send me to the FBI training academy in Virginia, but after an FBI check on me and finding out that my wife was a foreign national, from Malaysia no less, and that my brother-in-law and sister-in-law were both Mexicans, they changed their minds. Perhaps they found too many beer bottles in my trashcan or my amazing military record or talked to the CPA neighbors who didn't like me very much.

I was desperate and tried any and every job offer or interview. At some point in the process I had found an old application for admission to a graduate anthropology program in a State Universe in New York. Since I was filling out so many other forms, I decided that I would send in this one as well. I did not at the time take it seriously. I had aimed at admission into the UC system a couple of years earlier but received such negative and critical insults from a couple of arrogant male professors of one school that I gave it up without much of a fight. I filled the application out, got some letters of recommendation and sent in transcripts and promptly forgot all about it.

I got involved in building a redwood deck in the backyard of my Mom's house—a project that took about six weeks to complete. Then I continued looking for work. I got Rosie enrolled part-time in a few night-classes at an extension college nearby. She was learning medical terminology and other types of things. She was having good interaction in the course and seemed to be happy in it. Then that summer I received notice from State University Northeast in New York that I had gotten accepted to their PhD program for the coming Fall.

I was excited that someone in the world finally considered me worthwhile enough to take seriously. In the meantime I had gotten a part-time job as a janitor at a senior citizens recreation center in Orange County. It was a long drive and didn't pay very much, but I didn't mind the job and liked to interact with most of the old people there who didn't have many people to talk to.

I worked with a 16- year-old Chicano boy who was given a full-time position doing the same thing I was doing. He was a gang-member and there was a program that gave him double pay for doing the job. He did not last long on the job after he ended up breaking into the kitchen of the cafeteria and stealing some of their equipment. I remember distributing food under the WIC program to people who would drive up

Auto-Anthropology

in Mercedes Benz Cars and BMW's. The old men who helped out got a kick out of it.

Anyway, by August, almost one year after we had returned, I was off again to New York. I got rid of my old valiant and took a beat up Volkswagen beetle I had paid cash for from my own earnings out of High School, which I had repaired and repainted. We packed that Volkswagen full, and we drove across the country like that, with my seat moved fully forward so there were only a few inches between my belly and the steering wheel.

We drove across the U.S. in August during the final year of the draught, and so much of the mid-west looked burnt up. We went to Chicago and stayed overnight with the family of a buddy of mine I went through the entire Marine Corps with--a red-haired Irish-German who came from a big catholic family. He had died several years previously in a fishing accident, and his family had never gotten over it. I learned the details from his brother, and they kept his ashes in a coffee can in the closet in the room we slept in that night. It all felt strange to me.

The first two semesters in the program in New York State went well for me. I had made almost straight A's and I was given a Teaching Assistantship and an office of my own for the following year. I was vocal and opinionated and more than a little naive. It was a politically charged atmosphere and the social relations within the department could have been described as a bit frosty, if not down right frozen solid.

So I found it strange from the beginning and the second semester attempted a kind of ethnography of the department where I interviewed about 30 or 40 of the students and about 16 of the faculty. I discovered some of the internal tensions of the place and who was pulling whose strings. I did not know at the time that probably more than a couple of senior people probably wanted to get rid of me, and that my ethnography probably threatened the hell out of them.

During that summer I painted a two-story house for a few hundred dollars and built some oak bookshelves for a friend for another few hundred dollars. Rosie had picked up a baby-sitting job that added to our earnings. Near the beginning of the following semester one of the students in our program committed suicide by hanging himself. Some of the students voiced their anger to me about how they felt the department had kind of railroaded him and treated him poorly. They wanted to sign a petition of protest against the department.

The following semester some of the key figures in the faculty came down hard on the students and intimidated them into conformity. I spoke out against these people in the open forum of the classroom and pissed a couple of professors off. Needless to say that the semester was a busy year, but one in which we actually began saving money instead of spending it.

But by the end of the semester a handful of professors had officially ostracized me from their program, and tried to make me believe it was my fault and that I couldn't ever get into another program. I got the letter announcing that I had been denied my TA-ship for the following semester just around Christmas time, and that I was put on a conditional status in the graduate program.

Needless to say I was pissed off and never set foot in that department again, and after that only ever saw my primary advisor who encouraged me to stay within the program and fight it, and who, I believe, felt very hurt when I left the program.

That was just at the time we had our baby. It was snowing and icy, and our daughter came two weeks earlier than expected and at about 8 3/4 pounds. My wife was in the delivery room for almost 36 hours, until a rude Indian woman doctor finally pulled Mahala out with forceps. I was extremely disappointed at the program for having let me down during a time that we needed the most support.

About a month after Mahala was born we drove back to California in my new 1971 Chevy truck. At first we didn't know what we were to do. I was bound and determined to get into another anthropology program because I knew I was one of the best students and that I could do it. I ended up sending off two salvos of applications to different departments all across the country. The first salvo got one or two nibbles but no bites.

During the interim I installed a Jacuzzi on the deck I had previously built for my Mom, and then I went up north to help my brother move his practice and keep my grandma's house in Chowchilla while she went back east for a few weeks. I gained admittance to a small state college up in the valley with the idea of earning a second degree in some other field, and began getting involved with the Cambodian refugee community in the area.

But the second salvo of applications that I managed to get off by early summer time did the job and landed me in two different programs at the same time, for the coming Winter semester, so we quickly cut short our stay in Northern California and returned south post haste to get ready for moving again back east.

One program offered me a TA-ship right off the bat and entry in the winter semester with a full scholarship, while the other program offered me nothing and entry only in the following fall semester.

I was inclined toward the first school, but we ended up driving back out and visiting both programs in the fall. The first school was a small prestigious private college in the mid-West with some well-known faculty person's and pretty good connections as far as funding and hiring were concerned.

I attended it in the spring semester, but found myself treated so poorly by some of the people and so alienated by the stuffy and ultra-conservative social atmosphere that I decided I would go to the other school in the fall. So the day the school semester ended at the first school we had repacked all our belongings in our truck and were on the road again going to the other school where there was campus housing made available for us.

I found myself quite successful in this school, though I was not a part of any student network and totally outside its social life, and successfully completed four semesters and achieved my PhD. candidacy during the following two years. We moved in the middle of that period and found a better on-campus arrangement, and we soon made many foreign friends from other fields, most of who were married and with children.

I had taken out student loans to pay for the final year there, as I knew it was my last year, if everything went right, and we had several thousand left over. We used this to pay for plane fare back to Malaysia. Rosie was really missing going back, and she made me promise to take her back as soon as possible. So we threw most of our belongings into a small rental storage room, had a yard sale for the rest of our junk, and drove back out the long road to California one more time.

We got tickets to return to Malaysia on the 15th of July 1993. Rosie made herself busy the last week or so buying gifts for all her old friends and the few family she had remaining. And when we got back on the plane we had three bags, most of which were presents for different people.

Fifth

Sitting in a gold shop
Talking about old acquaintances
Of people long since passed away
Of names forgotten
With glassy looks in our eyes
Of the times since past
For an instant there is a strange silence
And stillness hanging over everything
Outside a baby is crying
And shoppers walking by in the hot sun
No one notices the spirits that hide in the sharp shadows
Who fill up all the empty spaces between the shop houses?
And who glide down the streets between the cars
Watching us from the infinite corners
In all the wall mirrors of the shop
We are not alone with our audience
We make a joke and smile
The gold seller makes me a special deal
On a small gold bracelet for my daughter
The door closes once again
Spirits rushing back inside
A few remaining
Stranded outside

Third Trip: July to September, 1993

The MAS ticket desk was at the same place in the airport as before, but the arrangement of the departure waiting area had been changed. We took an airport shuttle down. On entering the Bradley terminal I saw a middle-aged man who looked vaguely familiar—like an officer I had served with in the desert in the Marine Corps. I didn't think much about it. We checked our bags and had a five-dollar cup of coffee and a donut, and then went through the metal detectors and down to our departure gate.

There wasn't enough seating this time, and it began filling up. A large Malaysian family came, all eating a bag of chips, and spilling the food on the carpet. We had to sit on the floor with others. Then I saw the man that had looked familiar sitting on the end of a row of seats. Impulse made me walk over and ask him if we had met before. I was surprised when he knew my name and rank—Corporal Lewis.

I couldn't directly recall his name, though I remembered him well. We talked about the platoon we had been in together, and about the accident we had been in which one man was crushed beneath the tank. He surprised me as he remembered the names of the different people in detail. He was our former Platoon Commander, and was now stationed down at Camp Pendleton and was returning back East to attend the funeral of his father. He had gotten out and reentered the Marine Corps twice since I had known him in the late 70's. He was a Vietnam War veteran and was now a staff-NCO working in intelligence in relation to the US involvement in Somalia.

Soon we were all crowding onto a large square bus that had drivers at both ends to take us down the tarmac and load us on the airplane at the end of the runway--LAX had grown much busier, if not bigger, in the six year interim since our last trip to Malaysia. Meeting an old acquaintance left me with a strange feeling—the odds were against it, as I had not meet anyone I had known in the Marine Corps since I had been out. It was something to ponder as we took off and were treated right away to our first in-flight meal.

The food on the first meal was good and we ate almost all of it. Then we were treated to an in-flight movie—Rain man" with Dustin Hoffman and

Tom Cruz. I read a few articles in the Scientific American magazines I had brought with me.

This time we had our three-and-a-half-year-old daughter with us and it was enjoyable to share her first plane trip, as she sat by the window and looked out to see the water and clouds below. She was good the entire flight, falling asleep mid-way until we landed in Japan. The second meal wasn't as appealing to us as the first, and I remember the flight felt much longer than we remembered before. I began getting strong stomach pains and cramps of indigestion, and had to get up a couple of times to stretch and relieve the cramped feeling.

We came down at Narita at night and entered a terminal area that was different than the first time. The flight had been delayed over an hour due to a large storm off the Japanese Island that we flew over with some turbulence. We could see down and see a couple of great circles of gray clouds below in the evening twilight of the setting sun. We walked down long corridors and rode the conveyor belt that Mahala liked a lot.

We went down a flight of steps and found the toilets, where there was a long line from all the passengers on the flight. We waited a while and then went in and brushed our teeth and cleaned up a little bit, and then walked up another flight of steps and were directed down to another airport departure gate where we soon reboarded for our flight.

The second part of the flight felt almost as long as the first, and Mahala kept us awake the entire time. Fortunately we were entertained by a movie about a group of bus-passengers who were all killed as the bus careened off a bridge and into a river, and who became ghosts afterward attached to a young boy.

It was past 1:00 AM in the morning when we came down at *Subang* International Airport. I had diarrhea and cramps. We walked down another long corridor and came out through immigration, had our passports chopped and then picked up our bags and checked through customs. Mahala was playing with the luggage cart and the spring-loaded handle snapped up and hit her pretty hard under the chin and caused her to cry, but otherwise she was OK.

It didn't feel as hot and sweaty to me as it did before, and we went out and got a taxi into KL. We asked him to take us to a reasonably priced hotel nearby the train station. They were two Malays and they were driving a Proton Saga. The car made a funny humming sound from the tires while we were on the freeway. We talked to them and told them we

Auto-Anthropology

had not been back in 6 years. They were both very proud of their country and thought their Prime Minister to be the best. The hotel was a Chinese style one that was actually quite expensive for its lack of accommodations and Spartan furniture. We showered and took Pepto-Bismol and went to bed to get up early. It felt strange to be back in Malaysia again.

We got up early the next morning, before sunrise, to find a bunch of cockroaches inside the box of animal cracker cookies we had left over from the flight. As I picked up the box I felt something moving around in side and soon two or three of them bailed out the top and scampered under and behind our bed. We packed and went downstairs past the sleeping night watchman and hailed a taxi outside.

It was a Cantonese man in an old car. He complained to us right away about the government policies in the unfair treatment of the Chinese. The train-station was just down the road and we got out and wondered around to find the right ticket window. It was closed and so we had to wait about 45 minutes to get our tickets. We went across a road outside to a little cafeteria where we ordered some rice with *ikan bilis* and some fried *bee hoon*. It was our first Malaysian food for many years.

The train trip up was pleasant but slow. Mahala enjoyed the train ride and the scenery. We saw a lot of lotus blooming in the water along the edge of the railway, and Mahala really enjoyed going through the tunnels around the hills of Taiping.

We arrived at the Butterworth station late in the afternoon and we took the ferry across. As soon as we got to the other side Rosie called up her sister's residence to let them now we had come in, and then caught a Taxi to the same hotel on *Leith* street that we had stayed at the day we had left six years previously.

We checked into the room and soon fell asleep, to wake up about 1:00 or 2:00 in the morning wide awake. We took a chance and walked down the road that late and got some makan at an all night rice stall, and brought the food back and ate it. I still had diarrhea and cramps and couldn't eat much, and Rosie had constipation.

Early the next morning we took another taxi from the Hotel to Rosie's sisters house. This young Chinese taxi driver also started railing on about the unfair treatment of the Chinese by the Malays.

We arrived to find Rosie's niece sweeping outside of their small semi-detached terrace home. The first thing that Rosie's sister said to us was that we could stay a couple of days, but then her mother-in-law was coming to stay with them and we'd have to leave.

We stayed with them for about 10 days. I slept on the floor without a pillow and Rosie and Mahala slept on a small single-sized bed. We were pretty much jet-lagged for the first week, and would wake up very early in the wee hours of the morning when everyone in the household was asleep, and then get tired and fall asleep around 6:00 or 7:00 each evening. Each passing day we moved our schedule up one hour, so that after five or six days were back on a normal sleeping schedule.

Her sister and her family kept telling us how they didn't have any extra money and how they were so poor. I felt sorry for them and after about a week went downtown and bought them about **RM** $500.00 worth of furniture--a coffee table large enough to seat 4 or 6 people, with some chairs made of *Datu* wood, a large standup mirror, as the auntie had only one compact mirror for the entire household, and a large clothes cabinet for my wife's niece who let us use her small bedroom and who didn't have any clothes cabinet.

Rosie's niece had gotten a few days holiday from her work and one day we walked with her to the bus stop to see her off in the morning she hinted about doing something for the holiday. We stood at the bus stop in the rain, discussing where we could go. *Langkawi, Genting* Highlands, the East Coast. Finally we agreed upon checking into a hotel for a couple of days along *Batu Ferringhi* along the North coast of the Island.

So later that day we went down to our friend's office and copied the hotel numbers out of their telephone book, as Rosie's sister had a telephone book but threw it away because she felt she didn't need it.

So we called several different hotels until we got a pretty good offer at the Lone Pine. A professor friend of mine in the States had remembered Penang and mentioned the Lone Pine as a nice hotel to stay at. So we arranged to pay for two nights over the weekend and to take Bessie down with us so we could enjoy the beach with her company.

It turned out that the mother, Rosie's older sister, accompanied us the first day and night. The room we checked into was a large one and was old but nice. It had a nice balcony. Unfortunately it rained almost the entire time we were there, so we couldn't enjoy the beach so much, although I found the cool winds and the pounding surf exhilarating.

Auto-Anthropology

Rosie's aunt and niece returned on the second day, as it was plain they were not enjoying themselves at all.

I was kind of pissed off at the mom for not letting her daughter alone and convincing her to come back early. We wanted to get her niece on her own for a little while, without her nosy and nervous mother around to *kachow* us about every little thing.

I had begun finding Rosie's sister more than a little annoying, because she accompanied us wherever we went and she questioned every little thing we did. But if we bought groceries for her home she wouldn't even thank us, nor help us carry them or Mahala on the long hot walks back. More than a couple of times I got quite put off by her, and at the time thought her behavior was quite strange. I just dismissed her behavior at the time as a case of middle-aged neurotic housewife.

When we came back from the hotel we decided that we would find an alternative living arrangement, and tried to find a cheap and reasonable hotel to stay in for a while. So we stayed with Rosie's sister one more day, long enough to again call most of the hotels in Penang. Finally we decided to check into the YMCA because they had a reasonable monthly rate and a television and air-conditioning.

When we had all our bags packed Rosie's sister expected us to walk down to the bus stop and catch a bus, and then walk to the YMCA. I got pissed off at her because not only did we have three heavy bags to carry, but we had Mahala in a stroller to worry about as well. So I told Rosie to go down to the main-road and hail a taxi, and within 10 minutes we were at the YMCA.

We were at the YMCA for about three days and Rosie began getting desperate to leave Malaysia and come back to the U.S. She felt more immediately culture shocked than I had. So we went down to the MAS office at *Komtar* but the earliest flight we could get out was more than a five weeks later.

We didn't care for the YMCA because they were doing construction just behind our room until the evening and then there was Ballroom dancing just below our room until midnight, so the noise level was quite high. Also it was off any main bus-route and we would have to wait almost an hour to catch a bus to go anywhere.

We decided to bide our time and soon found a cheaper priced hotel with air-con and hot water for around $30 RM. per night. It was an old

Chinese style hotel built in the 1930s. When it was first built it was a first class hotel--famous personages of the era had stayed in it.

Japanese officers used it as their quarters during the war. The furniture in our rooms was of a dark exotic hardwood in the Chinese style of construction, and it was original to the hotel, having been built by a local *Hin Aik* furniture manufacturer no longer in business. We stayed in this hotel for almost a month, and by the end of our stay there we had befriended most of the Hotel staff.

We resigned ourselves to waiting a month before being able to return to the U.S., a month which at the beginning seemed like an eternity. Every day seemed to churn slowly by in the heat and the traffic of downtown Penang.

I hated the thought of staying so long downtown like that. We bided our time by reading and shopping at the bookshops and occasionally going to see one or other of the tourist sites around the island. About once a week one or other of Rosie's old friends would come and visit us, and sometimes take us out to somewhere.

The end of the first week we went back to visit Rosie's sister. She acted strange and didn't say much to us, almost as if we weren't there. So we left before too long and took the long bus ride back downtown. It was the middle of the following week when Rosie had gone down to visit her Godmother again, whom she had first met begging at the Goddess of Mercy temple and who then didn't seem to recognize us.

This time at her home the Godmother recognized us and we sat and talked with her and her friends. Behind her back her friend confided to us that Rosie's sister had come a year back and had borrowed most of Godmother's savings from her in order to pay for the down on the new home they had bought. Godmother had given her five hundred dollars that was meant for Rosie, and she had never returned the money.

It hurt and angered Rosie that her sister had taken advantage of an old woman and had taken most of her life-savings without paying her back. She told Rosie's godmother that since Rosie was not there nobody was around to take care of her or bury her when she died. So she told Rosie's godmother that she would take care of her and see to her funeral when she died if she put her name with Godmother's as a joint savings account.

We didn't care about the $500 dollars, as it didn't mean so much to us, but we were mad because her Godmother was now having to beg to make money for food, while her sister took her money--besides, she was not even Godmother to her sister.

It pissed me off because pieces fell into place and we realized that her sister had not only tried to hide the truth from us, but had actually lied to us about things. It also explained why she had been behaving so strangely, because she was trying to prevent us from finding out what she had done to Rosie's godmother.

Rosie got back to the hotel and a few days later had a spat with her sister on the phone and after that we didn't see or hear from her sister or her sister's family at all. They knew where we were staying at but never bothered to call us or come to see us.

The only time we ever saw her sister after that, or any of the rest of the family, was one day when we happened to meet her by accident walking down the road in downtown Penang, as she was returning from the bank.

She talked to Rosie and wouldn't even face me and turned completely away from me. It was showing me no face, as only Malaysians seem to know so well how to do.

A couple of weeks later, Rosie's sister had returned to her God-mum the RM$500 dollars that she had intended her sister to give to Rosie. We didn't want to take it, but she kept insisting. Finally, we took it and bought Mahala a nice gold bracelet as a keepsake for about RM$300, and we returned the balance to her.

After we had found out what her sister had been up to, we felt sorry for Rosie's Lau Mak and we went down a couple of times and bought her a sizeable quantity of food to keep on hand. We figured she had enough rice that she got for free during food distributions. She was even selling a little of this rice of extra cash.

So we bought her most canned meats--dried dace, curry chicken, sardines--packets of *Mee*, some *Lap Chan* (Chinese sausage). We bought over RM $150.00 for her over a couple of separate shopping trips. We figured she could stock up the canned meats to have on hand for a while after we left. All the food made her Godmother angry with us and she called us *"siow"* (crazy) and tried to hit us and scold us, but we knew that deep down she really liked it.

We spent the days for a few weeks like that, idling our time away until our plane was to leave again. In the evening we would sit in the hotel lobby and chit chat with other guests and with the hotel staff, who were mostly older Cantonese and Hokkien men and women. We befriended a young Malay man who had three daughters and who was away from home and feeling quite lonely, doing construction work on one of Penang's highways.

He was quite a nice man and he always played the jigsaw puzzles with my daughter that we had bought for her because she liked to put them together. When we left the hotel we gave him two bags of jigsaw puzzles and some clothes and other toys that we didn't have room for in our bags.

We did it at night when Mahala was asleep, and the next day when Mahala looked for her little toys, she found they were missing. We told her what we had done with them and she got really angry with us and we felt bad about it and decided that at three-and-a-half-years old Mahala had soon grown too old to arbitrarily dispose of her belongings without her consent.

We were itchy to leave the hotel and checked out about a week before our flight was to leave and went down and stayed for about a week at the Lone Pine hotel as they were still offering special rates and we got a smaller room.

There were a couple of holidays then and we planned it so that one of Rosie's friends could come and stay over with us for a couple of days. She had been nice to us during our stay there, and she came to confide to us about a lot of her problems, especially her somewhat rocky relationship with a Thai boyfriend.

We bought all kinds of snacks and sodas and a little beer, and we sat in with her friends and talked. I tried to get Mahala to go in swimming in the ocean. The waves were calmer than before and the days were sunny and warm.

She remembered the previous time when we were at the hotel when the surf was much rougher and a wave had broke and washed in under her feet and stolen one of her slippers. Now Mahala was mortally terrified of the sea, and screamed and screamed when I would go in swimming, or try to carry her in with me.

After that she wouldn't let me go near the ocean water, and if I wanted to go in swimming would have to try to sneak out without her noticing me missing from the hotel room. The first time I tried this she soon enough discovered what I had done and somehow figured out that I went

Auto-Anthropology

swimming. Next thing I know I saw her come running down to the water's edge screaming at me, with only my head bobbing up and down in the surf as speedboats would go racing by.

That night she wet the bed of the hotel three times, and we had all the sheets hanging up to dry and were quite embarrassed about it. From then on I only took her into the swimming pool, which she enjoyed immensely, riding on my back and splashing in the water. We would go in swimming like that twice a day--once late in the morning, and once in the afternoon.

It was a very relaxing week. We would take almost all our meals at some hawker stalls across the street from the hotel, that catered mostly to the employees of the hotels, and we didn't even get back to downtown Georgetown at all until the very last day when we went down to buy some inevitable gifts for people back in the US and to change a little more cash to travel back with.

The last day there a friend stayed overnight with us in the room to wake up early enough to carry us down to the train station to catch the train back down to KL. We walked out onto the empty train platform in the darkness of the early morning and waited for almost an hour for the train to come.

We sat there and mused about how much Malaysia had changed since we were there six years ago. There were so many more people, a lot of Indonesians. There was a lot more traffic congestion, and more high rises and luxury flats and hotels. It seemed to Rosie that Penang had changed more in the last six years than she had remembered it having changed in her entire previous lifetime. We mused also that we had changed a lot in the last six years without realizing it.

We took the bus back down and stayed in a hotel in downtown KL that we had stayed at while visiting the US embassy in 1987. It was almost the same, except now instead of $65 dollars for a large hotel room with too beds, we were paying over $105 for a much smaller room with only one bed--and that was a special business discount we had gotten through a friend of ours who booked the room for us in Penang.

We caught the plane the following morning. Another Chinese taxi drove us out to the airport along a new highway that had just been completed. He talked about all the Indonesians who were coming into Malaysia, many staying illegally, and about how much cheaper things were in Indonesia than in Malaysia.

Before long we were aboard the plane heading to Japan, and then to LA again. The flight was uneventful and therefore nice. We banked into LA on a rather clear afternoon, and the first thing that struck me was how much drier and browner LA was compared to the wetness and greenness of KL and Malaysia. We went through customs without any difficulties, declaring the package of salted fish Rosie wanted to bring back with her, and soon we were back in an airport shuttle van headed for my mom's home.

The van driver was an irate Egyptian. He circled the hotel terminus about six times with us in the van looking for more passengers until he gave up and got back on the main road. The whole way back he complained to us about how hard life was in the states, how he and his wife both had to work to make ends meet, and how, as an accountant back in Cairo, he had a limousine with a chauffeur of his own. Now he was sad because his own son was ashamed of his father bringing him to school in the airport shuttle van. Life indeed is hard everywhere I thought--he was just one more person in line.

Sixth

Such a long and difficult journey
Just so that I could be here now
To meet you face-to-face
So long to wait and so hard to struggle
Without ever knowing the reason
But here we stand together
And without words we know our intertwined destiny
The ways of the world wind all about
Whichever direction we decide to take
Still leads us to our final destination
We do not need to speak know the way before us
Though we soon part
The journey will have been worth the trouble
We may meet again next time around
And still require only the silence know each other's souls

Third Interregnum

We got back to LA to wait indefinitely to hear from the Malaysian Embassy about being given permission to conduct my anthropological fieldwork there. I had called the embassy in Chicago two times in early spring of that year, and had gotten no reply whatsoever. When we got back to LA I called the consulate in LA and received the application forms for social science research in the mail the next day. We filled these forms out in quadruplicate and then sent them back to the consulate.

Now we were back in LA without much to do until we heard from them again. In the meantime I completed several grant proposal applications to different funding agencies in the US, and I set to work on a constructing an artificial intelligence program in Hyper script--a project that I had been working on and off for over a year already. I thought it would be a good time to get it taken care of, because development of such programs require a substantial amount of time. It was slow going the first month or so, until things eventually began falling into place.

We got back just in time to help our friends whom we knew at our University to move into the new home they had bought down the coast near San Diego. He was doing an hour and a half commute from this home that he could afford to his teaching job at Cal. State Los Angeles. The home was nice and they seemed to settle into the community quickly.

We went back down to take their daughter and our own to the Wild Animal Park down in San Diego. It was a windy drive, and we noticed the smoke from several large brush fires along the route as we drove down. We were turned away almost at the gate of the Wild Animal Park because it too was on fire. We went to the zoo instead. We were shocked to see how many little Mexican kids there were on school buses on a field trip.

All the kids, their teachers and helpers were Mexican, and there were only one or two white kids in any group. Many of the kids would just push their way to the front of the line, and I scolded a group of young boys for doing it in front of us. Another group came and pushed Mahala

Auto-Anthropology

and her friend Sarah off a playground turtle that they were climbing on to get a photo.

When we got back that evening we found that we had traveled out to San Diego on one of the worst imaginable days, as there were seventeen major brushfires burning simultaneously in all of the Southland, and the worst was at Laguna, as it swept through all the beautiful homes of the seaside and the fire teams had a hard time fighting it because of the lack of water pressure and the high winds.

One of the fires was coming dangerously close to my sister's home out in the Walnut area. A week later there was a second, even worse fire that broke out in the Malibu area in northwestern LA, claiming quite a few homes.

We housesat for my Mom a couple of weeks while she flew back East to be with her family there. We took care of things while she was gone. When we picked her up at the airport we could see the smoke of the fire burning along the coast just to the north of us.

And then we were all awakened one morning by a major earthquake. It woke me up first and after I realized what was happening I called to Rosie and grabbed Mahala who was sleeping comfortably next to me and pushed her down on the floor under me at the edge of the bed. I frightened her more than the earthquake would have and left her shivering in fright for over an hour after.

I remember waiting for the quake to end, and watching things on the shelves above the bed begin to fall off. I was just waiting for the roof of the house to collapse. Then I heard my Mom calling from the hallway and I told her to get down low. She had run to see if we were OK and told me how the telephone lines outside across the city could be seen arcing.

We lost electricity and had candles and a flashlight in the morning. I went out and checked the gas main and found the streets eerily quiet and deserted and could hear only dogs barking and cats meowing. Soon electricity was restored and we turned on the television and at first there was no reception. Then a report came through and then another. Fires were burning all over the city. Soon they showed the death of a motorcycle CHP officer who rode his bike off a collapsed overpass.

Then we saw entire freeways collapsed, and a train derailed, and then an entire three-story apartment complex in which the very bottom floor was completely squashed beneath the upper floors. It shook us up the whole day and even the whole week after. It felt like the worst one we had ever experienced, including the Whittier quake the epicenter of which was nearby our home, and the 1973 Sylmar quake that had caused a similar amount of damage.

We waited until December to hear news from the Embassy, afraid to start anything that we wouldn't be able to finish. I got several rejections for funding from U.S. funding agencies, but was awarded a small grant from the Pacific Cultural Foundation in Taiwan. I called the consulate back and then wrote off three letters simultaneously to government departments in KL. Within two weeks the embassy called me to let me know that I had been given permission to do my fieldwork. They told me to mail them my passport so they could chop the entry Visa into it.

So, immediately after Christmas, we began racing around again to get ready to go back to Malaysia. I sold my computer to my brother-in-law and then bought a nice newer laptop computer to take with me. I hurriedly went to the library at my old alma mater and tried putting together as many materials for conducting research as I could find at the time.

Within a few weeks were on a shuttle again back down to the airport, and then soon we were back on board a MAS plane bound for Malaysia for the fourth time.

Seventh

Old aunt
Lights the joss stick and puts it in the urns
And burns the paper money
In the large pot outside
Spirit bound smoke
Sent heavenward

Old uncle kneeling on the ground
Shakes the joss toward the baby God
Mumbling a low monotonous prayer
Under his breath
The ritual fires are burning
The spirit smoke is curling
The ti koay is collecting mold
And ashes from the burnt joss

An old auntie cleans out the teacups
An old uncle replaces the wilted flowers with new ones
The winds blow through the open windows and doors
The paper lanterns suspended from the ceiling
Flutter and twirl and start spinning about

Old aunt is mopping the red tile floors
Old uncle is checking his ledger again
The same rituals quietly performed
A thousand and one times over
Only one day or one hundred years

Old uncle is dozing off
Old aunty has gone out to buy something at the market
The dragon slumbers
The phoenix has flown

Fourth Trip: January to December, 1994

Our plane flight was almost exactly like the one summer before, even down to the indigestion and diarrhea at the end of it. We left about mid-January, and wanted to get into Penang before the start of the Chinese New Year celebrations. This time we waited at the terminus until morning and then caught a shuttle bus to the other domestic terminal to take a plane to Penang. I figured that after taxis, hotel fare and meal and train tickets were all added in, that it was just about as cheap to fly and much more convenient.

So we had arrived at the airport terminal in Penang before noon of the same day, and we took a taxi from the terminal to the same small Chinese hotel we had been at during our previous stay. This time the taxi driver was an older Malay man and we talked mostly about the earthquake and the tragic collapse of the Highland Towers building in KL. He had a daughter living in San Diego. He drove the back route behind the University, a way that he claimed was less congested, and by the time he dropped us off at the hotel he had shown us the photos of his family he had in his wallet.

They gave us the extra room they usually didn't rent out for a night until they could get us another room. We stayed in this hotel again for about a month, through the New Year Celebrations. Early in our stay there I began playing with my new laptop computer and tried to set it up to the electrical system in the hotel.

I ended up shorting out all the lights and fans in the hotel when I plugged a small 120-voltage circuit breaker into the 220 outlet. The thing exploded in my hand and left black scorch marks on my palm and thumb, and it cost me RM70 to replace the circuit in the hotel and to buy a power converter to run my electrical things on.

One night I found small mice crawling on the cloth line just above our pillow to get into a plastic bag we had hung at the end of it. For the next couple of days I found several mice scurrying across the floor and one time in the middle of the night found two or three in the bag of bread we had brought back and left on the table. I repeatedly told the uncles and managers of the hotel about the mice but nobody did anything about it.

The manageress said it was not nice to kill mice so close to New Year.

Auto-Anthropology

So I went down to Komtar and bought a couple of mousetraps and baited them. Within 3 or 4 days I managed to kill 11 mice in our room and just outside by the television set. One day I was making tea outside where the condiments were kept and noticed all the mouse shit all over the top of the table and television set. Then I found three mice inside a plastic bag that had crackers in it next to the television set.

I grabbed the bag up off the TV and trapped them inside the bag, and showed them to the old Cantonese uncle who worked there. He grabbed a stick and opened the bag and managed to kill two of them, while the third one escaped. I quite baiting the traps after a couple of days as the blood from the mice was making them dirty and the last mice I got were small infants, and then one day I managed to cut a small *chi chak* (a small gecko) in half in our room.

We got to know the old uncles of the hotel quite well. The old man who had been in the hotel since the before the war and who loved the horses had gone into a retirement home to be with his wife. I managed to get a couple of interviews in and even some participant- observation of the New Year's celebration there.

A new manageress had come in, and was the principle shareholder in the hotel. She allowed two of her male companions to come in every evening and drink beer. They would sit and drink and act rude. Older Chinese men would come in and get prostitutes.

The hotel had gone down hill since we were there last and we no longer felt comfortable sitting in the lobby in the evening watching TV. A young Malay man was upstairs with an even younger Malay looking woman. He as so short and skinny but he acted so tough. He was a pimp and his girlfriend was a prostitute. They would go out every evening and then we would hear them coming back real late at night.

Later we found out that the two companions of the manageress would go into the back storeroom at night or into empty rooms, and drill holes through the plaster in the wall to peep at women who had checked into the hotels. We found this out after we saw them one evening going into the room of two American women who were an attractive mother and her daughter traveling together, and who had stepped out for the evening.

The next morning we told the Americans what we saw and they said that they found white powdered dust on their bags. They checked out of the hotel that night and left Penang feeling very uncomfortable. Later, the uncles and the old manager of the hotel confirmed our suspicions about these two characters. They would have to go into the rooms after they left and patch back up the holes that they had bored through the walls back up.

It seemed like a crude and childish thing for these two middle-aged men to be doing every night who were both married and had families. The old manager of the hotel was too afraid to say anything to them because they feared that they were in the secret society and knew people who would get them back.

They caused a great deal of consternation for everybody there, and news must somehow have gotten out about them, especially after an American who rented there died under mysterious circumstances nearby the hotel and the Malay couple suddenly split out of town on the same day without paying what they owed the hotel for back rent.

Talking to the old manager of the hotel about six months later, we found out that the two guys were still up to their antics almost every night and that they were finally selling the hotel. He had been manager of the hotel since the early sixties but had had enough of their nonsense.

The week after New Year ended I was desperate to find a more stable and suitable living arrangement, and had to use public phones outside the hotel to talk to real estate brokers. The first three brokers drove us around and showed us nice, new and overpriced flats on the thirteenth, seventh and fourth floors of large flat complexes.

A friend of ours tried getting us a low-cost flat for about a third less but everybody wanted a three-year lease agreement. Finally, one morning I called from the road a couple of more agents, with a beggar sticking his hand in my face while I was trying to hear what the Chinese gentleman on the other side of the line was trying to tell me above the din of the traffic on the street.

By the time I got back to the hotel this gentleman and his colleague were waiting at our hotel in the lobby, and we quickly rushed off to look at a nice second-floor apartment of an old Chinese-style mansion in *Tanjung Tokong*, where we had stayed in 1987.

It had a nice balcony overlooking the coast and sea of the North Channel and was semi-furnished. It was quite spacious, even though the Malay family who had lived in it before left it in a most dirty state I had

Auto-Anthropology

ever seen an apartment—at the bottom of a stair well sat an old rusted
refrigerator in a two-foot pile of filth and trash.

The walls were covered with handprints, dirt, *chi chak* shit and crayon
drawings.

The kitchen was covered in black grease. They took us to another
smaller, unfurnished flat in the *Ayer Itam* area, but it was far from a bus
stop and from any Makan, and we didn't like the idea of living in such a
tall building after having been in the earthquake.

The next morning we agreed to the *Tanjung Tokong* apartment and I
was to meet the broker and the representative of the landlady at 12:00
noon that day. Since I had only traveler's checks I went down to a
prestigious bank along Beach Street to try to open a savings account in
order to deposit my cash, which I needed to cover the down and
deposits and the broker fees, which had become quite considerable since
1987.

At the bank the tellers wouldn't allow me to open a savings account
because I had only a tourist social visa chopped in my passport. I told
them that I was there for a year to do research, but they didn't believe me
or understand me. Then I looked in my passport to discover that indeed
all that was there was a social visit chop that was to expire in another
couple of months.

With all my money cashed in my pocket, I walked out of the bank and
hurriedly went back to the hotel. I got Rosie and we took a taxi to the
immigration office in Penang. The rude officer at the window
discourteously told us there was nothing he could do and that we would
have to go down to KL. So we went back to the hotel, I called the broker
and postponed the deal until the following day; we hurriedly packed our
bags, took a silent taxi to the airport, and arrived in KL by three-thirty in
the afternoon of the same day.

We rushed in another taxi to the *Damansara* building and got there
about 14 minutes before they closed for the day. We were referred to
about three different windows and offices in different buildings until a
nice Malay woman told us that we needed to go to the Prime Minister's
Department in another part of the city to look up the person whose
name and address she wrote on a piece of paper for us.

We got up early the next morning to make sure we were at the office at
its opening time. We had to wait about a half hour at the police gate in

front, and were given special identity cards to wear when we went inside. I went to the office and told them my name. They found my name in a file and discovered that I had never received their instruction letter telling me to visit them when I first arrived in K.L., to take care of my visa and identity card. They had written the wrong numbers on the address and so the letter apparently was sent to the wrong address in the States, and never reached me.

We then had to go back down the hill to get passport photos made, which took about an hour and about a mile of walking and sweating, but we finished the entire thing by 11:00 and was back at the Damansara building by noon the same day, at which time I was informed to come back in two weeks time to have my passport chopped.

There being nothing else we could do at the time, we took the taxi back to the airport and caught the 1:00 o'clock flight back to Penang. We called the broker from the airport, and we settled the deal on the apartment by 3:00 **P.M.** We weren't scheduled to move into the apartment until a couple of days later, when the caretaker had time to come in and take care of a few plumbing and lighting problems.

The next two weeks we set about painting the apartment, finding a nearby day-care for Mahala, and getting the things we would need for the apartment--soaps, plastics, brushes, mops, a fan, an electric skillet, a refrigerator, a bed for Mahala, hangers, hose, rope, clothes pins and a few folding tables which proved essential for fieldwork.

By about the end of this period we took a bus back down to KL to have my daughter's and my own passport chopped for a year. The bus drove all night, and we tried sleeping as best we could on it, stopping up the huge air-con portals with rolled up newspaper. We waited a while at the busy bus-station, not able to find a seat on any of the benches, and ate at an Indian Muslim coffee-shop across the road, and then took a fast Chinese taxi to the *Damansara* building again where we again waited for about an hour for their offices to open.

We were the first people at the same lady's window, ominously marked "Experts," except for an older Malay couple who cut in front of us to whisper to the lady, only to be finally redirected to another window. So we rode directly back to the bus station in yet another taxi, and within 15 minutes were back on another bus headed back to Penang, which we reached by late afternoon, with it raining and all of us sick with severe colds from the air-conditioning on the bus.

Auto-Anthropology

The next day we were back in our routine. Mahala had missed only one day of school, and I was back trying to finish the paint job within another day or two.

For the next month we began mapping the shop houses of downtown Georgetown, walking along all of the streets and writing down the kinds of shops. Not really knowing quite what else to do, I counted people in coffee shops, trishaws, tourists, people on buses, cars, gravestones in cemeteries, and schizophrenics, and began taking black and white photos of anything unusual that I found. Toward the end of this month we began going to shop houses to do quick surveys. We were turned rudely away from about fifty percent of the shop houses we tried, and soon grew quite tired of the rejection.

Finally, one morning, we followed a large flock of tourists on trishaws to the Jetty area. Since they were all there, with policemen directing traffic around them, we figured we would walk over and check it all out too. A hawker we met on the street talked to us and told us to go over--the people were friendly and liked to talk.

My wife's only stereotype of this area was that they were all in gangs and criminals. She was very reluctant to go over to this area at first, and I listened to her, even though my anthropological experience told me otherwise and frequently tempted me to try it beforehand.

That morning we went over to the coffee shop and ordered coffee. We asked for the Headman of the place. He had just left. We could catch him before 8:00 AM most mornings. The next Monday we came back to see if he would let us come in to do a little survey work. He said sure, as long as we didn't *kachow* or bother anyone, there was no problem.

So the next day we got our forms ready, a blood pressure gauge, a weight scale and my skin-fold calipers, and we went down and started interviewing people.

One thing led to the next, and before we knew it we were down on the Jetty almost everyday weighing, measuring and checking people's blood pressure. The blood pressure gauge was a big icebreaker with the community, especially after I found several people there with high-blood pressure and they went to the doctor to have it treated. Soon we were doing household and nutritional inventories, and simple color tasks. Gradually we began extending the range of the tasks and inventories we were using.

We arranged to come in and give drawing tasks to some of the children on Sunday, and at first they allowed us to use their clan hall room for the purpose. We bought cakes and chips and packet drinks for the kids and I weighed them and took their heights and ages and had them do a number of drawings for me.

A couple of Sundays later we tried the same thing, with a new set of tasks and with extra cakes and drinks, promised as we were a better turnout. Nobody was around with the keys to the room and we ended up using the coffee shop outside for the purpose. It proved to be a frustrating day because some of the young boys were especially uncooperative and unruly, disturbing the better behaved children. Thus we ended up giving up and passing out the cakes early.

Then I began mapping the Jetty and pacing off the floor space of different homes I had been in, to get a sense of the population density of the area. About that time I interviewed a household with several young teenage girls in it who were keen to do whatever I had for them.

A couple of weeks later the older daughter of this family came out to the coffee shop to invite us back to their house to give them more tasks. The mother then asked me if I would give her daughter's English tuition. At first I didn't take her very seriously, but she said she was serious. It planted a seed in my mind and I got her at the coffee shop one morning and asked her if she was still interested. She said sure, especially as I wasn't asking any money for it, but just the cooperation of the students in performing the tasks I gave them, of which by this time I had quite a few.

Within a couple of months I had three different tuition classes I was giving to different age groups, and the size of the classes grew from a handful to over 20 students. Financially it got to be quite a burden for me, because I couldn't ask some students to buy books and others not to because they didn't have the money, so I ended up racing about town trying to find cheap deals on used English text books, dictionaries and readers, and started copying anything useful I could find for my classes. I reasoned that I now had a stable "control" group for my tasks, that I could then compare the results with the rest of the Jetty sample as well as with any non-Jetty Chinese I managed to interview.

About this time I figured I would try to enter into the Indian community as well as into a Malay Kampong or two that was nearby our apartment in order to get similar comparative samples from all three subgroups of the Malaysian population. After several days of walking around little

Auto-Anthropology

India trying to get interviews in, I found the Indians not only more resistant to being interviewed than the Chinese, but downright hostile to me. Since the Indians didn't have any apparent well-defined communities as existed on the Jetty for the poorer Chinese, and since the cultural resistance to intrusion among the Indians seemed extraordinarily strong, I abandoned the entire project of getting a substantial Indian sub-sample.

I next turned my attention to getting into a couple Malay Kampongs not far from where we lived. They were conveniently within walking distance and between them were of comparable size to the Chinese community I was doing. We first met the older ex-headman of the smaller Kampong. He was very nice and invited us into his small house. He told me that he had no problem with our coming in—he even invited it, but he had given up his headman-ship in disgust at how things were being run by people who no longer cared for the interests of the local people. So we would have to talk to the new headmen who were members of the UMNO party.

We walked down to the other Kampong that was about twice as large and had just missed the local party boss in charge who was having coffee. So we walked back and returned with our daughter in the evening when we were told we could catch him.

We introduced ourselves to a heavy-set middle-aged Malay man who was just getting on his motorcycle. We ordered coffee and sat down and talked for about an hour. He asked me what I wanted and told me he was in charge of the whole area. I tried to explain my project as best I could.

He told me that because of the impending election he wouldn't permit me to do any work there because the people would wonder who this "*Orang Putih*" ("White Ape") was. I thought his fears quite unfounded, but understandable from his political point of view. I thought it amazing how one arbitrary individual, selected from above, was allowed to make decisions affecting the lives of so many people.

He seemed to equate me in his mind with Peace Corps volunteers from the early seventies. He told me he thought the Kampong a dirty and ugly place, and that he wanted to see it torn down and the people in it living in flats.

I told him I was currently working with the Chinese down on the Jetty and he seemed interested in that. Finally, he told me that if I got permission from his boss who was the UMNO director of the Penang, then I could come into the kampong to do my research.

So early the next morning we dressed up and went down to *Komtar* to make an appointment with the chief UMNO boss of Penang. We got up to the front counter only to realize I had left my official research pass back at the apartment—I had been uselessly carrying it around in my billfold for several months now, showing it to disinterested Chinese who could care less, and the one day I might of needed it we left it behind.

So we caught a bus back home and then hurriedly took a *Sapu* (unlicensed taxi) back the other way, a young dangerous Chinese man who passed several buses on the left and wove in and out of traffic like there was no tomorrow. We got back to the desk only to be told that the UMNO director was at a meeting. We asked if we could make an appointment to meet him at some time. "Sorry, no appointments possible, come back again."

So we came back later that day, and then tried one more time on the following day. Each time was the same, and I figured he was too busy and too important a person to be bothered with such a trivial matter.

I thought about it and realized I had been thrown a big bureaucratic boondoggle. The more I thought about the local party boss I had spoken too the less I liked him and the less friendly and sincere I thought him to be. He seemed like a typical yes-man I had known in the headquarters in the Marine Corps, who put his own interests before anyone else's.

I wrote a long letter to the Prime Minister's department in KL thinking I could swoop over all this bureaucracy to get either permission or rejection from above. I got no reply whatsoever. Then I wrote another long letter, but still got no reply. After this I figured it was not worth the pursuit and found the Chinese, as stolid and money-faced as they may be, much more rewarding.

I did not give up hope of getting some kind of cross-cultural sample, especially as my tasks came to focus upon a single sub-set of tasks compiled into a single booklet. I felt the theoretical and empirical importance of trying this booklet out with an alternative cultural sample to compare with my Chinese sample was too theoretically important to let go of, so I next tried to go to the prison to speak to the people in charge there to be allowed to interview both the prisoners and the guards who lived in the barracks with their families just across the road.

Auto-Anthropology

After being referred from the guard at the front gate to another office, then to another office, and then back to the guard again, someone finally carried my ominous research pass and copy of my test-booklet into the warden of the prison.

We were left standing outside the main prison entrance for about a half-hour before the warden himself came out, with two other officers, to shake my hand and to tell me he would only permit me to come in if I had a letter of permission from the department of domestic affairs, which was independent of the department of socio-economic development under whose aegis of authority my card had any weight. So I went back to my apartment to hurriedly type out another long letter along with a draft of my test-booklet to mail to yet another office in KL for some kind of response.

In the meantime we continued with the Jetty sample. Things were slowing down on the Jetty overall, and my "control groups" became our main source of information, aside from a few sporadic odd interviews we could pick up from virtually anybody along the way. We waited and heard absolutely nothing from any agency in the Malay government. So I eventually despaired getting any more productive research done and instead concentrated my efforts to completing the Chinese sample as best that we could.

Unfortunately, the Chinese sample at the Jetty was beginning to dry up. I think the change came with the relationship to my daughter. We had stopped going down there frequently, partly because our daughter was beginning to have problems at school. She would refuse to eat her lunch unless some of the adults there would feed her—something she had picked up on the Jetty with everybody stuffing food into her mouth all day long.

At the same time, she began having crying jags. So we decided to switch gears a bit and to send her to school less—reasoning that it may be a little too structured, while at the same time taking her down to the Jetty just once or twice a week. But after this point it became more difficult to get much cooperation from anyone on the Jetty, and we began feeling like unwelcome guests who had overstayed our visit. Instead of greeting us with "have you eating rice today" people were now chronically greeting us with a double-sided "when are you leaving" or "you haven't left yet?"

By late October things felt finished. My sample sizes were not as satisfactory in a number of areas—but even my tuition classes were falling off in attendance. Many days only one or two people would show up, and I was lucky to have 50 percent attendance at any given time. We were spending more time again downtown doing participant observation.

We were lucky to be included in the 9th month celebration of the God of Hades by a local businessman's group in which were had become partly networked. I began taking a lot of photos of the shop houses and different sections downtown--especially the old wholesaler's market area that had been the focus of Japanese bombing during the war and that was now soon to be demolished by the Malay government in the name of development.

I began making some crates with some thin plywood and *Meranti* furring strips and simple hand tools in order to ship back our data and some of our belongings. The English couple who had lived upstairs liked my work and the young woman wanted me to show her how to do it, so that three boxes soon turned into five, with more wood, screws, glue and nails to buy. She ended up with a nice large box that she was very proud of. We got to know this couple very well. Mahala liked to go upstairs on her own in the evening and play with them—it was her first social contact without us—and she really took to the couple.

They liked their beer and we would sit out on our balcony at night until the wee hours of the morning talking of all the important social issues in the world. A few nights we cooked up some grand Makan and invited several of these young English couples over--with beer, rice, tuna, *bee hoon*, chocolate, etc. We had grown quite fond of the British and their relaxed and carefree spirit and healthy, amoral attitudes.

Seeing that we were not getting any more productive work accomplished, we moved forward our departure date by one month. The last few weeks we spent mostly by ourselves in a relaxed way. There was no point anymore in trying to gather in more samples, and I quit giving tuition a couple of weeks ahead of schedule. I accepted about a 33 percent loss on all the tasks that I had wanted to get done--but this loss had to be weighed against the cost of remaining there and the increasing lack of cooperation.

Some mornings we would go marketing. In the afternoons we would cook and I would organize my data. I had to arrange shipment of my crates and went through my old friend who was a shipping agent. He ended up being about three weeks late on the shipment, and it cost me about twice as much as the original estimate. I was a more than a little disappointed to learn that our English friends upstairs got about half the rate for their crate through another agent.

It seems my successful friend who had grown big over the years had also grown more expensive and less efficient. By the time the crates arrived at their destination, it had set me back on my schedule about five weeks--a delay which eventually caused a greater loss of a thousand more dollars and postponement of the completion and reading of my dissertation and my graduation date beyond the Spring deadline.

Once the departure date was set and the withdrawal from the field context was imminent, it was as if everything else just started coming undone at the seams, and the level of incentive necessary to continue to overcome the social barriers to gathering data drained out.

During almost eight months of fieldwork, we had not seen any of our old friends except one person who visited us one time. At first I became increasingly angry with them that they had abandoned us to our plight, but we had eventually become adapted to being on our own and not requiring anyone's assistance, and we had accepted our lot and learned to live privately by ourselves.

We grew to the point that we did not really desire their company anymore. During our entire time in Penang, we had only seen Rosie's sister once, unexpectedly in the street as she was coming from the bank. Though we ate many mornings at the same coffee shop where Rosie's niece took her Makan during her lunch break, we never once saw or spoke to her that year. They never called us or made an effort to see us, and I felt very bad for Rosie.

The last few days of our time in Penang, we checked into the Lone Pine Hotel down at *Batu Ferringhi*. I had been promising to take my daughter swimming in the pool for a long time—after nearly a year of bathing in red plastic buckets. I was extremely disappointed to find that their pool had been indefinitely closed due to leakage problems.

But my daughter took it better than myself and we ended up taking her into the ocean that she had become mortally terrified of. After a couple of hours she was swimming quite freely in the small waves, when she was stung by a Jellyfish that slipped through the old nets. We rushed her inside and the hotel management got some topical ointment that proved quite effective in quelling the pain. After a half hour she was acting as if nothing had happened.

I invited the students from my tuition classes to come and visit us, as well as the British whom we had befriended. The first day a number of the students came, bringing gifts. The next day some of the British came. The last day a few other Chinese friends came by. We all enjoyed ourselves and I took everyone out to eat hawker food in the evenings.

We returned to our apartment and collected our deposit the last day before our departure back to the U.S. The Chinese landlady was at first reluctant to pay us back, but thought better of it and pulled the cash out of her wallet. I gave her my task booklet that she took a couple of hours to complete. That afternoon we rushed downtown to do some last minute shopping. We bought a few gold presents for people back in the U.S., and a couple of gifts for the British couple upstairs. We were mainly interested in buying some books that were not commonly found in the U.S.

Our last day, we spent packing our bags and just hanging out. By afternoon, we became bombarded by a stream of visitors that we hadn't expected. Everyone brought parting gifts that filled up the remaining spaces of our luggage and stretched our weight allowances on the plane.

We ended up entertaining our different guests until after midnight--by which time I had become so tired I was falling asleep in my straight chair and barely responding to what people were asking me.

The next morning my shipping agent friend picked us up early and we squeezed our heavy bags into the boot of his car and he rode us down early to the airport. It was a pleasant, cool morning and it was a different view of the Island than any I had before. A student from my tuition group met us unexpectedly at the airport to see us off. We ate some breakfast at the canteen downstairs and soon we were getting back on board the plane and saying goodbye to Penang for the fourth and final time.

Eighth

Flotsam from a foreign land
Cast adrift upon the warm currents
Junk blown across by the winds
Rising and falling like the tide
Coming to rest upon the shore
A rotting, swollen plank of wood
Planted upright in the muck
Covered with barnacles and crawling crabs
Between the ocean and the land
Motionless against the rolling surf
Paper boats
Little white wind boats
Folded and fashioned by nimble fingers
Set into the lapping water
Floating off into the sea
Sun waves burning on the surface
Mysterious flames
Dancing deep beneath the water
Growing into dark stormy clouds
Rising upon the horizon
Lightning flashing
In thunderous heaven

After

The plane flight went without much event, except for the periodic bouts of twisting indigestion in my stomach and intestines. Within a few minutes we were at the KL airport and our departure gate for the long flight overseas was right in front of us. We shopped a little in the new international lounge, buying a book and some magazines for the trip.

We waited about four hours until we boarded the plane again. We were delayed by a sudden thunderstorm that covered the runway with diagonal sheets of rain and wind. About a half hour later we were in the air again headed for our Taipei stopover.

The rest of the flight was without much event. We ate one meal the first leg of the flight and I read a book and some magazines and newspapers, and soon we were all asleep. Luckily we managed to sleep most of the rest of the way, and did not take any more meals the entire flight across the Pacific, much to the chagrin of our hostess.

We landed, walked the long concourse to immigration, waited interminably for our luggage, which was the last to come off the conveyor belt, and then cleared customs without a hitch. Outside we found Mahala's Grandma and my sister waiting for us.

We returned in late November just before Thanksgiving. We spent Thanksgiving day with my family in a small and peaceful reunion. We did not have much to do for several weeks, awaiting the shipment of most of my data in our crates. We were pretty jet-lagged for about 10 days, with sleepless nights and sleepy, tiresome days. Our daughter Mahala overcame her jetlag in just a few days, but it was most difficult for myself, lingering on almost two whole weeks.

I was anxious to hear from the shipping agency about our crates. In the meantime we filled up our time with small things to do. We reorganized some of our junk in storage, and got our car back into driving condition. The battery was dead after a year. We met with some of our old friends, Bill and Charlotte, and spent a day with them. During this time I managed to collect a small American sample of my symbolic frame battery with which to compare to my British and Chinese samples.

Auto-Anthropology

We waited until after the deadline for the shipment, and if I hadn't made an effort to call and find out whether my shipment had arrived, and where it was, I doubt whether I would have been contacted at all.

I was doubly frustrated because I had not been given a contact number or address, and so was almost working blind. I finally found that my shipment had already been in storage a week and it cost me over a hundred U.S. dollars just to have to pick it up myself at a storage place not far from the docks.

I was very angry, as the cost of shipping suddenly doubled for no clear reason except for the fact that some greedy Taiwanese middlemen who drove Mercedes-Benz held my shipment and would not give it up unless I paid them first. The previous time I had shipped I went straight to the docks themselves and paid nothing to put the crates in my car.

This time I had to spend an entire day driving to three different places in Los Angeles, paying over 100 dollars and then twenty more dollars just so a forklift could dump the crates on the edge of the warehouse docking gate. I had to lift the heavy crates by myself, and found two of them to have been damaged—apparently punctured by the forklift. On crate fell on my leg and hurt me as I was trying to shift if from off the dock into the back of the Minivan. As it stood, I was about a month behind schedule and more than a hundred dollars short.

As soon as we got our crates we unloaded them and organized the data and encoded it. Then I set to work on the onerous burden of analyzing each page and entering all the data into spreadsheets in my computer and designing suitable databases for each kind of task.

This work came to fully occupy my time for the next 3 months, as much as 18 hours a day seven days a week, taking a break only for Christmas and then for a week when we had to relocate back to my university in Missouri before the semester started.

My main adviser telephoned me one day and offered me a teaching assistantship in a writing intensive course. This was a relief as it helped pay the expenses of the next four months at school, and it did not interfere very much with the production of the dissertation. We relocated back to the campus apartments where we had previously resided.

The day after we checked in a snowstorm blew in, dumping close to two feet of snow in less than ten hours. For the most part cars were snowbound, and I spent the day shoveling the snow off the sidewalks and from around my car. We had no furniture or covering for the cold tile floors, so fortunately we spent our first day shopping for a bed and a suitable card table and some cheap carpets for the rooms. We were just in the nick of time.

Work on the dissertation continued, and I finished the first draft in early March. My relations with the department, aside from my advisor and one or two other graduate students, could be described as nonexistent. I would sit for office hours in the department to have people not only did not acknowledge me, but to deliberately ignore me as if I were not even there. I felt like a ghost in the department, and grew to hate being there with each passing day.

I turned in my finished draft of the dissertation so that the faculty could have four weeks to read it. I would have gotten it to them earlier had I not been delayed in the shipment of data from overseas as was originally planned. I came back to the committee a month later to discover that no one had not only not read it, but hadn't even looked at it—so busy were they with everything else in their lives.

I became angry with them and let them know in no uncertain terms of my expectation that they get the job done so that we could move on with life without spending more money than was necessary. It meant that we had to miss the spring commencement and we were not to finish the dissertation until a month afterward.

It would mean the indefinite postponement of the end of more than 14 years as a student, almost exclusively of the field of cultural anthropology, and I left the department being treated essentially no different than when I had first begun my school days a decade and a half before, only a little older and more burned out and even disillusioned with my chosen field more than ever before.

Ninth

Then the barking dog was nearby
And the ghost was far away
Now the dog is barking far away
And the spirits are close by
The earth wind that carries all
From every corner
Penetrates every nook and cranny
Cleaning every crevice
Wearing mountains down to plains
Drying oceans into deserts
Souls howl in the barren trees
Dried leaf spirits twist and turn in the corners of the buildings
Wind spirits whisper to me plaintively
Through the closed window
The empty classroom is filled only with cold memories
The names of forgotten student carved in wood
The hallways still echo
With doors slamming and distant footsteps
Long since passed away

Postscript

Upon our return from Malaysia on the final trip, we had suffered jet lag and "reverse culture shock" pretty severely, at least for the first two weeks. My dreams were all back in Penang, and it seemed sometimes that though our bodies were now in LA, our heads were still back somewhere across the Pacific.

We kept odd hours, and it seemed especially difficult to readjust my sleeping habits back to a normal schedule. Our daughter fell right into a normal routine within the first three days. I was still waking up at one or two in the morning and falling asleep at four or five in the evening the second week.

It was the little things that we looked forward to most--the spaghetti, the Top-Sirloin, the *Lowenbrau,* the hot-showers and shave. It was the *nasi kandar* and fried *lor bak* and *rumpa hu* that we missed most about Malaysia.

The contrasts between here and there become most marked and apparent in those few weeks of readjustment. It was the cleanliness of the streets and the orderliness of the traffic and how damned expensive everything was on this side of the world.

It was mostly a deep-seated sense of regret that I felt in not being able to push the study further in the direction I had intended in order to collect a viable cross-cultural sample. I felt extremely disappointed with the Malaysian Government and the seeming total apathy towards the research, and this disappointment, I believe, undermined my motivation and determination to do more research in Malaysia.

I did not want to blame them for the shortcomings of my own research, but my hands were tied and I was frustrated. There was little to console this sense of disappointment, and all I wanted to do the last month or so, after I realized I would hear nothing from them, was to just get back as quickly as possible.

I never felt that I suffered much culture shock while in Malaysia, at least not as much this time around as on previous occasions. I knew the differences and knew what to expect and learned what not to expect of

Auto-Anthropology

Malaysians. Having been married to a Malaysian for seven years, I was quite familiar with some basic aspects of Malaysian character.

Culture shock is after all a function of one's character and deep-seated ethnocentric attachments and symbolic prejudices and little habits and I think in most ways we are probably some of the least ethnocentrically bound people on earth. I would rather call what we suffered during our time in Malaysia as a form of "cultural schizophrenia."

Whereas culture shock is considered to be the depression and disorientation attendant upon adaptation in a strange cultural milieu, usually due to subconscious resistance tied a strong attachment to one's own native culture—ours was a fundamental lack of attachment to any culture. It was a lack of a sense of cultural context in which we could identify ourselves and by which others could easily categorize us.

Consequently, most people seemed to have perceived us as a strange couple, uncomfortable, even threatening to be around. And we felt heavily the entire year in Malaysia a sense of irreconcilable alienation and loneliness in Penang.

It was a nonattachment to anything local or foreign, and a lack of a sense of focus about our own cultural orientation. We resigned ourselves to this sense of liminal and desocialized existence as part of the burden of the fieldwork and as something to be only temporarily endured until we once again moved on to greener pastures.

The only respite we had from this type of existence were in the fieldwork itself among acquaintances and informants of "our" communities who seemingly got along with us well, and hence we came to look forward to those fleeting moments where our identity changed from being nearly anonymous to that of a 'researcher' and hopefully a friend as well.

It was as my wife tells me, that every time someone asks sometimes where we are from in the U.S., we do not really know anymore what to tell him or her. It was a sense of not having a clear cut sense of attachment or belonging to any particular cultural orientation--the classic case of the inter-cultural pariahs—and thus did not feel strongly in a chauvinistic sense about much of anything at all.

I personally found most people in Penang too preoccupied with the almighty dollar to suit my own tastes. Among the Chinese I think it can be safely said that the more money they make, the more conceited and arrogant and class-conscious they can afford to become. I grew sick and tired of Mercedes-Benz cars and car phones.

But I rediscovered America as well—an America full of violence, inhumanity, and a counter-productive narrow-minded morality that continues to prevent American society from progressing in an enlightened way. It seems to have become increasingly a place where money is the most common denominator of everyone's existence. So all-important has making money become that it defines the exclusive basis for almost all human interrelationships in the world.

Changes had happened to us in the course of the fieldwork, imperceptible at first. One day we woke up and realized that things had changed for us. It is impossible to say really what these changes were--our relationship to the world had changed, and it could never be the same again.

These differences became especially marked in our social relationships upon our return to the university and department. The sense of being unaccepted and unwelcome, of not being given acknowledgement for having achieved something worthwhile in life, was about all that was waiting for us there.

Of all the people we were left missing, it was the company of the British that we had thought about and missed most. In hindsight this must have been due to their own cosmopolitan orientation that was noticeably carefree, accepting of challenges and privations, and lacking in any rigid moral prejudices besides perhaps a healthy self-respect. Americans by contrast now seemed so culturally inbound and naive about the larger world. But such are the different ways of the world, and the dilemmas of finding our own way within it.

It has been five years since I first wrote this manuscript. We have sojourned a year in China where I tried with only partial success to carry forward my doctoral work in comparative, cross-cultural research, and we lived a couple of years in Wyoming where I conducted another kind of research that proved quite interesting and where I got in touch with another side of American culture.

Auto-Anthropology

Five years later, we are perhaps less culturally oriented or attached as we were upon our return from Malaysia. Conditions in Anthropology departments generally seem to be deteriorating, as the call for genuine fieldwork has often been met only with multicultural hype and hiring preferences.

We are more Pariah that even before, and the sense of exclusion from Anthropological forums especially seems almost total and absolute. I doubt we will be sojourning back to Malaysia except perhaps as tourists only to eat the makan.

We have turned a couple of corners in our lives, and look forward now to greater stability and another form of productivity. I have intellectually outgrown anthropology, and thus now seek to leave it behind. I will always remain an anthropologist at heart, though I no longer measure myself or my world by any anthropological yardsticks.

As I edit these pages for their on-line publication, I cannot but help relive the many moments they encompassed in our lives, and to reflect once again upon the motivations and circumstances that drove us forward in life and made us what we were. I do not really regret having chosen Anthropology as a career, as impossible as it has been. I am a natural anthropologist, of sorts, and think of myself as better than most.

I laugh to myself that I will be allowed, as a middle aged white man, to teach my first introductory course in Anthropology by the age of my retirement. It must make me a failure as an Anthropologist in someone's eyes at least, if not in my own eyes—but I did not fail myself, my system has failed me.

This is all a self-fulfilling prophecy, a by-product of 30 years of affirmative action and class closure of academia. To deny this is to contradict my life experiences and to contradict everything I worked for and stand for as an Anthropologist.

I see the world and do not rate humanity very highly in it any more. We are violent and selfish creatures--no culture is immune from these kinds of limits of our character, though it has taken different expressions in different times and places. As I recently heard Sidney Mintz say culture is now more of an obstacle we must learn to overcome in order to get along in the world with others.

I have come to a conclusive understanding of cultural realities, and though it is important to celebrate diversity and heritage, when this is politicized ideologically and exaggerated beyond its normal importance in our lives, it is used as the justification for the unequal distribution of resources and resource opportunities.

This is as true in the U.S. as it is in Malaysia or China. No society can afford forever to maintain double standards among its own people, and for all societies charity must begin at home. If we do not take care of our own, we are only inviting the rest of the world only to take more advantage of us and ultimately to do violence to us.

But beyond the big and the small, I see anthropology as something I married myself to, for richer or poorer, better or worse, in sickness and in health, a long time ago, just as I married my wife and stuck by her all that time.

I've seen many other people, with much more support and opportunity, bail out at the first hard-knock, only to seek the vain promises of more lucrative fields. Many, many other anthropologists climbed into comfortable academic armchairs with almost no fieldwork experience and often only because their academic connections.

More than one friendship has ended for these reasons. For me, in my lifetime, commitment has not been an intrinsically dirty word, except what other people have made it and turned it into. It did not have to be this way. It could have been a wonderful thing, a beautiful thing. Instead, it has been marginalized and thus delegitimized as a valid form of experience and a worthy way of life. This is as unfortunate as it has been unnecessary.

I carry forward in my life without envy or great regret. I am happy for all those people who are succeeding in their own way, and I am sad for all those who still suffer the privations of poverty and prejudice. I have come to realize that I am both an anthropologist and a human being, in spite of our pariah-hood, and in this I find no more contradiction. I do not celebrate the self or the other any longer--I do not put the other upon some pedestal, nor do I seek to aggrandize my own ego.

Rather, I think it is the other way around. I live by certain minimal standards about what it is to be a decent human being in the world, and I've come increasingly to expect others to meet me halfway at least on those standards. Many of these standards are meta-ethical and post-conventional, and therefore are construed commonly as unrealistic for the mean everyday world. But they are important nonetheless to follow if we are to construct a better world for ourselves and our children.

Tenth

Within the labyrinth
Of many twists and turns
Hunting for the Minotaur
Becoming lost within its guts
In many different directions traveling
Without a clear sense of beginning or end
Guided only by fear and uncertainty
By the instinct for survival
Stumbling somewhere in the middle
Upon the beast behind the barred door
Its bloody fangs want to devour all human flesh
Forced to fight and die or else to flee
In madness and insanity
Without even a spot of light to illuminate the way
But once dimly discovering the way
Finding the distant light
Slowly growing in brightness
Around every corner
Finally leaving its internal corridors
Forsaking whatever is left behind
Forsaking illusion and suffering
Forsaking hope and promises
Forsaking love and friendship
Forsaking understanding
Forsaking knowledge
Forsaking existence
Forsaking all
Even self

Missing Minutes
Auto-dotes & Auto-Graphs
& Aphoristic Alter-notes

Hugh M. Lewis

1992

AUTODOTES
Self-Cures and Home Remedies in a World of
Words
(1991)

THE WORLD

The world has become, as far as we are concerned, an increasingly and almost exclusively human world. Humankind emerged from a world dominated by nature, and human civilization became predominant in place of nature. As human civilization has developed, nature has been steadily reduced to a sterile remnant of what it once had been. Whereas previously human civilization was always surrounded by and encapsulated by the wilderness, it is now human civilization that surrounds and encapsulates nature. Nature survives only in the interstitial cracks of human civilization.

Because the world is predominantly human, it must now be measured in terms of its human dimensionalities rather than in terms of its natural vistas. It is an artificial world of human-made asymmetries, straight lines, sharp angles, and continuous curves rather than the natural bilateral symmetry, jagged edges and chaotic twists and turns of natural design. Because of its humanness, it is a world to be measured in terms of its social differences and human living spaces, and in the many ways in which humankind has adapted the earth's natural environments to its own needs and how it has adapted itself to the resulting world.

It is futile to try to turn back the pages of history to a pristine period before the predominance of human civilization in the world. Our natural reaction to the civilized abominations of our own doing is to seek a primordial world—a perfect, unsullied paradise—that is both before and beyond the eruptions and corruptions of human time. But any such attempt to return deliberately to a world before time and outside of the confluence of human history is, at best, bound to end in pathological regression, destructive isolation and social sterility, and, at worse, in unnecessary destruction and disaster for the human world as a whole.

The most we can hope for now is to try to brake the forward momentum of modernizing historical change long enough to cause a general shift in its overall direction in a way that will prove less costly and devastating for the natural world. Many human actions and activities that were unconsidered and done with complete abandon just a few decades ago are now becoming increasingly taboo and even immoral from a human and natural ecological point of view.

There has been a steadily rising human awareness, almost a worldwide collective conscientiousness, about the importance of fundamental environmental issues. This increasing awareness of the state of the world is the necessary corollary of our own human sense of history. We can no longer freely trespass upon the natural world with the impunity and immunity of its indirect consequences and unexpected reverberations that our forbearers of civilization once had. We are becoming increasingly subject to the consequences of our own machination in a fragile, delicately interdependent earth.

The human world is one characterized by its lack of balance, its substitute artificiality, its social and natural asymmetry, its historical linearity and lack of evolutionary ecology.

The natural world is composed of a delicate and intricate web of living and evolving interdependencies. It is an elaborate system of checks and balances and of mutual systemic controls that evolved over many millennia—gradually and toward increasing stability.

Natural selection worked against the long-term survival of evolutionarily extreme forms and designs that tended to threaten or upset the balances and controls of life on earth.

Exceptions to the rule were either modified or eliminated. Evolution has long had an inexorable kind of selective, systemic rationality—a natural logic of its own that promoted the survival of the whole and the many over the interests of the part and the few. As humankind wrests control from the natural world, it would serve as well to heed the earth's ages old, worldly wisdom.

We have developed a civilization that is increasingly beyond our control in a world that is increasingly under our control. In this new world system, it is the few and the exceptional whose interests are parasitically promoted over the needs and interests of the many and the whole. The choices have long been recognized and available to us, and yet we have consistently failed to meet the challenge that our own human survival and human nature has posed for the world.

The man-made logic of our own world system of civilization is proving to be fundamentally pathological because, in its own pursuit of development, it systematically destroys the basis of its own growth and survival in the natural world.

We live in a human world of mass production and mass consumption, mass media and mass ideology, mass bureaucracy and mass organization, mass money and mass psychology, mass education and mass mobilization, mass needs and mass solutions.

Our mass oriented world is fundamentally impersonal and alienating of individual subjectivity, systematically substituting artificial symbols for natural needs, satisfactions and inclinations.

The individual is confronted existentially with the success imperative of 'participate or perish' in the mass orientation of the world. Few if any alternatives remain viable to the individual rather than this imperative for participation, that are not becoming increasingly co-opted and restricted by the mass oriented world system.

Almighty money, and its pursuit, is becoming the secular symbol of this mass oriented system in place of the emblem of God, which has been declared dead by nineteenth-century existentialists. Money buys the passport of entry into the system. It is the ticket for citizenship and participation within the world system. It is a paradox that though everyone is engaged equally in the pursuit of money within that system, the poor only become perennially poorer and the rich grow chronically richer.

Auto-Anthropology

The only things that their hard earned money can buy for the poor
people are the very things that the rich profit from, while the entire
energy and lifetime of the many poor people is virtually consumed in the
processes of production of those very things that they spend their money
on and that earn a profit for the wealthy, who in turn produce virtually
nothing in the world or for the world except words, wastage and mass
human need and desire.

The pathos and the fundamental irrationality of our world system are not
too difficult to discover. In spite of the tragic prospects of a world
population bomb, international family planning and birth control
policies remain poorly underdeveloped and, even in many cases,
blatantly disregarded or even resisted in practice.

Though pollution grows at a daily rate in every aspect of the earth's
environment, the basic processes producing this pollution remain
unrestricted and even accelerated in their growth and developmental
promotion. The earth's finite base of nonrenewable resources are being
quickly consumed, and for the most part, un-recycled, while viable and
more healthy alternatives have long been known to exist, and the
technologies to develop and exploit these alternative resources long
available.

Those few resources that are considered renewable, the water table and
the forest stands, the earth itself, are being consumed faster than they can
be replenished. Perhaps the earth's most valuable and precious resource
of all, life, is being rapidly obliterated in its biological, evolutionary
potential and in its ecological coordination. All this in the pursuit of
money and the corrupt kind of power that only money can buy.

These trends in the development of the world system are increasingly
out of control, and ultimately only a very small minority of humankind
are actually benefiting from these net developments. The ultimate
madness of the mass oriented system is that even those who most benefit
from its development will also be the very ones who have the most to
lose from its inexorable breakdown. The madness of such a world
system is its mutually assured destruction—a destruction of the whole
world in which no one, no matter how wealthy, can escape.

It is something of a unhappy coincidence that the impending world crisis lends itself readily to millennial and apocalyptic prophecies. It is almost as if such prophetic visions were ideologically self-fulfilling or were based upon some fundamental, predictive understanding of human nature and human history. It is unfortunate because it is liable to be these very analogies that will blind us to the realities and prevent us from seeking reasonable solutions to our world problems.

But there is more than a single grain of truth to these prophetic histories in that it is the very values that they preach—frugality, humility, spiritual purity, faith and devotion, as well as brotherhood, love and charity—that are likely to be the most missing, needed virtues, and least common vices, in our global climax.

Though Protestant and puritanical, such values are not necessarily laconic and militaristic. People preoccupied with the production of weapons, with the power of weapons, with the arts, sciences and strategies of war, have little time left over for the development of the arts and science of life and living. It does not need to be reiterated that the production of weapons in the world has contributed nothing of net and lasting value to the welfare of the world, but has only led to unnecessary destruction and waste.

To combine a Protestant and puritanical spirit with a pacifistic political orientation is a much-needed formula for salvation in an increasingly human world. We have only to witness the modern development of a democratized Japan to see how well such a formula may work.

It is imperative that we begin teaching our children how to value life and living, and how to make the most of peace, rather than making of peace merely the preparation for yet another bloody, useless war. If we do not begin soon, not only can we blame ourselves, but our children will grow up to blame us as well.

We must recognize and acknowledge the intrinsic merit of the cultivation of any and all forms of artistic production, as well as the intrinsic value of improvement of human development, no matter how subjectively and qualitatively defined, and no matter how poorly measured by quantitative indices.

It is a paradox that the vast amounts of human time, energy and money wasted upon the production and improvement of weapons contributes virtually nothing to the improvement of the general quality of life of humankind, while next to nothing is left over for the cultivation of human arts that take nothing from life and living that it does not give back in a qualitatively improved form.

It is only the military minded and money mongering who fail to see anything valuable in human arts that cannot be counted and which cannot be used as a means of controlling, exploiting and destroying others. It only speaks of the warped values of a modern humanity that sees art as a waste of time and weapons, not only as a means for making money and protecting property, but also as a legitimate means of self expression.

Because it is becoming an increasingly human world, its dimensionalities must be increasingly measured in terms of the general human condition and of the consequences of human stress and response, initiative and reaction within the world.

Old formulas of human nature and of a kind of social Darwinism must be given up in favor of newer formulas that do not equate the ethno-cultural traditions and patterns of human history with the dynamics of human evolution, and that do not confuse the causes of cultural change with the consequences of biological predisposition and genetic heritage, which in general only results in war and conflict arising from competition.

It will do us little good to see the modern developments of the world as a by-product of human evolution, and it may well be the case that these kinds of ideologies even promote and legitimate the kind of status quo and may prevent the positive kinds of historical changes that may help to resolve our modern world crisis.

We can ill afford to continue promoting ideologies that hold that human historical developments in the world are basically predetermined by human biological and evolutionary destiny. If anything, historical civilization had led to the destruction of human nature and its own evolutionary platform.

If we destroy nature, then we are destroying ourselves, because we are an intrinsic part of nature.

The frustration of human creativity must eventuate in human destructiveness. The frustration of human love results in human hate. The frightening aspect of modern machineries of destruction and death are not that they depend upon human aggressiveness and hate for their functioning, but they are largely impersonal and indifferent in their design and operation.

The tyranny of modern evil is not the same kind of rational tyranny that depended upon the promotion of basic human aggression and hate for its function, but it is a tyranny of the fundamentally alienated and anomic.

Its irrationality is its very rationality. A person can be a creative lover of humankind and yet still feel compelled by reason to push a button that leads to the distant destruction of a faceless human enemy.

The role of aggression and hate remain mostly only symbolic and ideological in the cultivation of popular support for modern machineries of death—it is at best a displaced aggression and distant hatred, indirect in destructiveness. Modern tyranny is cold and calculating, corrupt and controlling, and yet it remains mostly invisible in the daily lives of people.

We are faced with a fundamental existential alternative for the future. If creating order from chaos and pattern from randomness is what is constitutive of life, and making the ordered chaotic and random is what is constitutive of death and destruction, then creativity is anti-entropic and life giving while destructiveness is chaos producing and death making.

It follows that a creative world is one in which more is produced from less, and something comes from nothing. A destructive world is precisely the opposite, where less is produced from more, and nothing comes from something.

We have a mass existential and evolutionary choice, to become more creative in our world, or to remain destructive of it.

Though we must act in the world, we can never know all of the consequences of our actions. Nothing that humans do is ever completely condemnable or completely condonable. There is no human motive that is pure and unmixed. There is no person without two sides, and no system without contradiction and double standards.

There is neither all good nor all bad in the world, but that people make it seem so. Because we must act even though we cannot ultimately know either the causes or consequences of our actions, we must not be too quick to presume to know or judge the actions of others in the world. It is in the recognition of the inherent possibility of our own evil in the world that we come to understand, and to ultimately forgive the evil of others.

Poor motives are frequently thinly disguised, and it requires little insight of wisdom to see through the veil to the human substance beneath. Under the skin beneath the veil of illusion there is always a veritable mine of human potentiality and virtue.

Imaginary visions of human possibility always hide in the shadows cast by the light of day.

Between the black and the white is an infinite field of gray composed of a rainbow of colors.

Those who are blind to their own illusions are susceptible to the illusions of others. Those who are convinced of their own importance are subject to the suggestion of superiority and power of others in the world. In this way we can say that in a world so composed of illusion, the blind lead the blind, and the one-eyed person would surely be king.

When people learn to see themselves for what they really are, they then inevitably become ashamed of their own nakedness. It is always sobering to laugh at the irony of the common nudity of the human condition. Beneath all our clothes and all our illusions, we are all the primitive children of nature.

The nearly overwhelming sense of security and solidarity of a mass oriented society is that everyone seems to be doing the same things no matter how foolish it may really be.

This is an utterly false and dangerous illusion that justifies the method of social order by the blind madness of the crowd. Principles of social organization can be simply reduced to the problem of crowd control.

It is obvious where such principles come from—the social psychology of crowds and theory of behavior modification. The masses of people across the world are rendered increasingly susceptible to the inducements and incentives of the world system, at the same time being rendered increasingly predictable and controllable as well.

Human civilization emerged from the darkness of the natural order of things. It gradually dawned with the light of a new age. Civilization came to superimpose a human made order on top of the natural scheme of things.

Analogies to these metaphors of darkness and light are the corresponding metaphors of night and day, the sun and the moon, sleep and wakeful activity, birth and death, the blindness of vice and the virtue of vision, the darkness of ignorance and the light of understanding.

Frightening unknown creatures of the imagination stalk the nighttime darkness by the light of the glowing moon, while it is the human being toiling, sweating beneath the bright sunlight who commands the day.

Upon these basic metaphors and their somewhat fortuitous associations we have built a world civilization. What difference might it have made if our mythos began instead as "in the beginning was the circle of fire."

MY WRITING

Writing is the crowbar of the mind, prying open the problems of the world, letting in the light of knowledge and letting out the hidden elements of understanding.

I use my words more like a crowbar in the world than a sword or a foil. My writing lacks the skilled refinement and the touch of finesse that is the mark of a good writer. I must depend upon the brute strength and basis vocabulary to move, bit-by-bit, inch-by-inch, the mountains of the world.

Because words do not usually flow easily from my mind, my writing is labored, typically difficult, strained and consuming of much time and energy. I must count the rewards for my writing not in terms of money earned, but only in terms of the number of mounds of meaning that have been moved.

I would trade off my whole compendium of poetry for a single simple poem that's profound enough to be published and read in the world. I must content myself with quantity rather than quality.

Better a single word to summarize a thousand pages than a thousand pages to summarize a single word.

Excessive verbosity, verbiage, loquaciousness and 'logorrhea' are the mark of mediocrity in writing—the sign of uncertainty and the lack of credibility, that the writer does not really know what she/he is talking about, and it is talking more around the point than to the point.

Written words must be more like deeds than mere words. They must act upon the imagination of the reader rather than just communicate intentions or meanings. Words must get things done with the least amount of excessive effort. Only in this way can an author be taken seriously enough to be read and reread with any interest and earnest.

Words written for mere self-expression go out but do not ever come back to close the hermeneutic circle. Such words may communicate mostly one way, but seldom do much more than this in the world.

Written words must move mountains, not make mountains out of molehills.

The world is so replete and inundated with written words and printed trivia that few people can afford to take the extra time required to sort through the junk to find the jewels of literature.

People can hardly be blamed from editing from their existence so many mixed up messages that assault their minds and insult their intellects. Our world suffers as much from the word pollution of the collective mind as it does from any other kind of ecological contamination.

It is wise to wonder whether the vast majority of printed or published material is worth the paper it is printed upon, especially when the few remaining trees of the world's forests are becoming so precious.

There is little intrinsic about my own growing mound of printed-paper that represents the compendium of my writing that should set it apart from this mountain of mental verbiage.

Because of this, it is becoming increasingly difficult to justify my writing purely in its own terms, especially when its investment grows more onerous and less rewarding with each additional page, and with each passing year.

Auto-Anthropology

Making Paper Mountains may only be my biographical and historical compulsion. But even so, it remains a very human preoccupation, and what but history and biography itself would pass judgment upon what will soon pass away and what might long remain.

My small mound grows daily because too soon in my tedium and my medium I can find nothing better to do with my time.

My poetry is closely like my painting, so close as to lead me to believe they have a common connection in my creative and active imagination, and fulfill a common normative need in the expression and external production of my being human in the world.

The purpose of both poetry and painting is not to persuade the human mind, but to induce the human imagination to experience new states of being and new possibilities of becoming in the world.

Poems and paintings enrich our experience of the world much more they cost to produce. Poetry and painting is not merely intellectually interesting, but imaginatively intriguing and even spiritually stimulating in life. The power of the poet and painter is to convey the same experience and sense of fascination and wonder of the world to the reader or viewer.

If I can with my words just open one other mind, jarring it loose from its prejudices and preconceptions to let in the light of the wider world view, like a crowbar that pries loose a bent and rusty nail, then my paper mountain will have been worth the efforts in its writing.

The air is free and printed words are relatively cheap—perhaps this is way so little money is to be made in writing.

Better one word of truth than a thousand words of deceit.

The true meaning of a text can never be read directly from the words, but must be found somewhere between the lines, between the pages, between the covers, and between the shelves.

To live entirely in a world of words is to live in a stuffy, interior world of illusion without a window to open to let in fresh air and sunlight and without a door through which to pass onto the wider pathways of the world.

One must learn to read with one eye upon the word, and one eye upon the world, and with one's head in the clouds but one's feet upon the ground.

Better to be completely illiterate than to lead a life of boredom stringing together trite clichés. Words can imprison the mind as much as they can liberate it.

There are no words that do not reveal as much as they conceal, which do not tell lies as they speak truth. Words are always half true and half-false. They are always the vessels of ignorance and prejudice as much as they are the vehicles if wisdom and enlightenment. This is their myth, paradox and their power.

I started writing because I felt I had something important to say when nobody else was listening to me. It was my method for dealing with the madness of my loneliness in the world and became my madness for methodically treating that loneliness. Now, thirteen years and twenty odd manuscripts later, I'm still writing and people are still not paying much attention to me. I guess its time to try to publish something.

What I would give for the volume of poems that I have dreamed of only to awaken and arise to suffer a loss of words, or that I have put away for a later date only to become forgotten and irretrievably lost. One must learn to 'grasp the moment' of inspiration, or else relinquish the preoccupation of plying poems composed on the fly.

If talking it all out is therapy for the soul, writing it all out is therapeutic for the mind—relieving it of the mental clutter of confused conceptions, contradictory notions, and nonsensical meanings.

Writing clarifies and sharpens the intellect, exercising the brain's analytical and imaginative powers, jogging the memory and one's power of reason.

It is little wonder that writing can often be frustrating and difficult experience.

Writing mediates the gap between the word and the deed. Writing may either prove to be a precursor to action or a substitute for it and an excuse for inaction.

One person's fact may be another's fiction, and there is nothing in writing it that doesn't make it seem so.

If I had a quarter for every page I've written, I would have enough to at least put a down upon a small house. As it is I must content myself with feeling at home with my typewriter. It is better if one's words dwell in the world than to have one's world dwell in words. Better to live in the words of the world than in the worlds of words.

I prescribe heavy doses of writing for anyone who feels the least bit foolish, ill at ease, or confused with the world. There is no quicker or more complete remedy for the inanities of the world that the illusions of words

Writing has always been for me something of a transformational experience. I emerge from the wilderness of a new manuscript somewhat altered in character than how I entered the forest. It is something like a journey that which there is never any returning. It is never a journey without some cost or trade off in terms of one's time, energy, flexibility, and alternative opportunity in the world, and too much such transformation inevitably leads to burn out of one's resourcefulness and involvement. I get writer's block on a regular basis with little else to do except wait for the percolation of new ideas and words.

Words are the trees of the forest of the world, and books are like maps, that chart the pathways in small sections of the wilderness. The wilderness of the world is vast and its trees are too many—writers are but helpless wanderers of the woods, marking out different trails between its many regions.

It is fitting that my stormy creativity should at last come to rest upon the rock of writing. More than in any other form of creative expression, writing provides an anchor to the restless world.

My first manuscript was written on the top of a wooden footlocker in an open squad bay. It was a very difficult and frustrating process at first, but soon became an obsession that consumed all my extra energies and spare time.

Auto-Anthropology

No one during that year bothered to ask me what I was writing about. It must have seemed to the lifers in the open squad bay such an incredible absurdity that they could not but doubt its value. For me it was a separate reality, an escape from the intolerable stresses and strains of the mindless situation of a never-ending moment.

Now I can complete a manuscript in several weeks and though it consumes the main part of my time and energy, I have extra to spend on other things. Writing does not come now as hard as it used to be. But few still bother to ask me what I'm writing about, and I think most must still not believe in it. It remains a separate reality from which I can regularly escape from the vicissitudes and problems of everyday life.

Writing creates a world in which I have supreme mastery. The author always has the final word, and it is this absolute authority that is both the corruption and the power of writing.

Ours has long been an age of literacy. We are creatures of the written and printed word. Our signatures carry the legal authority of our whole life, and are the basis for all legal transactions, the possession of property and public authority and identity in the world. Whatever the many implications of literacy for the transformation of the human mind and world, we cannot now easily escape the consequences of these historical transformations.

As long as humans remain human, there will always be interesting books to be written and read.

Books and words have been the building blocks of human civilization and the flagstones of the way of human history. Without them we would have neither history, civilization not humanity in the same sense that we know them.

My will to write, and my many unpublished manuscripts and collections of poetry, have always symbolically represented a kind of intellectual and spiritual declaration of independence in the world.

My writing has been a way of silently but positively asserting my will and my own way in the world—speaking our silently without fear or recrimination or retribution or persecution for my words and thoughts.

If we value the freedom of speech as the guarantee of the freedom of thought, then we must value equally the freedom of the press as the only guarantee of the freedom of speech and thought.

Politicians will always depend upon the publication and dissemination of propaganda by which to persuade and warp the will of the people to the politician's own ends and against the people's own best interests.

People may burn books but their fires can never be destroy the truths which the words represent, nor take away the freedom of mind such books symbolize and which led to their creation in the first place.

Though there are copyright laws and patents pending, no human being or corporate group has a monopoly or a corner on the market of the

Auto-Anthropology

human mind or of collective knowledge that is the common stock of the construct of panhuman civilization.

The idea that ideas and thought can be a privilege of private ownership the same way that material possessions are is inherently antithetical and destructive to the very freedom of mind upon which the creation of new ideas depends. Such practices can only be regarded as fascist and anti-intellectual in the final analysis.

The virtue of the human mind is that it is ultimately and necessarily free from social control, and the written word is both the primary instrument and expression of that freedom.

I had a kind of writer's block for a few years. I felt as though I couldn't write well what I wanted to say, and whenever I actually started to write, I felt as if I had nothing at all to say. Neither the thoughts nor the words to express them by were available when I needed them, though I had off moments of literary inspiration.

This was sometimes a maddening, frustrating, stultifying and ultimately deadening experience, but I continued to force myself to write as much as I could stand, in spite of many interruptions, distractions and existential interims in my life, and though finishing a piece frequently proved even more difficult than starting them, and many things were left unfinished, I eventually broke free of this bloke and gradually loosened up enough to feel at ease with my writing and only then did writing begin to be a genuinely enjoyable experience for me.

Looking back upon this period, I am not sure what the sources of this block really were. One important factor seemed to be a susceptibility to a kind of authoritative criticism and influence in my writing as well as in many other areas of my life, by people I then regarded to be my "significant others," but who proved in the long run to be my 'fair weather friends' and acquaintances of circumstance and convenience.

I could call them, in hindsight, more like Minotaurs of the academic labyrinth than real intellectual mentors. Needless to say, these people are no longer a part of my life, nor are the kinds of intellectual-emotional-social interdependencies that our relationships represented.

Breaking free of my writer's block had something to do with breaking free of the kinds of social bonds in the world kept my sense of self identity in the world as a writer bound to other people's petty prejudices and preconceptions. It is unfortunate that in Academic arenas of authorship, such dependencies seem to be the norm rather than the exceptions to the rule. My best writing has never been academic.

My writing over the years has only improved by small increments and has moved only gradually in some directions while in others it has changed only slightly if at all. I sometimes read some of my earliest stuff and am struck by its freshness, directness, its unsophisticated strength and vitality of style.

I must admit that a great deal of my writing has been roughshod and only first draft, and often not written with the view of the readership in mind. My writing has represented for me more of a personal, psychological odyssey through my life than any kind of social trip in the world.

Birds of a feather flock together...different strokes for different folks...the pen is mightier than the sword...between the cup and the lip there is many a slip...etc. etc.

Auto-Anthropology

Books are just like tools. Everybody wants to borrow them but no one likes returning them. I have lost many books and a few tools this way.

Any longer, my life lesson has been to simply "donate" a book rather than to "loan" it with the expectation of getting it back within a reasonable time without asking repeatedly. Same with fools.

It is necessary that a writer be well read. A person who always writes but rarely reads is one who remains unable to read her/his writing in the way that others will read it. It is like a person who believes she/he is experiencing the world by sitting in front of the television set. I've learned my lessons the hard way. Reading remains the only counter-balance a writer has to keep from going too far. There are so few good writers in the world because there are so few good readers.

ANTHROPOLOGY

Anthropology is by definition the holistic study of humankind. The drawing of disciplinary and sub-disciplinary boundaries in its specializations and territorial demarcations of professional interest is antithetical to the general and synthetic basis of the whole field.

There is something wrong with such a field when its professional members no longer identify themselves primarily as anthropologists with the implication of disciplinary holism and breadth of interest, involvement and intellectual understanding, and instead become identified as being primarily one sort of specialized person or another. This has been neither a necessary nor a desirable state of affairs, though wholly understandable from the standpoint of its structural relationship with its domain host society.

Of course, specialization is the basis of bona-fide expertise, but it is not the exclusive source of authority or credibility in knowledge.

Professional anthropologists would do well to remember their lessons in introductory anthropology.

I have been pursuing the study of professional anthropology for almost ten years now and honestly feel little further ahead that when I began, even though my understanding of the world has increased enormously. I have never been in any anthropology class in which any other student has ever out performed me or shown more or better knowledge of the field than myself, and yet I have over the years consistently seen other, younger students getting ahead with their careers while I seem to be running in place.

Many people ask me why I keep investing my time, energy and money in the pursuit of a profession that has given so little compensation in return.

Auto-Anthropology

With a wife and a child to worry about, I can no longer give them any honest excuses. In this matter I can only ultimately blame myself, though I do not thereby condone the values of American society, the politics of Academia or the professional prerogatives of the anthropological elite who are for the most part conservative, classicist and ego-centric in orientation. If there is great hypocrisy with the world, then it begins with the basic lack of honesty with the self. Honesty begets humility and makes us immune to the infliction of hypocrisy.

My minor contributions to the field and my devotion, authenticity and sincerity of commitment to the pursuit of anthropological understanding in the world no longer requires the legitimization of the professional in group or the justification of the power elite. I would continue to pursue my own anthropological interests, via my writing, as both a scientist and a humanist, whether anyone else calls me an anthropologist or not.

I figure I will be deemed capable of teaching my first Anthropology course by the age of my retirement.

The most pressing problem in the world today are primarily human problems, and the most intellectually challenging puzzles and paradoxes that confront human understanding today are basically and irreducibly problems of human reality. On this anthropological ground, I stake my claim as an anthropologist.

After making A's in four field-methods courses, several general theory classes, and two or three history of anthropology seminars, not to mention the host of other, interrelated topics, I seem to still not have gotten it all right. I'm beginning to wonder whether I ever will, or even if there really is a right way of going about being an anthropologist.

The most important thing I have learned from my anthropological studies has been to recognize amongst all the differences of humankind the same basic common ground and sense of identity and dignity of each human being.

Professionals within the field hardly impress me at all anymore, with their long list of publications, their self-centered sense of smugness and self-importance, and their academic party lines and their sea stories.

It is the common person, in whichever cultural corner of the world, with their basic dilemmas and interests and involvements that I find most interesting. These things are not found in a book or in photography—they are to be found only in other people. How much basic equality can an anthropologist establish with other people of the world if they do not confront or resolve those structural asymmetries in their own lives?

If you want to get rich fast, go to law school and become a lawyer. The world can always use another lawyer. But if you want to remain poor, over qualified, and discriminated, then become an anthropologist. Though anthropologists have always desperately needed the world, the world has seldom the need for an anthropologist.

I've met many professional anthropologists who think they are perfect; at least in private, and who would like to believe they are God's gift to humankind. They can become quite frustrated when they come to realize that hardly anyone around is paying much attention to them, and that they are probably are not, after all, God's chosen on earth.

Auto-Anthropology

I used to be a true believer—a committed anthropologist—until I passed through its back door one too many times. The view from the rear does not look as pure and sacred as the perspective from the front. The biggest career disappointment of a professional anthropologist is not that they have failed to solve any of the world's problems, but that the world has failed to solve any of their problems.

The nemesis of Anthropology will be weighed not in terms of its failure to provide any important answers or solutions to the problem of human reality, but in its failure to ask nontrivial and interesting questions about that reality.

As to the anthropological question of whether there are really any significant barriers of difference separating one person from another, or cultures, or nations, or different periods of time, I must say that there are few if any that are not made by humankind itself.

The most important lesson to be learned from social anthropology is that rules were always made to be broken. No human-made rule would be worthy of being obeyed if it could not be honored in its breach, or defined by a growing list of exceptions. But the paradox of anthropological knowledge does not end here—this is only where it begins.

Yuppie anthropology has become the pursuit of anthropology for other ends. While it may have the virtue of lacking the commitment of 'authentic' anthropology as an end in itself, it suffers the shortcoming of prostituting the study of anthropology to whatever circumstance or convenience that comes along. What used to be a well-regarded neutrality of anthropological science is quickly becoming a vested interest of a-scientific territoriality.

Between biology and technology little remains leftover for plain humanity. Between the brain and the computer, there is little room for the mind and its culture. For the true scientist bent upon closing the gap between nature's secrets and technology's power, the interests and problems of the human being cannot but be seen as an obstacle interfering with progress.

The interests of the human science of anthropology will not be well served if all of human nature and culture is reduced to a severe logic of genetic determination, or if the mind and its social history are merely mimicked by computers and systems of structural explanations. While biology and technology may be nothing but a matter of machines and genes, human anthropology has always been something more.

Anthropological science is not based upon literary criticism (or on comparative literature.)

Show me an anthropologist who has all the answers and I will show you a veritable menace to the profession. Anthropological administration adds nothing to the stock of anthropological knowledge but takes away a great deal of human freedom. The net consequence of anthropological administration is academic mediocrity.

Auto-Anthropology

The mind of anthropology and the anthropological mentality are not the same—the former is the collective genius and understanding of the common problems and paradoxes of human reality, while the latter represents the simple solutions of a rabid intellectual extremist who foams at the mouth at the thought of her/his own ego in the world.

The mind of anthropology is to be found in the field among the peoples of the world, while the anthropological mentality can be found dwelling securely in the departmental forums among all the professionals, hypocrites and pseudo-intellectuals, vying to get some media time and a few scant research funds.

Professors of anthropology no longer bother with me because I no longer supplicate their egos. Students no longer talk to me because they are too preoccupied with supplicating their professors' egos. Though I remain marginally attached to anthropology, I am no longer strictly identified either as a 'student' or as a professional.

I once overheard an indiscrete conversation between my main advisor and one of his other students. They were talking about myself in the third person within my earshot. For all my knowledge gains, my advisor said, it somehow falls out the backside. I replied: "Only until it's needed."

I don't know when the transition actually happened. It was when I lost faith and trust in the authority of all too human anthropologists and in what too frequently passes for 'friendship' between students. It has struck me as a double paradox to become a stranger among professional strangers who are supposed to have as their primary objective getting to know other people in the world.

I can no longer identify myself as one particular kind of anthropologist or another, nor even as strictly an anthropologist. The general domain of anthropology has itself become too confining for my breadth of intellectual interests. The mind is inherently interdisciplinary and humankind is inherently cross-cultural. I know call myself simply an independent "Alternative Anthropologist."

It is not too long before one outgrows even the generality of anthropology, feeling some of the frustrations of its intrinsic and extrinsic limitations. One eventually begins to wonder whether there is not possible a more general, embracing and realistic point of view to be adopted beyond the merely anthropological. The one explores the sociological, the psychological, the educational, the theoretical and the methodological.

The principal anthropological fallacy seems to me to be the paradox of inferring a probable presence from a definite absence. Statistics seems to come to the rescue in this problem, but its concreteness of numerical quantification always conceals the initial and final arbitrariness of its qualitative and normative evaluation. All areas of anthropology founder upon the problem of bridging this critical difference between what is and what isn't but may possibly be. Whole anthropological mansions are built and entire intellectual and anthropological empires are carved out from the world upon the basis of what amounts to the 'astonishment' of the anthropological imagination which must always fill in the gulf between the fact and its fiction, the datum and its idea, empirical reality and rational truth.

Whatever the relative distance between the known and the unknown, it cannot be but spanned by at least one leap of faith. Between the said and the done there is always a virtual infinitude of anthropological possibility and plausibility. If anthropologists took no risks, they would achieve no gains.

297

Auto-Anthropology

The more I learn about anthropology the less I know about the human world. The net outcome of an anthropological education can only be a tremendous appreciation for the variety and versatility of humankind, and a correspondingly tremendous intellectual humility towards the always encompassed but never encompassing horizons of one's own ignorance and prejudices.

In this regard it is striking how anecdotal so much of the evidence in anthropological discourse really is, and how cliché and trite many of its paradigmatic exemplars. Humankind would do well to be spared the intellectual hubris and arrogance of the anthropological know-it-all.

I am more and more astonished by the analogous parallels between the culture of anthropology and the anthropology of culture. One must have lived and worked as an anthropologist for at least a year in some departmental setting to come to fully understand and appreciate how like other human beings anthropologists really are, and how tribal-like and petty such settings can become in terms of their factionalisms over limited resources, their status hierarchies and cliques, their gossip networks and background machinations, and their rituals and myths.

The student of anthropology becomes twice born as an adult child in a strange and alienating cultural world—at least once in the field and once again in the department. This is so often so much the case that it is to be legitimately asked if the "escape to the field" that is so much the source of anthropological romance, authenticity and reality, does not also become sometimes an "escape from the escape." Becoming a life-long professional stranger in different world is possibly an adaptive response to the failure to become very familiar with one's own world. Anthropology has always been an acceptable and alternative avenue for the strange and unfamiliar.

If this is sometimes so, then it may also be legitimately asked whether the emphatic desire of some anthropologist's to make the strange familiar and to bring the whole of anthropological enterprise into the more familiar regions of science in our own society, do not really represent the unconscious wish to become more normal and familiar with the world. As such it is possibly a wish to return to the repressed by the repressed.

The history of anthropology has always been constituted by an academic question and answer dialectic between the thesis of collectivizing tendencies of science to see the human world organized upon a common set of universal laws and the antithetical and contraposed relativizing tendencies to emphasis the many differences between people and to play down all the similarities. It has been the basis of this rational dialectic that has led anthropology to develop as a coherent and relevant field of human understanding.

It has long been unfortunate that so many professional commitments and involvements for the advancement of mutually egoistic and egotistic interests has tended to popularize the profession to one extreme position or the other, instead of cultivating the kind of attitude and ability to step outside of the entire dialectic itself while keeping one foot each on both sides of the dividing line.

It is the fact of the dialectic itself, and not the involvement in either of its extremes that makes anthropology interesting and authentic in the world and that links it critically to other general intellectual paradigms like philosophy, science, art and religion.

The biggest threat to the anthropologist's sense of professional objectivity is her/his own most personal sense of human subjectivity. Maintaining the veil of anthropological authority in the world depends upon the illusion of such objectiveness achieved by implicitly denying and explicitly controlling the subjectivity of those people whom the anthropologist studies and upon whom the anthropologist is supposed to be an expert authority.

Auto-Anthropology

Cultivating such an illusion and maintaining the anthropological veil is much simpler if the only forms of evidence are material artifacts and biological traits and if the people represented are not allowed to speak for themselves and talk back to the anthropologist.

It sometimes seems to me a much wiser course to simply make a science of subjectivity instead of trying to transform subjectivity into an objective science. For so many people who seek simple solutions and pat answers to the complexities inherent to understanding human reality, this would render anthropology seemingly too soft, to loose and too much like an odd humanity rather than a hardened science. Such a threat of subjectivity is a threat to their sense of authority in the world and a threat to the kind of physical science upon which such a sense of authority is based.

I personally have never once doubted the profound relevance that the study of anthropology constitutes for the world, though I may have always misunderstood the relevance. The question of its possible irrelevance in the world has never once vexed me.

It is paradoxical that so many professional anthropologists who seem bent upon demonstrating that anthropology is in fact a hard and respectable science, so often strike me as unconsciously doubting the intrinsic relevance of anthropology and thus in their chronic insecurity are searching for some pat formula, some model, some structure, some law of discovery, that renders the anthropological profession as predictable, paradigmatic, and puzzle-solving as what the profession of physics has come to epitomize in the world.

They are engaged upon a never-ending quest for an anthropological El Dorado or QED, some elemental touchstone that will demonstrate unequivocally to themselves and to the rest of the world their authority as a science and thus their profitability from that science. They seek some solution to the perennial and common human problem of selling themselves and their profession to the world in a way that the world wants and is willing to pay for. It is a grand paradox that those who would seek to render anthropology most certain, secure and scientific in the world are those who may hold the belief in its ultimate irrelevance closest to their hearts.

Beware the rise of an anthropological aristocracy. These are the few who seek to turn their profession into a guild or a union and to prescribe for everyone the rules of conformity and the price of admission. They are elitist, hypocritical, pseudo-intellectual status mongers who would do virtually anything to get ahead and who remain hung up on the horns of their own authority complex. None of us can but help spill over into the authoritarianism and asymmetries of the field, or end up distorting practically anything and everything that comes back from the field as an authentic article of anthropological faith.

Otherness is a condition of not knowing ourselves well enough.

There is a way of seeing others—of looking squarely into their faces. It is as Vincent Van Gogh must have seen others—every line, every feature, the very character and soul. One does not come by this way of seeing easily. It takes strength to penetrate the veil, courage to face the darkness, especially when the face is in the mirror.

First impressions often prove to be the final impressions, but usually for reasons converse than might at first seem. Knowledge may be power. It may be power to create or destroy, to exploit or to make equal, to constrain or to liberate. The paradox of anthropology is that it offers both these sets of possibilities in the world. To promote anthropological wisdom in the world is to promote greater realism of worldview by which to temper our ideological precepts and prejudices. It promises a better understanding of our world such that it will become increasingly difficult to promulgate illusions that profit only the few at the expense of the many, while it may facilitate the advancement of more optimistic values that will increasingly benefit the many.

ACADEMIA

Academia is a paradise of mixed blessings. It has always demonstrated that nothing that is perfect can ever be had without some human cost. It is as much the neurotic's escape from human reality as it is the center of the intellectual pursuit of the 'really real.'

Academia is a place where people gang up on one another and where the loner is bound to become a loser. People form cliques and small parties, not merely for the pursuit of mutual intellectual interests, but for the pursuit of power, as well as for the sake of mutual protection.

There are always more than a few academic sharks on the prowl of university corridors preying upon hapless and helpless victims. It demonstrates how great and ideal humanity really is in Academia when everybody watches but nobody comes to the aid of the victim. Unfortunately, I've been both victim and eyewitness.

The values of academic competition and success can only lead to an ethos and pathos of success rooted in an obsessive fear of failure. In such an atmosphere, one person's success becomes interpreted as another's failure, and in order to better one's chances of success and to assuage one's anxieties over the prospects of failure, many people become very adept in making other people's losses their own gains.

People have sometimes told me this, but I have just never believed them or bought their wares.

In Academia, there are people in positions of authority whom one will never meet but who can and will make completely arbitrary decisions regarding your future success or failure within the system. A person can be shot down without much cause by someone completely anonymous for a reason that has little to do with that individual's life. People can invest many fruitless years of their life within the Academic System without ever being told that they never had the slightest hope of success from the start.

Class structures Academia as much as Academia reinforces the class structure of our society. Academic equality, opportunity and fairness become empty rhetoric when one takes into account the influence and implications of class in the ethos and pathos of Academia. The ideal of Academic social mobility becomes then an exception rather than the rule for the lower classes, and the benefits of receiving a higher education becomes the prerogative of the wealthy and well connected. Academics, if they are any good at being what they are, know what class they owe their allegiance to and who's who among themselves.

Academics have been quick to point their fingers in blame and easily criticize virtually anything under the sun that suits their convenience. A great deal of their liberalism and radicalism amounts to so much false consciousness, and in the last analysis becomes mere hypocrisy when one considers their cooption within the System and where they get their pay checks from. The espousing of values contradictory to the predominant society can only be allowed in forums where they make no difference in the larger world and where they can be shown to be false anyway.

If all professors genuinely practiced what they so often preached, few would survive very long in the Academic marketplace or in the world beyond. This academic dichotomization between the said and the done even becomes more contradictory when some of the most popular and liberal acting professors turn out to be some of the most fanatical upholders of the status quo of the Academic System. Almost a decade of successful academic work has only led to increasingly reinforce these beliefs, and almost no contrasting evidence has served to disconfirm any of these views.

If Aristocratic values, class snobbery and feudal relations survive in modern industrialized societies, then it is in Academia where they may be found most to flourish. In this regard, Academia represents one of the most conservative social institutions of human civilization—even military machines must of necessity reform and renovate their social organization in order to keep pace with the development of modern warfare. Democratic values have hardly entered into the way things get done within Academia, and academic authority, even if severely circumscribed and limited by even more autocratic administration, nevertheless remains virtually absolute and autocratic.

Academia remains a realm of social contrasts and ideological contradictions. It combines the best and the worst, the most open and the most close-minded, the most liberal and the most conservative. Great talent, virtue and humanity are to found alongside of mediocrity, hypocrisy, minion-ship and fanatical true believers. It is frequently the case that things, and people, in Academia prove to be the opposite of what they appear to be.

It is especially true that in Academia, its cover cannot judge a book.

The end of self-honesty and social humility is the beginning of hypocrisy and egotistical hubris. Academia is the proving ground of human character and spirit, where everything is only hypothetical.

Auto-Anthropology

Any school is only as good as the people who compose it. Great resources, great reputations, great test scores and great plans can mean next to nothing if the average student remains disinterested, uninvolved and distracted in the normal curriculum. A school may be poor, lacking in renown, with few good students or high class administrators, and yet still out perform the best and accomplish great things if its faculty are able to tap into and mobilize the fullest potential and spirit of the student body. Nothing is more defeating of human potential and deadening of the human mind than the run of the mill and 'business as usual' routine and attitude in the classroom and corridor.

It is proving to be a grand paradox of my life that though I've always hated and resented Academia, it remains practically the only arena of the world in which I have much hope of accomplishing anything significant. For me Academia has always been something of a love-hate relationship—rarely have I been able to experience its everyday ethos with neutrality and disregard for the things going on around me. Almost everyday I come home from school I've been bothered at something somebody did or said during the day. Only on rare occasions do good things occur, and it is usually for reasons which I could never have predicted or planned for. I long for the day when I can sit through the whole class period without utter disinterest in what is going on.

An 'A' professor is one who invites open discourse in the class, does not mind criticism or contradiction, and always takes the time to talk. 'B' professor expects all students to tow the same line, doesn't really like too many questions, and always seem to be in a hurry. 'C' professors have a small following of a group of students, never quite remember your name, never have the time to talk, and seem to be trying out for popularity contests in the corridors. 'D' professors are young, bright, upwardly mobile, highly motivated, and seem to be trying to win a beauty contest. 'F' professors are divorced, frustrated and treat all students like misbehaving children. In my many years as a student, I've come across only very few professors to whom I would give an 'A'.

In Academia, the nice person will finish last, and everyone else will come in second to last.

During the last decade, schools have been organizing themselves increasingly along the lines of big business. For these schools, the goal of academic administration is minimizing costs and maximizing profits, and the job of education itself becomes of secondary importance. It is unfortunate that in a business world organized around a military industrial complex, the business models that the schools have adopted for their own administration come straight from the models of military organization.

It is unfortunate that because Academics have usually not been in the military themselves, and usually despise the military, that they are blind to the parallels of some of their own practices. In this regard I found the student rating scale and evaluations and the file kept on each student by the department in one university to be very similar to the same kind of evaluations officers of the Marine Corps regularly made of their men of their command.

After about four years of such evaluations, from at least half a dozen different officers, I came to conclude that the decisive factor of such evaluations was not my own behavior, which remained fairly consistent, but depended almost entirely upon the subjective opinions of the evaluating officer.

Auto-Anthropology

Evaluations turned on whether that officer liked you or not, which in turn often depended upon how many affinities you shared with that officer and how much you kissed up to them. Now the same kind of thing has been happening in universities, with the decisive criteria of a person's grades and evaluations being increasingly the subjective opinions of the particular professor. More than once I've attended classes in which I knew that no matter what I did, I would receive at best only a B because I crossed the professor on intellectual issues or there existed a basic conflict of personalities.

It is unfortunate that universities should fall into a blind routine following a principle of organization coming from a domain of social order that has long been noted for its anti-intellectual orientation. The most that can be hoped for in such institutions is the cultivation of spuriousness, blind obedience and student sycophancy, and ultimately, the leveling of an insufferable mediocrity that holds 'routine operational efficiency' as its supreme value. When professors become more concerned about deadlines than with discussion of ideas, we have ended up by putting the cart in front of the horses in higher education.

The most dangerous intellectual is the self-righteous reformer who has all of the answers to the world's problems but none of the worldly wisdom to get us there. Academics may be more enlightened than the lay public, but certainly they are not necessarily more emancipated.

Nowhere else is the dichotomy between the mind and the body, knowing and being, ideal ends and practical means, the said and the done, greater than in Academia. As nowhere else, it is in Academia that the intellect and ideas of mind become systematically and purposefully separated from the real world context in which intelligence and such ideas have their primary reference and ultimate origin. In Academia good thinkers and true believers do not necessarily have to be great human beings.

Academic organization is not that much different from military organization in its promotion of conformity and preservation of the status quo. The main and most basic difference is that where military organization promotes conformity of the body and turning off the mind, academic organization is oriented toward promoting conformity of the mind and turning off of the body.

In the marketplace of knowledge and good ideas, even if increasingly online, the competition can become vicious, cutthroat and unrelenting.

Besides this basic contrast, the only other essential difference seems to be that military organizations must occasionally fight wars, while in Academia it is just an everyday battle of the ego. The thing about aggression is that the student just doesn't know quite what to do with it at the end of a long school day or at the end of a long week or a long semester or year, just as a soldier doesn't know what to do with his mind at the end of an exhausting day of drill, exercises and field operations.

It used to be that higher education was an important investment in one's future. In contemporary American culture at least, it seems that education has become just one more thing to be consumed. We can always use our diplomas as bumper stickers on our shinny new cars that we use to drive to the end of the unemployment line.

American Academia, like most sectors of American society, has become characterized by an increasingly top heavy administrative super-structure that accomplishes nothing except increasing the controls and constraints upon people's freedoms and that costs a great deal to maintain.

Auto-Anthropology

Education for independent thinking cannot but become compromised by such unbalanced administrative overhead.

Thoughts cannot be spoken freely in open forums when everyone is afraid of her or his job or grade. Fairness becomes a fiction of those who fail.

I have been on five different university campuses in different parts of the country during the last five years. In all five I saw the same things occurring—less money in the budget, increasing costs of tuition, the building of parking lots and new expensive facades of buildings by private contractors, and the taking over of vital academic services by national chains and the private sector of the economy.

In all this 'development' very little has been done to develop human potential or new teaching techniques that will better tap into the unlimited potential of the human mind. The universities may be improving physically in their appearance, but mentally they are quickly becoming an administrative quagmire and a professional nightmare. The education of the intellect cannot profit by becoming a big business.

Like the military, Academia is quick to punish and often painfully slow to reward.

Educational equality has been compromised for the sake of enhancing political economic efficiency of what amounts to pen pushing, paper piling self-legitimization, instead of meeting the very real and substantial needs of the ultimately incalculable human mind.

The paradox of this is that educational efficiency has been traded off in the name of greater social equality, which rhetoric itself is based upon the blanket administration of double standards.

My accumulating GPA has been my piling up of special credits to get into Academic Heaven rather than the piling of money to buy my way into the establishment. I've been waiting at the gates for several years, and no one has yet come to open them for me.

In education there is always some point of diminishing returns beyond which the extra effort and investment has decreasing net effect. The trouble has always been trying to figure out exactly when this optimum point is reached, and if surpassed, whether one should continue playing one's hand or just retire from the game. In Academia it is all or nothing.

I have found little to compare to the experience of sitting in class after class, day after day, hour after hour, semester after semester and year after year just waiting for it all to end. Students sit silently, directed towards the head of the class or in a circle towards its center, constrained in one place so that they can move about very little, if at all, and can only speak when spoken to. More often than not lectures are half-baked and boring to listen to. I have found little more effective than this except perhaps television, and increasingly, the Internet, in systematically eroding one's active involvement with one's effective environment, encouraging passivity and stultifying the creative imagination.

Auto-Anthropology

The best thing that can be done is to open up all key administrative positions to periodic general election by the faculty. Only in this way can the real academic interests of the students and their professors be best served, and the cooption and direction of school policy from above be effectively prevented. It is a paradox that our society has rather middling managers who earn as much or more than most national presidents and high-level government officials. The answer to improving the quality of our education and the freedom of our society has always been in achieving more democracy and not less.

American academicians and administrators would do well to pay less attention to the welfare of the 'student body' that has always managed to take care of its own needs, and to give more interest to the condition of the 'student mind,' the needs of which commonly go increasingly unsatisfied.

The most rewarding intellectual experiences I've had have been when I've been in a genuine dialogue with professors or other students on ideas and things of the world. I have learned as much from such discussions as from any monotone lecture or stuffy textbook. The interests of the young students are not well served if they are not permitted enough "quality time" in interpersonal contact with their professors.

Administrators impose superficial cattle classes and distance education with an eye to account books, but do not weigh the immeasurable. The measure of the quality of any education is directly proportional to the amount of time each student gets to spend talking with her/his professors. Not much is going on if everyone acts like they are too busy to take the time to talk to one another.

The social needs of students are inseparable from their intellectual requirements. If a student's body and emotions and psychosocial identity won't co-operate with the Academic system, there is little the student's brain or behavioral discipline can do to control the situation. Growing up, becoming an adult and seeking wisdom in the world has always had its own independent schedule that must be heeded regardless of the Academic deadlines.

The most successful and highly rewarding students are those who are able to put the maturation of their social and personal life on hold long enough to get their degree in hand. More than anything else, this requires that the student have come from a background of socio-emotional and economic security and stability that fosters a healthy and unthreatened sense of ego identity to be developed soon enough to keep the student in check and on schedule until they are able to finally finish their degree. Non-discrepant socialization supports healthy ego-development.

The best students are returning "nontraditional" students who have been in the world and have some measure by which to weigh the teacher's words.

Professors should be allowed to pick their own courses and schedules, and should not be subject to a popularity contest.

Auto-Anthropology

The virtue of having to teach is that we are forced to learn—often for the first time.

The academic priesthood is but one pathway to enlightenment. It is frequently a very straight, narrow and hypocritical one. There has always been another avenue to seeking wisdom in the world. This is the way that is seldom straight, never narrow and always full of disillusionment, but it is always open and unending. Needless to say, the two paths rarely intersect and learning to walk along one road in life tends to make one ill suited for traversing the alternative route. The paradox is that the road less traveled might be the most rewarding intellectually.

One should not underrate the role of serendipity and intuition in the quest for understanding. Our noses follow our pathways of intuitive interest and curiosity as much as our noses lead our interests.

The mark of didactic education, whatever its external trappings, is that it teaches its students to say nothing rather than to risk making a mistake that will bring punishment or a poor appearance. In any such system, students are encouraged not to make mistakes, and not to learn anything by making mistakes. In our own Academic system, the encouragement of conformity of belief and behavioral obedience goes far in advancing a student ahead of the class.

Perfection of performance is rewarded in competitive contexts versus the acquisition of new skills, and the fear of failure is frequently the primary motivation for getting anything done. It is to be wondered that, given such an ethos, our own Academic system has advanced very far beyond a prescriptive, didactic approach.

To know is something of an illusion concealing all we don't know. Learning always dispels that illusion of our own ignorance.

The more I learn the less I know. The more I know the less I learn.

The hardest part about living is not knowing that we will eventually die, but in not knowing how best to use the limited time we are blessed with in life.

Everyday I sit in class, I learn something a little more about the world I didn't know before. Every school day is a lesson in my own ignorance and narrow mindedness. Everyday I sit in class, is a day I miss in the world.

Thoughts are absolutely free until they are voiced. Once spoken, thoughts become imprisoned in the words that speak them. Words are the chains of the free mind. That is why a loquacious professor is often one who thinks the least (and a quiet professor(ess) may think the most and deepest.)

AUTHORITARIANISM

It is a small person who counts success by other people's failures, and their strengths by others weaknesses. These same people will regard others success and strength as their failure and weakness. Unfortunately, the world is not lacking in such small people.

The slave owner may be harsh and unforgiving, or kind and generous, but remains still a slave owner. A slave may be a good worker or a worthless one, but still remains a slave.

Fear is always irrational, though it may be put to extremely rational ends.

First we fear, and then we fear our fear and feel guilty and ashamed because we are afraid.

It is one thing to preach tolerance in the world according to one's own standards of right and wrong, but it is altogether something else to become tolerant in the world of others' standards. Each new generation on earth must learn this lesson anew, and each generation must be taught it over again by the next.

Auto-Anthropology

The greatest human capacity that can be acquired is the capacity for tolerance of human differences in the world.

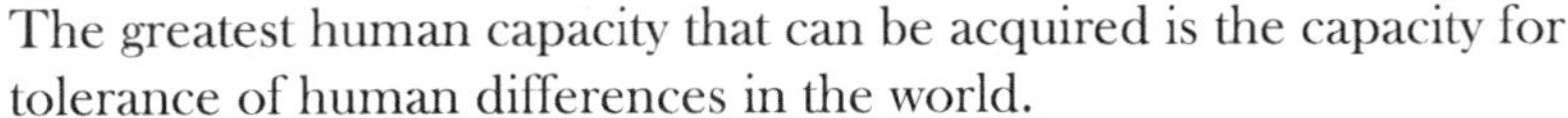

Authoritarianism is the "dis-ease" of authority. It is due to the inevitable human corruption of power in the world. All Authority casts a dark shadow of authoritarianism. Americans have never been immune from this disease, and it has frequently been of critical influence in the perpetration of injustice in all spheres and phases of social life.

Humankind must take seriously the appellation 'Homo auctoritas' as indicative of a universal proclivity towards the power and corruption of authority in the world. If evil comes from the arbitrariness of Authority in the world, then no human being is completely free of its possibility or influence, and even the notion of an Arbitrary God must cast such a shadow.

Self-skepticism is the only antidote to such disease—the possibility of our own evil in the world must be discovered and recognized in everything we think, say and do. It is when we begin taking ourselves too seriously that we are led to trouble with others in the world. Being too serious about ourselves in the world leads to an incapacity to deal with others in a realistic way. The practice of regular self skepticism leads to becoming equally skeptical of others in the world as well—the proclivity to accept ourselves too seriously leads to our taking others in the world too seriously as well.

The quest for perfection in the world must always end up in frustration. When the need and drive for Perfection becomes an obsession and a compulsion, it becomes dangerous. When we cease making mistakes by always doing the right thing, we cease to learn anything in life, and we become then anti-human by definition. The intolerance of imperfection leads to a need to stomp it out and deny it wherever it is found.

Show me a perfect person and I will show you a perfect fool.

One person's vice is another's virtue. One person's failure is another success. One person's weakness is another's strength. One person's folly is another's wisdom. For each action, there is an opposite but equal reaction.

When we fear failure we then need to find it in others we do not know. We then need to avoid getting to know those others who we treat as our own symbolic failures lest such knowledge refutes our own preconceptions. We end up avoiding what we fear and fearing what we avoid—we fear the unknown and end up avoiding it instead of taking the only route, which would ultimately dissipate our fears in the first place.

We even go so far as to collectively set aside and systematically segregate certain categories or 'types' of people as socially sanctioned symbols of failure. Because we are taught to fear such people, we learn to see them symbolically in terms that are dangerous, dirty and unpredictable—terms, which then in turn justify their social discrimination and control.

There is a self-reinforcing closure about this kind of belief and behavior in life, which remains effective until we experience such discrimination ourselves. When we must walk in the footsteps of failure, we come face-to-face with the projective possibilities of our own fear.

Inordinate fear of failure leads to an obsession with failure, which begets a gambling compulsion—the uncontrollable need to take inordinate risks that are normally unnecessary.

It is not coincidental that any society, which highly prizes and rewards well achievement and success at all costs, should beget a great many failures who have unwisely gambled away all their resources for the unrealistic promise of success.

Unfortunately, the very values most worth living for are those that are also most worth dying for. It is a tragic irony of human history that so many have died for values and causes that prove to be hardly worth living for.

It is not too uncommon or too difficult to face death bravely—but it has been unusual and extremely hard to go on living bravely in the face of death. The common weal, the crowd, and the wicked fight with weapons and fear—the courageous and faithful fight with words, freedom and peace.

There is no person so perfect as not to be in need of some improvement. There is no human strength without its hidden weakness. There is no armor so complete as to be without its vulnerable spots. The best protection in life is the well-kept illusion that hides the bestial nakedness of humanity beneath the veil of greatness. The best weapons are truth that pierces the armor of illusion, and honesty that lifts the veil of ignorance.

As surely as the night must follow the day; and the moon must rise in the shadow of the sun; great weakness must accompany great strength, grand mistakes must follow great successes; great depths make great heights more pronounced. Without the darkness and shadow, life and light would be flat, uninteresting, and without the necessary contrast that gives it depth.

Life is meant to be taken seriously, but never too seriously. When we begin to take things too seriously we lose sight of the fact that though life is serious business, it is also a grand joke we play upon ourselves.

It is difficult to find it in ourselves the same kinds of negative qualities that we so facilely attribute to others, but seeing such similarities can be a sobering experience to the ego, and having the romantic illusions we ascribe to others fade and turn ugly can have a chilling influence upon our hearts.

One person's illusion is another's reality. One person's destiny is another's fate. One person's myth is another's history.

It is easy to envy what others seem to have and we do not. But to have compassion enough to find in each person what is most valuable is compensation for our jealousies.

The fear of failure frequently leads to a Pyrrhic victory, for in our desire to succeed at any cost, we become willing to risk everything.

When we fear, fear, we end up denying our fears, and in our denial we become trapped in our own vicious circle of deceit.

Auto-Anthropology

We fear that which we do not understand, and because we fear it, we tend to ignore it, to avoid having to face it and get to know it. Then we fall victim to our own prejudices. We end up avoiding our own ignorance and blaming others for the fear that is in ourselves.

The first lie begins a long chain of deceit, when we have to cover over one lie with another until we've forgotten what the original lie was. Lying is inevitably a self-defeating strategy. It may be effective in the short term, but it eventually backfires upon the chronic liar who must cover lies with other lies until reality is lost sight of.

Lying undermines trust, which is the basis of mutual respect in interpersonal relationships. Without respect, there can be no love or friendship (and honesty gives way to deceit.)

Those who live by fear of the truth learn to become good liars, and those who lie learn to live in fear of the truth. Fear and lying are always closely connected, where one is found, the other is sure to be nearby.

Fear is the fate of the coward. The courageous cannot live well with fear and are too troubled by lying. They must sooner or later grab the bull by the horns and wrestle it to the ground.

The world is full of fools. To be foolish takes no special talent or skill at all, but to call the fool's bluff takes wisdom, and to free ourselves from the fool's spell, takes strength and courage.

We develop a need not to know that which we fear. To confront our fears face-to-face entails a challenge to our own sense of identity in the world. We would rather bury our heads in the sand and believe whatever lie and illusion we need in order to keep us from having to face, and learning to live with what we most fear.

No other person can know better than ourselves what it is we most need and want in life. Sometimes another person can help us to see what it is in ourselves that we fail to see, but it is only upon ourselves that we must lay the heavy burden of responsibility for success and failure in our own life. It is all too easy and common to seek solutions to our own dilemmas from others, and then to blame them when they prove to be wrong.

People see what they wish to see, and cannot be made to face that which they do not want to.

Auto-Anthropology

Authority tends to blind people, creating its own aura of power until inevitable contradiction reveals the human being underneath the badge and uniform.

When we hate, we become imprisoned by the thing we hate. In our attachment to hate, our hate comes to control our consciousness and undermine our own sense of freedom. To not like or care for something does not mean that one must hate it. One does not have to love that which one does not hate, or hate that which one does not love.

We blame the world for our own weaknesses, and blame ourselves for the faults of the world. The only salvation is the release from our sense of guilt. But such release is not found in sociopathic absence or freedom from responsibility, but in its saintly embrace.

The sense of security in a mass-oriented society is that everyone seems to be doing the same thing no matter how foolish and nonsensical it may really be. This is a false and dangerous illusion that justifies the method of social order and behavior by the madness of the crowd.

The mass mind is an oxymoron—the crowd has only a herd mentality.

It is never wise to underestimate the deliberate cunning of people who have the quest for power as their primary motive and ultimate goal in life. They will be the first to attack and the last to retreat, and will go to any end imaginable to accomplish their designs, and though utterly defeated, they will never relinquish their goals (except in our dreams.)

I am proud to claim that I have never treated another person in the same ugly way that so many people have felt appropriate to treat me. I have come to have little patience for the kind of deliberate ignorance and prejudice by which others misappropriate one's identity in the world for their own convenience. I no longer regard with great compassion people whose sense of success feeds upon the feelings of failure by others. It is saddening to know how many different kinds of people in the world do this very thing without a sense of self-conscious guilt or shame.

People only feel ashamed or embarrassed when they are afraid of the consequences of their actions and the reactions of others.

We choose our own values in life and then judge others in the world according to those choices, without realizing that not everyone makes the same set of choices, or even that if they seem to share similar values, they may well have chosen them for very different, even contradictory reasons. People either choose the values they live by, or if failing to choose, then inevitably have them chosen for themselves by others.

Auto-Anthropology

The fear of persecution is the source of guilt. Freedom of the mind demands freedom from fear and guilt, which depends upon not been threatened by persecution or violence. The only way to gain such freedom is by becoming non-violent and non-authoritarian oneself, and by seeking out and cultivating non-violence and non-authoritarianism in others. Fear, violence, or guilt are all social chains which imprison the mind. A prisoner of the mind is still a prisoner even if the body is emancipated.

It is unfortunate that authority and legitimacy is increasingly co-opted and mandated within the World System, and is measured in quantitative terms which frequently has little or no nothing to do with human qualities and virtue.

The world will become more human and humane, more subjectively satisfying and less alienating, when there is less mass and impersonal exploitation and greater individual equality and interpersonal compassion.

If we have a certain existential investment in our illusion in life, no matter how ill founded they may really be, we will tend to act in ways that will maintain our illusion in spite mounting contradictory evidence.

If the investment in the illusions of our own identity is very strong or dear, then we may perseverate in reinforcing our fictions in such a manner unrelentingly, piling illusion upon illusion and denying anything that does not support our identity in the world.

In such a manner, we will suffer an unending chain of crisis, each connected to the next, and how we manage to resolve these crisis, or fail to, will determine the net outcome of our realistic adjustment to the world.

We take advantage of whatever opportunities we can get, even if it is often at someone else's expense. We pay attention mostly to those who receive the same advantages as ourselves and disregard the rest. We call any person a fool who passes over opportunity for another's sake, and honor as heroes those who take the most advantage of any situation.

Perhaps all this stems ultimately from an "UR" version of humanity of warriors in a conflict-prone world in which it is either win or die.

If aggression comes from and leads to the need to proclaim and reaffirm one's identity in the world, then authoritarianism is a consequent and a cause of the need to control that aggression in the world.

The illusion of authority is always some superhuman ideal, idea or idol. We cannot value the lives of others too dearly when we subordinate the value of our own. If we hold as most sacred that which is beyond our own lives and humanness, then we cannot regard the lives and humanness of others as sacred enough not to be violated.

Auto-Anthropology

Predictability is the primary weakness of the authoritarian.

The authoritarian is married to her/his unconscious obsession with authority. All other relationships in the world are secondary and subservient to this. The authoritarian is the most adulterous monogamist and monogamous adulterer in the world.

Authority is the only religion of the authoritarian. It does not matter really what the symbolic trappings of the ideology and ritual really are, as long as they feel the perverted power and violent force that authority represents. One religion's prophets and saints are another's heretic and rebel.

No human being is free from authoritarianism of others but we all remain blind to the possibilities of our own authoritarianism. This blindness is the very symptom of our own authoritarianism. When we say emphatically 'Screw Authority' we are really announcing to the world a love hate dependency upon the very thing that we must so emphatically renounce and deny.

Authoritarianism is the obsessive preoccupation with Authority. Can we have authority without authoritarianism, and power without moral ethical perversion?

Authoritarians are blind to their own Authority. Authorities are blind to their own authoritarianisms. For them it is more a matter of routine and of regimen—a taken for granted matter of course. This transparency of authority and authoritarianism is rooted in the unconscious control that authoritarianism has upon our lives. We act without being fully aware of the unconscious causes and consequences of our actions.

Because it is mainly unconscious, our preoccupation with authority becomes expressed symbolically and transforms our lives into a vicious circle of obsession and compulsion. We seek to find and control in our external world what we cannot face and control in our internal world. Because authoritarianism controls us, we seek to control the world.

It is amazing how conscious like and deliberate what is basically unconscious authoritarianism can seem. This is so perhaps because unconscious authoritarianism seeks to frame and constrain the conscious mind which therefore cannot act independently from such control, but which must then act in such a manner that is consonant with and reinforcing of the unconscious. Though authoritarians are fundamentally closed minded, their unconsciousness can be read like an open book.

A person can serve only one master, and can be master of only one person.

Auto-Anthropology

Our World System had long promoted and rewarded a kind of political economic authoritarianism. Colonial fascism has always been the dark side of the coin of Imperial Capitalism. When we are successfully authoritarian, we call it "high achievement" motivation and fail to acknowledge the dangers of its exploitative, victimizing, aggressive, competitive, and acquisitive characteristics.

Authoritarians are quick to dismiss the liberal attitudes of others as a problem of authority. Because they themselves lack much imagination or the ability to entertain questions or tolerate doubt, they find people who have such capacities as a threat to their own sense of order, and people who exercise their freedoms as 'breakers of the law' and irresponsible. Authoritarians see their restricted version of authority as being necessary to their sense of the world and therefore as fundamentally unquestionable. Non-authoritarians regard such blind faith in Authority to be basically a personality problem of freedom.

The most significant factor about modern 'mass' authority and authoritarianism in the world system is that it is impersonal. Victimization and violence have their own logic in the world that is not fully logical but pathological. The pathologic of violence and victimization is that the victim is regarded as guilty, responsible for the violence, the cause and not the consequent effect of the violence. The kind of pathologic is the ultimate repression of an authoritarian's own responsibility and projection of guilt onto others.

AMERICA

Being born an American may have been a mixed blessing, but a blessing nonetheless. Americans grow up under the deadening weight of crude materialism, and must later in life unlearn many of the trite truisms they were taught to believe in.

Americans typically have egos several sizes too large, a bottomless stomach and an insufferable gullibility to swallow almost anything fed to them by others. Americans walk the way of the world only to wake up from their naiveté to learn that they are not immune to the evil of the world.

Americans may have been spoiled by too much affluence, convenience and freedom to pursue their own pleasures. But Americans are not the only 'ugly' people in the world, and not necessarily the worst, the first or the last set of imperfect human beings to have come along. Indeed, in spite of their own attitudes of over achievement and others' criticisms of their life-styles and their weaknesses, it is amazing that Americans have accomplished anything at all in the world (and far more than most others.)

Most people do not learn to prize their freedom until after they have lost it. Many others never have had the freedom to lose. The weak and insecure would just as soon sacrifice their own freedom as well as that of everyone else for just about any spiritual illusion that promises their salvation. For them, freedom is not a prize to be won, but a prize to be paid for by the false promise of their protection.

Auto-Anthropology

Freedom is having the opportunity to learn from one's own mistakes while taking heed of the advice of others.

We cannot be genuinely free until we have learned to grant to others their freedom, even if it means forsaking our own. Learning to give for other's sake is just the beginning of the long pathway to freedom.

The first step taken, all else then follows.

It has not been military might, political power, economic achievement or scientific or technological success that has made America a Great Society. It has been the promise of its freedom, human rights and equality that it has offered to anyone seeking a better life and to escape persecution. It has been this promise that has made the United States a model for worldwide emulation, even if in name or in paper only. And it has not been either a false or an empty promise.

It has been unfortunate that so many new Americans seem to have forgotten or never grew to understand this fact in their pursuit of the unprecedented power, prestige and personal aggrandizement that success in the American system rewards.

Young Americans cannot be blamed for having been raised with a false sense of values and unrealistic expectations and thus failing to adapt themselves to a quickly changing world. Nor can they be faulted for failing to carry the torch and catch the baton when their own leaders have extinguished the flame and lost their way.

It is this fact of its freedom and its promise of equality that has long made America different from the rest of the world. It has been a difference that is rapidly diminishing, not because the rest of the world is catching up with the United States, but because Americans are falling behind in its own promise to the world.

In this sense we can say that its Empire has come back home to America, and it has come to stay.

America has never been a perfect society, but it has also never been a pigsty. The progress of enlightenment, social emancipation and the realization of human equality have been slow but steady—a step backwards for every two forward. Americans have rarely been as pure of heart as they would like to see themselves. Paradise cannot be had except at great human cost, and if it is founded upon the pleasure principle, it is liable to be a paradise for the few and a living hell for the many. It is fitting that America should move slowly and be short sighted in its prospects for paradise—anything too far and too fast is bound to end in disaster for everyone.

America's lesson in Vietnam, one that it has seemed to quickly forget, is that it is never necessary to destroy the village in order to save it. Freedom does not follow the path of bullets and bombs, broken bodies and burnt homes. The only thing found at the end of a gun barrel is fruitless destruction and the involuntary servitude to one's own possibility of evil in the world. Too many paid too dearly for the mistakes America made in Vietnam for us to forget too soon the lessons that our own history has taught us.

The road to freedom leads through a vast, drought filled desert. The promise of spiritual salvation from all human troubles hovers above the

<u>Auto-Anthropology</u>

far-off horizon like a mirage of a blue ocean shimmering above the hot, dry sands. People thirst for freedom but do not know what will quench their thirst. The source of freedom flows deeply underground.

The tyranny of aggression is that it compels the peaceful to defend their freedom. Though aggression is frequently promoted in the name of freedom, freedom is seldom won in the name of aggression.

If the best defense is a good offense, the best offense is none at all. The prize can only be lost if it can only be won by war.

Calling the vast American military machine the 'Department of Defense' barely disguises its offensiveness to the rest of the world. Freedom gained through 'enforcing the peace,' whether this be a Pax Romana, a Pax Britannica, or a Pax Americana, can only be freedom for the few at the expense of the many. At best it can only lead back to the corruption of the very society that created such unfreedom of violence in the first place.

Common virtues have given way to contemporary vices. In the name of modernity and civilization, basic human values have been forfeited for empty symbols of strength solidarity, security and superiority. Fashion and status dictate people's behavior, and these are manipulated by the large commercial interests and by government itself.

Americans have had their basic character altered and modified by a mass media and a warped, uneven and exploitative incentive structure, to become gross materialistic consumers and media junkies. We are brainwashed to feel guilty for being Americans, and compelled to rush to the shopping malls to temporarily alleviate our guilt feelings.

Freedom and salvation will not be found in a Sears' mail order catalogue.

Americans value the possession of private property more than they value their own freedom or even human life itself. Inordinate physical attachment to physical things in the world is precisely the opposite of the definition of human freedom. Freedom is the license to spend one's own time and energy in one's own way—owing someone else lots of money or paying rent for the possession and use of property can only be a vital restriction of human freedom. Any freedom upon which our society is founded can only be in name only if its promotion is ultimately based upon practices and principles of possession, unbridled profit and private property that must lead fatefully to human unfreedom.

The only ultimate bottom line is that there are no bottom lines in human reality. One must always beware those who claim to know and to have the bottom line—especially if they are trying to sell it to you.

A person may only speak for one's self, but no person can justly speak for any other. We must beware those people who claim to speak for all people, or those of a certain kind who claim to speak for all of that kind. In any such claim exists a dangerous and tacit denial of the freedom for other people to speak, and ultimately, to think and know for themselves.

It is only the simple minded who seek simple solutions to complex human problems and who chronically claim to speak for others when they are only selfishly thinking of themselves, and who unconsciously and uncontrollably choose symbols of solidarity and strength over antithetical symbols of peace, compassion, love and tolerance.

People, who are themselves exploited, must find someone else to exploit in turn. People who allow themselves to be used and dumped upon must in turn find someone else to use and dump upon. People who live beneath some shadow must themselves cast their shadow upon other's lives. What goes around comes around, and we eventually reap what we sow. No matter how hard we may try or wish, we can never escape the lasting consequences of our own choices.

To deny the role of class in American society is to deny the very basis of social inequality itself. In our ideology lies the very basis of social inequality itself. In our ideology of natural rights, we ascribe psychopathology to the poor and the failed, and psychological spirit and virtue to those who are most successful, all the while blatantly ignoring the background social context in which both success and failure are situated and configured.

This being the norm, it follows that the predominant social collective consciousness is class consciousness—and unmarked but very deliberate awareness of an individual's social background and relationships in the world, and these pre-understandings more often than not form the criteria of our attitudes, projections, opinions, beliefs, values, and judgments regarding both ourselves and other people in our lives. Class categories, differences of background and situation, and relative social standing and entitlement, form the basis of social significance and human valuation.

It follows that class always tends to reinforce, and reproduce itself. People make deliberate decisions in relation to what will promote their own class interests over those of other classes and individuals who comprise these classes.

The rich help one another to stay rich, and the poor keep one another poor. It also follows that upward mobility will be the norm for the upper class—that no matter how mediocre and average a person might be, if they are born into the upper strata of a society the availability of opportunity and of rich reward and positive social reinforcement will tend to keep them afloat no matter how personally failed they may really be.

On the other hand, a person born into an impoverished class background may demonstrate superlative skills, steady and unbending drive, and superior talent and abilities, but will nonetheless be consistently driven downward in society by the many, more often overwhelming, checks and controls arrayed against that person's chances for success.

The undeniability of class inequality and function of class in perpetuating social structure in America makes American society fundamentally not very different from any other national or multi-ethnic society in the world.

The elites of one country have more in common with the elites of other countries, in terms of their interests, prerogatives, values and views of the world, than they do with their own poor people. This commonness among the elites is recognized internationally as human virtue. Being born poor in a world of increasing social inequality is to have been born with a social disease—a 'corruption' of class.

People, who live by appearances, judge others on the basis of appearance. To live by the principle of appearance is a sort of magical formula for social success—that like produces like. One must dress in the most expensive clothes, drive the most stylish car, and talk to all the right people in the right way, and social success will follow.

The surprising thing is that this formula sometimes works. One can possess all the talent in the world, but without the appropriate style of social presentation, will be foredoomed as a social failure. But to live by the basis of appearance alone is an empty, shallow, and eventually self-defeating strategy of social mobility.

Ignorance, prejudice, repressive discrimination and deceit, to the extent that these policies in life reinforce inequality and unfairness in social relations, will lead to success. But any such success will be ephemeral and short lived—those who live by the lie, die by the lie, as there are always bound to be competitors with superior advantage in the world. Honesty, though slow and inefficient, still remains the best policy, and

Auto-Anthropology

tends to make one immune to the arbitrary vicissitudes of merely
meretricious appearances.

Class-consciousness is the normal form of social consciousness
informing our experience with the subtleties of social difference,
solidarity, and significance upon both conscious and unconscious levels
of understanding and feeling. Try as we might, we really cannot escape
its structuring influence upon our attitudes, values and worldviews, either
in how we see and treat others, or in how we are seen by and are treated
by others.

It also tends to constrain in decisive ways how we see and feel about our
selves—tending to invade, interfere with and eventually take over and
control our private, inner subjectivities. It is class that thus tends to
simultaneously and contradictorily both socially revitalize and to
collectivize everything we see and do in relation to others in the world.

It is perhaps the ultimate paradox that because class-consciousness is
based as much upon the illusion of appearances as it is upon anything
substantially real, it becomes both the dialectical antithesis to which false
consciousness is compared, and a basic form of class-consciousness
itself.

The complicating fact of the matter is that there are few if any non-
arbitrary standards of alternative or genuine consciousness by which we
can compare and evaluate the concept of class-consciousness. We can
claim that as a social phenomenon it exists in the world, but we can
ultimately never prove it and may only indirectly ever point to it and
say—this attitude is true and this one is false.

It is this paradox that makes such consciousness so easy to deny and to
falsify.

Charity and equality do not go very far in America. Few gifts are given
which are not penny-ante, nickel and dime, token or without strings
attached. The American Indians learned this lesson well in their

transactions with the White Men, summing it up when they said 'White Men speak with forked tongue.' American society is the greatest consumer society to have ever existed. It typically aggrandizes Greed and makes of selfishness and egotism a reward virtue of personal success and achievement.

The formula for success has been reduced to competitive striving for one's own profit at someone else's expense, and the American legal structure promotes and protects the property, profits and prerogatives and privileges of the wealthy while systematically discriminating against and dispossessing the rights of the poor. Americans love any and every winner, and hate a loser. As Edgar Allan Poe well knew, Americans especially despise the poor. The trouble with this twisted social values are that ultimately only one person can become a winner, and that person must live in a very lonely and empty world.

Freedom must always be fought for, as there are always enough people in the world who are deliberately trying to take it away, the best of intentions notwithstanding.

Beyond any other inventions or feats, human rights remain the most important contribution American society has made to the world. Few other societies in history have ever made the democratic doctrine of universal human rights the foundation stone of its social order.

It is unfortunate that this foundation is being undermined and eroded by the pursuit of power, pleasure and personal aggrandizement. Foreigners in America frequently have low regard or little appreciation for such a doctrine so alien to their own hierarchical values, and Americans who grow up in the fold of freedom and the lap of luxury never suffer its loss enough to appreciate what they have.

Auto-Anthropology

One important factor in the decline and fall of the Roman Empire was its persistent failure to pay back the debt it owned to its own citizen soldiers who literally built Rome by their toil and sacrifices only to return from foreign campaigns and conquests to find themselves dispossessed and impoverished plebeians of the streets. The Pax Americana can learn an important lesson from this Imperial History.

The real loss in America is in terms of its rapidly deteriorating quality of life. The limited availability or relative lack of opportunity among any but the upper rungs of the class structure means that there has become less and less to go around for everyone. When people have talents, skills, abilities and energies that are going to waste or left unrewarded because there are fewer and fewer job opportunities to utilize these capacities, then we must ask who has been most responsible for the loss.

The political economic and socio-economic shortcomings of our Great Society are due in part to the general loss of cultural confidence in our own values and orientations. The complex of inferiority and failure should never be underestimated in terms of its power as self-fulfilling prophecy in our collective life.

When we see foreign competitors who, by strength of their own social organization, cultural confidence and solidarity, seem to be getting ahead of us in the market place, it is almost automatic that we should begin seeing ourselves as born losers and them as born winners. When we begin to believe this, we begin behaving in ways that tend to reinforce these ideas, as if they were true, and little can then be done, short of complete reversal of roles, to change our attitudes about ourselves.

People sometimes seem to be subconsciously aware of these attitudes and their consequences upon our lives, and will almost deliberately set out to attack our self-confidence and to undermine our basic faith in our values, abilities and beliefs.

MILITARISM, PACIFISM, POWER AND PEACE

The best defense is a good offense. The best offense is none at all. The prize can only be lost if it can be won by peace.

The balance of power can only be upset. Peace cannot be permanent if it is promised by the threat of war. Any weapon has only one purpose in the hand of its wielder, and this is to murder others in the world. Once forged, a weapon will eventually be used.

The Power of Peace is the appeal and appreciation of what is most commonly and mutually human in all of us. The Power of War is the threat to what is most common and mutually human in all of us. War and Peace have the same source in the human heart, but in each the heart serves a different master. War in the world follows war in the heart.

The cowardly of war are the courageous of peace, and the courageous of war are the cowardly of peace. We honor our war dead as sacred heroes, and think of those who wish to continue living in peace as fools. The coward dies a thousand deaths, soon forgotten; the hero dies but once, when passed long remembered afterwards.

Our earthbound age is discovering the preparations for and consequences of war are increasingly expensive, unaffordable, and destructive.

We are learning indirectly the hard worn lesson learned and forgotten on thousands of fields of battle that no one wins in war and everyone loses. War and its machineries of death, are quickly becoming barbaric anachronisms in an earthbound age, that in the long run has no net profit for anyone and yet which is increasingly costly for everyone. It is a grand paradox that permanent and lasting peace in our earthbound age will not be won by victory in war, or by its threat, or over the bargaining table of the powerful military nations. Peace will be achieved when the common soldier simply throws down her/his weapon to let the earth and the sea reclaim it.

Better more mouths to feed and more babies to breed than buttons to push and triggers to pull. The world might become an over populated place, but at least it doesn't have to be a violent one.

Militarism is ultimately an anti-human disease in which the social preoccupation with the fear of death leads to a compulsion to project and cause death upon others. The main problem with this social pathology is that it is extremely contagious and pernicious—the need to beget death in ourselves leads to the same needs in others.

The thing the military mentality fears most is peace and freedom. Peace depends upon the realization of freedom in the world, and freedom depends upon peace. In a world that is peaceful and free, there is no room for the military minded, and this is the worst possible threat to the warmonger.

Auto-Anthropology

As long as we seek to define empowerment in narrow and unequal terms that divides humankind into different camps, such empowerment can only lead to its own corruption and the perversion of violence and war. Only when we seek panhuman empowerment through the realization of human rights, freedoms and equality, can we speak legitimately of our own empowerment as well. Such empowerment can only be had through the promotion of pacifism in the world—a live and let live ethos of love, charity, tolerance, and forgiveness in a world of evil.

It is a paradox of pacifism that its power can only be had in the individual's renunciation of the pathos and nomos and obsessive-compulsive preoccupation with empowerment in the world. The power of pacifism comes from the renunciation of power hence its dialectical transcendence in the realization of the power of the human heart.

It is also a paradox that such empowerment also constitutes the ultimate connection between panhuman interests and rights and individual interests and rights. The pursuit of our own rights, freedoms and responsibilities in the world is concomitant with the pursuit of universal human rights, responsibilities and freedom in the world. One cannot be had without the other, and one cannot be taken away without taking away from the other.

Those who pursue the path of pacifism cannot but help be led sooner or later to the same conclusions regarding the paramount importance of human rights, responsibilities and freedoms in the world defined in both the broadest, panhuman sense as well as in the narrowest of individual senses.

To relinquish the preoccupation of power and violence in our own personal lives, and to gain the upper hand in the control of our existential fears and uncertainties, is to gain access to and release a vast hidden reservoir of human potentiality in both ourselves and in everybody whose lives we touch.

The cultivation of creativity, in our selves and in others, goes hand in hand with the promotion of pacifist values and worldview in the larger world. Human creativity is the opposite of human destructiveness. That which is creative, if frustrated, must become destructive. That which is destructive, if constrained, can become creative. Peace is to war as creation is to destruction.

If we wish to find our worst enemies and our most dangerous threat to our freedom and future security in the world, then we have to look no further than on our own neighborhoods, our own backyards and in our own mirrors. The threat is there, like a shadow we always cast in the light.

The preoccupation and fantasy of violence and aggressive power in the world is a symptom of our own immature and regressed development. It is to be well wondered how much the promotion of aggression in the world doesn't rely upon the repression and frustration of human sexuality in the world, when so much violence of obscene proportions is replete in our television programming while even the most innocent and natural images of sexuality are taboo and perverted.

Human development can only be advanced when as both individuals and as a world society, we learn to give up our dependent and neurotic attachment to such violent and immature forms of power in order to cultivate greater human capacities and to pursue more worthwhile interests in the world. In our global militarism, humankind has become

<u>Auto-Anthropology</u>

like dependent and retarded children in the pursuit of its own narcissistic developmental interests.

MAD-ness equals 'In order to save the world, it was necessary to destroy the world.' In order to assure peace and freedom, it is necessary to control peace and freedom by the threat of war. This madness continues to grow hardly abated in the world.

The victimization of children in war is parallel to and an extension of the victimization of children in peace. The former relies on weapons to amputate, burn and break the bodies of children, the latter relies on poverty to amputate, shock and paralyze the child's soul and spirit.

In this sense it can be genuinely said that war is a kind of politics of enforced inequality between different classes and categories of people.

There is no greater or more sobering lesson in the horrors and unnecessary realities of war than to see and smell and hear the screams of a child that's been burned head to foot by white phosphorous or napalm. This is a tragic if sometimes-unavoidable way to be taught the value and virtue of pacifism.

Too bad that no one has yet thought up a kind of inoculation to the horror and violence of war that would render humankind immune to the threat of its infectious disease. It seems that sometimes we can only get pacifism under the skin when we can become sensitized to the suffering of others and aware of our human heart of darkness in the cause of such suffering.

If war is the pursuit of politics by another means, then peace is the pursuit of war by another means. In war, there is always a better way.

There is only one kind of development, and this is human development. Any human action, which does not ultimately contribute to the improvement of the human condition in the world, either directly or indirectly, must be considered as unnecessary or antithetical to the long-term interests of panhuman development. In the human world, there are no neutral words or deeds. Neutrality is only the guarded disguise of the pursuit of power. The best index of human development in the world is the relative health, happiness and opportunity of the average child within a healthy family context.

Though there are many consequences and causes in the historical and cultural explanation of how and why war happens. Within context of the modern World System we cannot overlook the central importance played by the history of political economic development in creating the conditions as well as the means for virtually every major war in modern earth history.

Economic affluence at home has often entailed economic imperialism and exploitation aboard. The promotion of capitalistic development is interdependent with the control of colonial underdevelopment. When armies are marching and whole nation states are mobilized for war, it is the captains of the armament industry, weapons manufacture and the military industrial complex that profits the most. Capitalistic enterprise often makes alliances with fanatic fascists and bureaucratic officials, even by communist or former communist nations.

Auto-Anthropology

There will be peace in the world when so few are no longer allowed to profit from the suffering of so many.

Peace depends upon the realization of human freedom in the world. The realization of such freedom depends upon the education for responsibility to exercise and realize such freedom.

The realization of such responsibility depends upon the promotion of the values and views of non-violence that entails the realization of human equality in the world.

The basis of violence in the human world is the creation and promotion of human inequality, by class, race, religion, nation, caste, age or sex. It follows from this chain of associations that if we want to attain peace in the world, the best thing we can do is to promote human equality and the responsibility of freedom.

For closely related reasons, it takes money to make more money just as poverty begets yet greater poverty. Similarly, and still related, we may say that just as violence leads invariably to more and greater violence, so too does peace promote greater peace.

The escalation of world war has been a vicious cycle of the growth of global militarization, which has been fueled primarily by the capitalistic interests of the armaments industries as promoted by authoritarian state regimes daring more open and democratic nations to struggle to keep up the armaments race. It is the epitome of evil in the world that so many should have been made to suffer so terribly so that only a small proportion of humankind can have its cake and eat it too. Outlawing all weapons would not stop these parasites of human pain, but it would prevent them from acquiring the prestige and glory, that they do not deserve.

Our earthbound age is one in which many things stand for their opposite. We promote war in the name of peace, aggression in the name of defense, fascism and totalitarianism in the name of freedom and democracy, death in the name of life, deceit in the name of truth, poverty in the name of affluence, hierarchy in the name of equality, underdevelopment in the name of development. It is a testament to the power and authority of official verbiage and the mass media that can turn black to white and white to black, and obscure all colors in the world beneath the veil of gray.

It is the epitome of the evil and unfreedom of the human mind when such instruments and devices as the television, radio, newspaper, education, and magazines (and the Internet and wireless communications) can be used to rationalize away any problem or paradox, no matter how fundamentally nonsensical, irrational or inherently pathological such rationalization may really be.

It is all the more remarkable when it is considered that what is taken as the basis of social scientific fact is really fiction, and there is no such thing as the average John and Jane Doe Public.

We have created an illusion of world power by the make believe magic of virtual, paper realities, and as long as it seems convincing and credible enough to the un-inquisitive and gullible, the world will continue to conform to the lie, and turn a mythological prophecy into an ideological history.

<u>Auto-Anthropology</u>

Educating our children for peace and teaching non-violent and pacifist values in the world has never been an especially problematic, or un-efficacious proposition except that we've made it seem so. Because it has rarely been tried, it is believed that it cannot be done. But if we can prepare our youth to be good warriors then it seems possible also to be able to be able to prepare them for being good peacemakers of the world. The means for such pacifistic education has long been available, but the motivation has always been lacking. Its benefits for humankind far outweigh its costs.

War is a situation for which everyone is responsible for their own small part that is played, and yet no one is to blame for the entire thing. Whether we work in a munitions factory, buy war bonds, or we pull the trigger, or drop a bomb on an anonymous enemy, we are all ultimately responsible for our actions in the war. Nuremberg has instructed humankind that it is no longer merely enough to blindly follow one's orders without ethical consideration of the moral consequences of our own involvement and actions.

If all participants and combatants accepted their fullest human responsibility for their own involvement in the perpetration of its violence, then there would be no war in the world to judge. The tyranny of aggression and violence is that it forces the innocent and the good to commit evil and atrocious acts in defense ultimately of their rights and freedom. In war, as in peace, the buck stops at the center of each and every person's soul, and we cannot legitimately point our fingers at our enemy to blame them for our actions and decisions.

Though in war everyone is responsible for their own part that they play, and no one is ultimately to blame, some people share more responsibility and blame than others because they play a bigger and more critical role in the perpetration of violence. In this regard, we must look to the politicians and high ranking military commanders who are most influential of the decision and directions of aggression and violence in war, but who rarely if ever suffer the first hand consequences of such violence.

Only naïve and gullible young men can be made to readily die for a false cause. It has been unfortunate in history that the arena of conflict and combat cannot be confined to include just those instigators and warmongers and profiteers who are most responsible for the war and yet who suffer least from its consequences. Such leaders might be less likely to wage war and more dissuaded from entering armed combat if they had to confront the very real prospects of their own possible death from such a decision.

Peace comes from the capacity for compromise and competitive cooperation. The world will not meet us halfway if we are not willing to meet the world more than halfway. Compromise is an art, that is learned in adaptation to life. Its capacity comes from patience, tolerance, and the willingness to adopt the point of view of one's opponents. It does not come easily. It does not come without struggle, risks or courage. It cannot be had without a sense of loss and only partial gains.

The groundwork for war is laid when people raise some symbolic form to a level higher than their own. It comes when people who are otherwise good and common, commit acts that are evil and uncommon because they are not held responsible for their own actions, but are able to defer that responsibility onto something beyond themselves, superhuman, absolutely and ideally good.

Auto-Anthropology

The foundations for a secure and lasting peace cannot be laid in the preparations for war that leads inevitably into another vicious cycle of war.

EARTH AND NATURE

It is the earth that will adapt humankind to her needs, and not we who will adapt the earth to our needs. In our transformations of the world, we have become transformed by the world. Neither we, nor the world, can go back to our original separate states of nature. We were originally never separated from the earth, except that we sought to isolate ourselves and dominate nature as the basis for our own collective survival.

Because of humankind's predations, the evolution of life on earth has once again entered upon a contraction phase. In every concrete crack and crevice of our civilization, nature is struggling for survival and return. We must not underestimate the recuperative and regenerative power of the natural earth.

The never-ending forces of erosion work steadily away upon the edges of our grand civilization. They work so slowly and gradually that they are imperceptible to our greater and intelligent vision. It is the great and certain patience of Nature's ways that will eventually conquer over the insolent impetuousness of our own blind human progress. Human greatness and evil, vice and virtue, hubris and nemesis, will make no difference when lying side-by-side in the grave of the earth, covered over by the sands of time, buried beneath the regenerative soils if decomposing life.

Auto-Anthropology

Archaeologists and paleontologists of the distant future, if there are any, will dig beneath the earth's soils to discover a layer of irradiated concrete rubble and piles of broken and shattered bones buried in shredded plastic concrete.

They will have soon discovered a worldwide base line for early human civilization, and wonder what forgotten historical events caused this massive level of destruction. They will discover the ages old lessons of human nature and human history that has been learned the hard way in one age only to become forgotten in the next age. Hopefully our remote heirs of human civilization will by then have learned these lessons well enough not to repeat the same old mistakes. This will be the final evidence of humankind's real progress.

Nature has a sense of order, and a mysterious mind of its own. Our involvements in the processes of nature can only interrupt and interfere with these patterns and their products in a dissonant and destructive way. The best we can hope for is a neutral relationship between our civilization and the natural world upon which it depends.

What a curse upon the earth it has been that the spirit of humankind should remain perpetually insatiable, and their souls always searching for vicarious salvation in the world, in the mythological escape from mortality.

How is it that one species among all the forms of life on earth has come to so dominate the earth and destroy or dominate most of the other forms of life in its quest for power and security from the forces of nature?

In anything we do, we cannot escape the ecological imperative of our earthbound age, that the human destruction of the world's natural habitats and ecosystems are the most consequential challenge of survival that has ever confronted humankind except perhaps during our earliest era of evolutionary adaptation and struggle for naked survival against the forces of nature. Could it be that humankind learned its first evolutionary lessons too well, and adapted too much?

Could it be that the needs of humankind's own destruction are too deeply rooted in the first evolutionary steps of human nature? Historical civilization may have been humankind's elaborate way of postponing the inevitable—a sophisticated way of usurping nature's control over our destiny because we are maladapted from the start to fit well into the larger scheme of things. Everywhere we go and settle, we become like an species ever invasive upon earth

Humankind evolved as a phylogenetic freak of nature, and human civilization has developed as an infection upon the living tissues on the earth's skin. The few brief Millennia that this infection is playing itself out within is but a momentary ecological episode in the natural life span of the earth—an episode that is nonetheless producing catastrophic and long lasting consequences.

Auto-Anthropology

Destruction is always a faster, simpler, more chaotic and easier process than construction. Creation takes time, patience, and trial and error. It is a sign of our earthbound age that despite all our rapid developments of world technological civilization, we are accomplishing in a few brief moments of mad destructiveness what required many millions of years for nature to achieve. We are taking away so much from nature after she has given so much to us.

Our war making tendencies, our violent and aggressive capacities and our basic destructiveness towards nature can only be taken as a sign that as a biological species, we are like children who have not yet grown into our place in the natural scheme of things.

A fully developed species does not destroy its environments because such ecocide leads to destruction of the species as maladapted. A more mature species has incorporated into its nerves and veins the organic experience and evolutionary wisdom of natural karma, and has found and seeks to maintain a fragile balance of power in its universally manifest relation with the natural order of things. The development of our civilization has been but a premature precociousness—as a species we are trying to grow up too fast, and cannot feel at ease in our childlike condition.

It is possible that nature itself is yet young on earth—that in its evolutionary exploration of its own possibilities and limitations, in the dinosaurs, in the great mammals, in humankind, it is slowly and steadily trying out and figuring out the most suitable arrangement and patterning for its myriad diverse elements.

When it hits upon a correct answer—like cockroaches, sharks or other primordial species—then it stops and moves on to the solution to other elements of its grand design. If it frequently makes mistakes, it does not hesitate to tear things back down and start all over again. If this is true, then we must begin to see our own presence and purpose upon the earth as perhaps constrained, ultimately controlled by the designs of nature. Our existential being upon earth may well prove to be extremely tenuous in the long run.

Death is meaningless to nature except as a natural process in the lifespan and realization of forms of life. It is inevitable because it is necessary and so natural. To humankind, death has come to mean everything, as the ultimate thing we cannot avoid no matter how hard we may try to control outcomes. On this basic difference, rests almost all the problems and paradoxes of the human condition on earth and of the unnatural condition of an increasingly, exclusively human world.

Time has been a purely human construction in the natural world. Nature has its rhythms and cycles of birth, regeneration and death, which have been happening time immemorial, but it knows little of the timing, that we ascribe to her. It has its schedules and its seasons, but it has always been a never-ending, continuously changing moment of the present.

Nature remembers little of its own past, and thinks nothing of its own future, except as these become organically incorporated and consequential to the development of its own evolutionary being on earth. Otherwise the pathways and trajectories of past and future have no meaning like what that they have to us. Perhaps we measure time so carefully and exactly because we are so aware of our ultimate mortality and ephemeral presence upon earth, after which time means only nothing.

Auto-Anthropology

We must not underestimate the delicacy of the balances that have evolved in nature. Minor causes regularly lead, however indirectly and extenuated the chain of linkages, to major and long lasting consequences.

The complexity of nature's interconnections, webs of relations and pathways of change are so great and so random as to be completely unpredictable by our science. There is no telling exactly what or how our actions of today will reverberate and resonate upon the earth and rebound upon us tomorrow, eventually and inevitably. We can only be sure in our understanding that consequences will come.

When the earth shakes, the wind blows, the waves rise, and the rains fall, there is little humankind can do to stop it. It is in these moments that we are most reminded of our own being in nature and of our own natural helplessness before the forces and elements of nature. It is in these moments that we are reminded of the real power that moves the world and all things in it. And these moments are also often the most beautiful, resonate and memorable in our lives.

To see our sui generis origins in the earth itself is to remind ourselves of the primordial volcanism and fundamental electromagnetism of our bodies and being. It is possible that our bodies, as all life on earth, has a kind of force field or natural aura of life that all life is sensitive and remotely aware of. The common hysterias of our uncontrolled aggression, violent perversion, and crowd madness may have its roots in the mesmeric power of these autochthonous of life. In our transformation into civilized human beings, we maybe deny and tune out this kind of hypnotic spell of nature, which becomes domesticated and taught to be cast over our being. It is a power that charismatic and violent political leaders have learned to master.

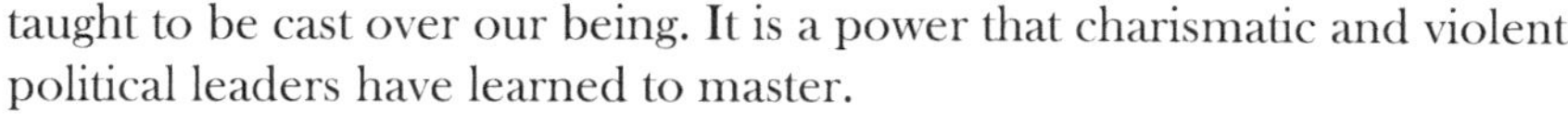

Earthbound is a modern condition of our own existential awareness of and in the human world. It is a collective consciousness of our own ecology of being upon the planet earth. It is a way of discovering ourselves in our natural environment.

Earthbound is a human state of being that has become increasingly bound by the earth. It is a paradox that earthbound being did not really rise in our collective conscience until after humankind first escaped the imprisoning pull of the earth's gravitational field.

The view from space offered humankind a conception of the earth as a lonely and solitary, but beautiful living planet in the vast depths of space. As long as we had our feet firmly planted upon the ground, we took the never-ending boundaries of the earth's horizons for granted.

Now we have only the vast emptiness of space to remind us of our utter isolation in the larger universe.

Like being culture bound, earthbound has come to mean dialectically its own contradiction upon earth—the previous geo-centrism of our imaginations and our conscience in which we saw the earth exclusively in our own terms, put there for the sake of our own development and aggrandizement, has given way to an enlightened appreciation of the importance, and limitations, of the earth as a living space system, an entity itself, in its own right. The paradox of earthbound being has come to ultimately usurp and relativize our own anthropocentric worldview and value orientation toward all life on earth.

Auto-Anthropology

We are no longer the dominant species, the apex of the hierarchical pyramid or the top link of the Great Chain of Being. We are becoming better able to appreciate the point of view and intrinsic importance of all other life forms on earth, especially when our civilization has plotted their destruction and extinction. Other plants and animals have their own separate evolutionary purpose and reason for being on earth that is separate and not subordinate to our own narrow human purposes and designs, and because the water and force of life that flows through all the veins and channels of the earth also flow through our own veins, the loss of any and all life on earth, becomes inevitably our loss as well.

The winds blow for our own common being, and the waves roll and crash upon the rocks with the vitality, that flows through our veins. The distant, strange sounds hidden in the conch shell are the echoes of our own beginning on earth. The yelps and howls of the coyotes in the moonlit night are the beckoning and calling of our own primordial nature. The owl that hoots in the darkness of nights shadow talks of our own shadowy darkness and our own destiny. The silent beauty of a flower and the rolling landscape is the silence of our own death. In everything, Nature calls us back to our own being and our own beginning.

Humankind has become earthbound as never before—the existential uncertainty of our own condition upon earth is the direct consequence of the development of our civilization running head long upon a collision course with our own sense of earthboundness. We may speak of our earthbound karma and our earthbound dharma, our earthbound imperative and our earthbound ecology and ethos, in a relevant way that would have made far less sense even a decade ago, and utter nonsense a century ago.

But now earthbound being is coming to increasingly shape and define our own identity upon the earth and to have an increasing influence upon many elements and relations of our everyday lives. Nothing we do any longer does not have some kind of indirect effect upon our larger world in long chains of relation that we barely comprehend, but we can no longer afford to ignore these indirect kinds of consequences of our daily activities and involvements, as they will eventually come back to haunt and plague us in unexpected ways. The circularity of the earth's surface and the seasonality of life have become our own circularity and our own seasonality.

Earthbound enlightenment is the dawning of a new consciousness in the human world. It is awareness of our environments and of the dependence of the human conditions upon these environments in new and revolutionary ways, ways that our own being and becoming upon earth, in terms of human development, has hardly yet caught up with.

The most valuable resource we now have is the human resource, and the most critical constraint we have upon this resource is the limitation of time. If we can learn to just slow down the pace of our working rhythms and cycles in everything we do, then we can give to ourselves, our children and our world the extra edge of time that is most needed in order for us to resolve our earthbound predicament.

In our earthbound age, less is more, small is beautiful, and the slower the better. There is no need to do today what we can safely put off until tomorrow, or the day after.

Auto-Anthropology

No one really knows what the carrying capacity of the earth really is, or what the long-term promise and potential of our scientific progress will really prove to be. It is too soon to yet tell, but it is certain that the most pressing problem and predicament of our earthbound age is that of global over-population and the corresponding depopulation of the earth of other forms of life.

In bringing evolution on earth to a standstill, is stopping nature's clockwork, and in continuing to reproduce our own kind at an exponentially uncontrolled rate, we are creating for ourselves a global crisis and climax of unprecedented proportions. The prospects of our world cannot be bright if we continue along our way as blindly as we have so far been. It is perhaps too late to reverse the wheels of history or to prevent impending holocaust, but no one has the bottom line on the future of life on earth.

We are upon the verge of a new era, the dawn of a new epoch, the birth of a new age on earth. In the twilight of our earthbound awakening, we do nit yet know if we are at the dawn of a new day or at the dusk of a new night. We can no longer afford our unquestioned old values and worldviews in the same naïve and innocent way as before. We have become bound by the ecological horizons of a round earth. In its roundness, we have always implicitly understood that the earth was a finite resource, even with the infinite progress of our science. Our earthbound awakening is upon us, and it inadvertently influences everything we think and do in our common world. It has come to increasingly frame the external contexts of our everyday life, constraining our beliefs and behaviors in ways, that were rarely understood before now.

Earthbound is the only bottom line of our modern moment and our contemporary human condition. Earthbound being is the key conceptual metaphor of our moment, our nature, our world, the earth and our condition upon it. We might be able to escape the gravitational pull of the earth, but we cannot escape the prospects of our own earthbound being and becoming.

It is not our selves or our father figures, leaders, commanders, statesmen, capitalists, and parental authorities who will inherit the earth ad all the problems of our human world. It will be our children and our grandchildren who will inherit the future earth and who will hold the key to the future of all life on earth. If we cannot instill in them a new respect for all life on earth, including human life, and teach them the lessons we ourselves have learned the hard way, then our failure will become their failure, and we can only blame ourselves for the final scene.

BEING and THE WAY

A bamboo is suppler than a gnarled old limb—the bamboo bends in whichever direction the wind blows, while the limb is sure to break in a heavy storm. But the old twisted limb is sure to make the more dependable walking stick.

Truth resides in the dichotomized whole, and is revealed in the relations between the many parts. The way is always a paradox—a dilemma of alternative avenues, many in different directions.

We seek what we cannot know and we know what we cannot seek.

When we exhaust all our answers, only questions remain. There is no solution that does not give birth to yet a new set of problems.

Every path leads to the way, and the way follows every path.

In a world of proud princes, it is the humble pauper who is king.

In a world of big Chiefs, it is the little brave who would carry the day.

In a world full of captains and commanders, it is the peacemaker who conquers

In a world of the beautiful and sophisticated, it is the plain and simple that is most sublime

In a world full of the unusual and the extreme, it is the commonplace and average that is most outstanding

In a world of prophets and visionaries, it is the blind mute who points the way.

In a world full of many winners, it is the loser who counts success as a lesson well learned.

In a world full of complicated words, it is the simple deed that speaks the loudest.

Nothing is, that also is not. Everything that seems to be, is really something else. The art of living is always an art of indirection, and the way of life is never a straight line.

It wasn't until I walked the way of the world that I came to understand how much of a homebody I really had been. But, upon returning home, I soon realized how much of a discontent wanderer I had also become.

A never-ending source of paradox is that although our illusions must always be dispelled, our life is full of illusion that sustains us in the darkness of disillusionment.

The way lies in waiting for the hapless wanderer who comes stumbling along searching for it. It is ever patient and ever present and ever silent. It never tells the wanderer when or if the wanderer has found it.

There is only one way, though it comes from many corners of the world and leads in many directions. If you happen to meet someone along the way going in the opposite direction as yourself, neither traveler is wrong. Both are just upon different parts of the same path.

The way that is, is never the way. The way that isn't, is always the way. Neither this way nor that way is the way, nor is the other way. The way that isn't the way always winds between the other ways.

The way has no beginning and no end, but is always between both beginning and end. It is an eternally moving moment that never comes to rest. To follow along the way is to make a journey without ever reaching the journey's end. The destination of the journey is to be found along the way.

There is no wrong way, because there is no right way. There is no best way, because there is no worst way. There is only one way, but it leads in an infinite number of difficult directions. Though there are an infinite number of directions, they all lead in the same way. We cannot lose the way that we cannot find—we can only lose the way that can be found.

The way always leads in only one direction, and the way is without any one direction. We cannot turn back along the directionless way. The way is always forward, though there are many dead ends. The directionless way is always long and winding, twisting and turning in many directions, and though each direction is the way, the way remains only one directionless direction.

To follow the way is to lead the way is to follow the way is to lead the way.... until we've finally lost our way. And once having lost the way, then we will finally find it. And finding it, then we eventually lose it forever.

The directionless direction cannot be found by any map or compass. It is the direction that the wind blows and the water flows. It is the direction that the earth moves through the universe, and the direction the human takes through the forest. The way is always a grand circle within a circle, encompassing yet other circles. The directionless direction of the way is infinitely roundabout and circular.

We cannot ever change our way, though the way is always changing. The power of the way is its paradox, and the paradox of the way is its power. The direction without direction leads in all directions and yet goes nowhere. The directionless direction leads nowhere, and yet can be found everywhere. It is somewhere and anywhere. And there is here and this is that.

Auto-Anthropology

The way is silent, and silence is to be found along the way. Words are like stones in the way—they mark the path but make the path difficult to follow. Words are strung together by silence and the way of silence is strewn with words. Words may need the way, but the way does not need words.

The wise person knows the way though s/he has never seen it. The fool is blind to the way though s/he may have long lived beside it.

The way passes through this world, but is not of this world. It is of another world. This world is full of petty people who think they are important, but travelers along the way are few and far between. The way begins at the end of the world, and the world begins at the end of the way.

The way ends at the end of the day. The way is not a matter of distance, but of duration. It is not a sense of place, but one of process. Where the sun rises, that is where the way begins.

The moon is a bridge for the night. The moon is a night-light upon our pathway between dusk and dawn. Wherever we are at night, the moon waxes and wanes upon our shoulders.

Night overshadows the way, and clouds our senses. We fear the night because we lose our way, led only by moonlight.

To lead the way is to follow the way. To follow the way is to lead the way. To see the way is to seek the way. To seek the way is to see the way. To find the way is to lose the way. To lose the way is to find the way. To learn the way is to travel the way. To travel the way is to learn the way.

Like a long tunnel that never ends, the way always leads through darkness to a distant source of light. Which star in the nighttime sky is not the way?

We cannot ever know what is in the minds of others, but only what is in our own minds. We can know what is in our minds only imperfectly and with uncertainty, for our minds area always playing tricks upon us and fooling us—hiding and changing. And if our minds are always hiding and changing, then knowing the minds of others is thus doubly treacherous. It is a miraculous wonder that we may know anything at all except our own illusion.

Humanness is the source of our being, and our being is the source of our humanness. As human beings, the evolution of our experience and the experience of our evolution has gone hand-in-hand with the creation of the uniqueness and paradox of our condition.

Auto-Anthropology

With each new generation born, this evolutionary experience of humanity is recreated and relived in both the parents and their children. As such, our species are but one linkage in a long chain that stretches back time immemorial to the very beginning of life on earth. And each generation is the next and newest link, in that long, long chain with billions of links.

Being is a frame of mind and mind is a state of being. It follows that if the sense of being is environmental in nature, then so too are the senses of the mind. Both mind and being are organically rooted in the evolutionary experience of the natural world.

Being is always decentered. As such it chronically lacks the sense of balance that only comes from the possession of the center. Being is always upon the outside looking in, and never upon the inside looking out. The state of being and the frame of mind of the view from the inside is fundamentally different from the sense of being of the view from the outside.

The view from the outside is subject to the vicissitudes and vagaries of nature—to its changes of weather and the predation of the wild. It suffers the cold and wet of winter and the heat and sun of summer. The view from the inside is one based upon the control of nature, the protection from elemental forces and hazards. It is an artificial point of view.

The sense of being is not to be gained through vicarious experience.

Vicariousness substitutes illusion for the reality of being. It is difficult not to live vicariously in a world that so conditions our experiences by vicariousness and illusion, by hedonism and fantasy rather than refrain and concreteness.

The existential problematic of modern living is not the same imperative of survival that made earlier humankind's sense of being in the world so sharp and acute.

It has become the imperative of learning to live non-vicariously by seeing through the illusions that come between our experiences of the world and our own sense of being in the world. It has become the imperative of recovering a lost sense of being in our world from the flood of illusions that inundates our experiences.

Being begins in the bare bones of basic experience. The raw state of its reality works its way from the surface of our skin deep down underneath like an infection that spreads throughout the body. Being begins in honesty. It is free of illusion because it cannot lie. It ends always with the equi-finality of our own mortality.

Along the way of being, we give up our innocence for wisdom. Being does not come with disillusionment, but before the illusion. Disillusionment suffers the loss of being upon the road to becoming. It represents a return to the place where we started, with the experience of what was left behind, without the original innocence with which we started.

Our return to natural being can never be complete. It must always entail a sense of loss, of imperfection, of unfinished business, and of unfulfilled feelings. The recovery of our own natural innocence can only be had through the discovery of the darkness of our own hearts from which the

possibility of our disillusionment and the disillusionment of our
possibility both spring simultaneously.

Nonbeing is to be found in the denial of death, as something dark,
unnatural and evil. Being is to be found in the embrace of the existential
inevitability of death, in our ephemeral presence, momentary, our
fleeting experiences of life, and final mortality of our own existence.

Being begins in the experience of death and ends in the experience of
birth. In each birth is the beginning of another death, and in every death
is the ending of another birth. We cannot be and deny our own mortality
at the same time, not without illusion and self-deception.

Our being in the world has become increasingly defined and constrained
by the earthboundness of our contemporary condition on earth. Because
we cannot escape our earthbound being, we cannot escape the existential
consequences of its ecological imperative upon our lives.

It is a paradox that the salvation of our own being in the world is based
upon and in turn forms the basis of the salvation of our world itself, just
as the destruction of our world is rooted in and leads to the destruction
of our own sense of being in the world. Human reality and being are
inextricably related with its earthbound environment. Human destiny will
be the fate of the earth, our fate the destiny of the earth for when we are
bound and ultimately dependent.

The way changes with the world. What it was yesterday is not what it will become tomorrow. Today it takes us this way, and tomorrow it will take us that way. The way is always some other way.

The way is not well served by hurrying along without smelling the flowers and not appreciating the picturesque sites along the path. The way is therefore always slow and steady, sometimes stopping and often turning. It is made for walking and not for running.

We may sleep and rest, and yet still journey along the way. Our dreams area always journeys along the way. We may spend all the days of our lives working and traveling to one place or another, and yet never once make a single step along the way. We may journey along the way by standing still, without traveling anywhere, and we may move unendingly and yet go nowhere. The way moves mountains closer to our feet, but it does not move our feet closer to the mountains.

The way is always the vision of a mountaintop hovering above our horizon, and it always leads through a dense and dark forest that never seems to end. The way ends at a still and silent lake at the bottom of a mountain valley that is hidden somewhere in the forest. When we come to the end of the way, we will know its view not from the mountaintop but by the clearness of its reflection upon the surface of the water.

Auto-Anthropology

Of the many different paths to follow, which way on earth does not eventually lead back home to where we began?

All ways lead finally to the same end—that is death.

If there is a will, there is a way. The heart can have only one master, but the way can have many hearts. Being serves the human, the human serves the will, the will serves the heart, the heart serves the way, and the way serves the being. To follow the way is to lead the way, and the way always leads from and back to being human.

ODDS and ENDS
(Children, Migration, Mixed Marriage and other Marginalia)

I find most children quite interesting and enjoyable. It is their parents whom I find too snobby even to say hello, and too hung up on their own egos to really enjoy life. It is too bad so many children have so little choice in the matter of their parents.

Growing up is learning one has choices to make. Better to remain an eternal child than to have to become a frustrated and repressed adult.

In their innocence, children are without the pretensions of the adult world. In their ignorance of the world, they are without the prejudices that make the adults so sure of their world.

It is the natural openness and unabashed inquisitiveness that makes childhood such an interesting period of life. Children do not become embarrassed or ashamed of themselves as adults have learned to become, though they may be shy or become confused. Children meet the world with one hundred percent of their being, adults with less than half.

Auto-Anthropology

The world of the child is not just a simpler version of the world of the adult. It is a different kind of world in which the quality of experience is very alien to the adult world. Children do not make the kind of normal distinctions that so order the adult world and that are usually taken for granted. For a child, it is very possible that a dinosaur could be in the backyard, or that Bambi can be in Snow White's forest. Cartoons, in their Carroll like animation of normally inanimate objects, capture some of the sense of the child's reality very clearly.

It was not until I became a father that I really grew up. It is not until people have children of their own and become full-time parents that they become full-fledged adults, and give up the illusionary vanities of their own lost youth for the sake of their children's future adulthood.

My daughter has taught me so many things I never really understood before. She has taught me the joy of simple pleasures seemingly inane from the adult point of view. She has taught me the meaning of patience, tolerance, responsibility and selflessness. She has taught me the true meaning of love, friendship and companionship. Most importantly, she has taught me many of the neat things of my own childhood that I had somehow forgotten in my struggle to grow up.

Children learn about the adult world by tearing everything they can touch down to their own level. By tearing apart the adult world, they are learning how to eventually put it all back together again. Though they may make many mistakes, they will also compose a new sense of order much different, and in many ways, far better than the world of their parents.

Mixed marriage really puts to the test the faith that, in the face of universal human nature, differences of gender, class, nation, "race," culture, language, and history are of little importance. We frequently fail this test in our own faith.

When we were first married in my wife's homeland, rumors spread quickly that I was a "California Abalone Diver," or a "Confidence Trickster," or a "C.I.A. agent," but nobody ever came forward to see if these claims were true or false. The people who started some of these rumors were people bent on exploiting my wife for her money and labor before she married me.

Being married to a Chinese wife has often reaffirmed my faith in anthropology. Chinese are not so different from Americans, as both can be rude, mean, selfish, prejudiced and ignorant.

Though there is little romance about mixed marriage, romance is sometimes the only common illusion that will save the marriage.

Auto-Anthropology

Mixed marriage is a funny situation, everyone seems curious about you, but after their curiosity is satisfied, they seem to feel uncomfortable to be around you. Being married to a person from another culture is to live between two cultures, and to become a full member of neither one. It is truly being an odd couple. About the only way out of this situation is to become quite wealthy, and then you can become honorary and privileged citizens of either culture, rather than just outcast pariahs.

There are some facets of my wife's Chinese character that I shall probably never really understand. There are some traits of my own that I have little doubt seem quite strange and abominable to her. These differences can sometimes be quite subtle and on the surface at least be covered over by similar resemblance, but they can often become major stress points in the relationship for the slightest, most petty reasons.

When you are an odd couple, everyone stares but few speak, and though everyone is quite polite, few are very friendly. So many who think they are superior to you for some reason or the other can become quite rude and arrogant towards you. Everyone talks behind your back, and few talk in front of your face.

Our daughter, the product of "miscegenation," knows little about the differences between "Chinese" or "American." If left on her own she and her kind would quickly create a new hyphenated "Creole" culture that was genuinely "Chinese American," and perhaps she really will anyway in spite of her parents' purposes and prejudices. It is good to know that, though she will never be just one or the other, she will always have a choice between both worlds. When she fills out an employment application form, she can check herself off as either one or the other, or as nothing at all, or as just another human being.

* * *

Mixed couples are citizens of a country of their own making. It is a country whose only territorial boundaries are the earth's oceans that separate foreign shores. It is a "multi-cultural" society in which racial differences are effectively undermined and serve no obvious purposes.

* * *

My Chinese-American daughter is living proof that the ideology of racial purity is a myth that defies the natural reason of evolution. She has brown hair, almond eyes, tan skin, my wife's toes, and my stubborn disposition, and she is about as cute as can be. She is the proverbial dragon girl.

* * *

Our Chinese-American daughter shares the best and worst of both worlds, and she will be free to choose between them.

* * *

Mixed marriage and children of miscegenation form a new racial and ethnic category in the world that has little to do with any previous distinctions. When the world becomes one, people will be free to move about as they please and to marry only those who come closest to their hearts. Their children will inherit citizenship to the world and the keys to the future.

Auto-Anthropology

The migration experience involves an unending sense of personal displacement and estrangement in a foreign land that is often threatening and sometimes hostile. The migrant never fully resolves these feelings, but represses them in the interest of adapting to demanding new situations. The migrant longs for a return to their homeland like an old person longs for lost youth, or an adult longs to return to childhood, or an unhappy "has been" longs to return to a more glorious past. It is in the existential paradox of the migrant's life that the world that used to be "home" will have subsequently changed in such a way that things no longer seem the same and there is little room remaining in which to fit.

Immigrants find themselves fitting in nowhere in the world, even if they wish to they couldn't comfortable return back home, even though many do anyway.

The child migrant has adapted to the new environment as if it were their home. Lacking the experience and wisdom of the old world, these children grow up to out-perform their parents in a world that's largely taken for granted. This is often the source of an intense kind of generational conflict.

Migration has been the rule, and not the exception of human history. Migration has been going on time immemorial. The portrayal of humankind as permanently settled in one local region and as homebound in worldview defies the anthropological wisdom of human culture history.

Humankind has long been getting around and mixing things up much more than we, in our semi-sedentary existence, would give them credit. The rise of human civilization has always depended as much upon the exogenous influences of trading, trafficking and traveling, as it has upon locating the individual to a permanent and fixed place, especially for purposes of taxation.

Human beings are prone to move about and to be over the long term quite transient, because the grass always seems greener on the other side and in their perennial unhappiness they are always left unsatisfied and unfulfilled by what they have in their present circumstances. This need to move on is fundamental to human nature, ingrained in our evolutionary experience. It has been time immemorial since we rose up on two legs to walk and descended from the trees to run long distances.

There is a tendency for a host society to exploit, ridicule, discriminate against, take advantage of, and to stereotype the newest immigrant. Immigrants are often seen as childish, ignorant, barbaric, dirty, dangerous and immoral, and even though they often begin at the bottom of the social ladder, they are seen as a political-economic threat to the status quo. This kind of paranoia toward the newcomer happens even among people who were them-selves previous newcomers. Everyone at some point in history has descended from migrants.

The American Academic and Professional "Brain Drain" has been going on for a long time and represents a curious kind of conspiracy of an international class of intellectuals that neatly cross-cuts other racial or ethnic or national or class or gender boundaries.

If America used to be the land of the free and the home of the brave, it has since become the marketplace of the international elite and the technocracy of the professional class.

If there have been many ugly Americans abroad, there have since been many "ugly Foreigners" in America, with the only thing being on their minds their getting ahead at everyone else's expense.

Auto-Graphs
Autobiographical Aphorisms

Hugh Lewis

The Universe

We cannot imagine an infinite system that extends forever in all directions. We can imagine a finite system, but we cannot imagine what lies beyond that system, even if in truth and fact the cosmos appears thus endless and infinite in scale.

Infinity of the universe is a question we may never scientifically answer.

There are imponderable questions in science that we must nevertheless try to think about and take into account, even if we cannot sufficiently answer them one way or another.

The dilemma of being human is the dilemma of being aware of not just our own existence, but of the existence of the entire universe, and of our diminutive place in that vast world.

The universe, as vast as it is, happens instantaneously, everywhere at once. Not just this, but it happens instantaneously, everywhere at once, upon multiple, possibly infinite levels, at the same "time" even if this time is relative and not simultaneous.

An object of mass moving in space will travel forever in precisely the same direction, until acted upon by some external counter-force. We may call this perpetual motion.

Auto-Anthropology

The only perpetual motion on earth that is possible is the motion of the earth itself.

Just as we have a paradigm of thermodynamics that is inviolable, so also are there other inviolable paradigms governing motion, gravitation and information in the universe and that are equally inviolable.

The paradigm of motional dynamics for instance tells us that all motion is essentially chaotic and it takes energy to change the trajectory of an object in a desired direction. It also assures us that there is no object or force that is without motion and therefore discrete finite direction.

It is something of a grand paradox that the deeper in space we peer through our earthbound telescopes, the deeper back in time we may see, but though the Cosmological Principle by logical extension promises us a simultaneous universe out there in the universal "Now" (general relativistic considerations not withstanding) the further in depth we look, the less we can know what the universe looks like in any instantaneous sense.

Thus it is a paradox that we may see the universe depth of time, but never in depth of instantaneous space.

There is nothing in the universe, either of force or mass that is not in constant, continuous motion through the universe. Absolute rest, like absolute zero, is a physical impossibility. What is even more strange seeming is that the same object, as part of larger gravitationally unified systems in relative equilibrium, may actually be moving in complex trajectories described by multiple motions and directions at the same time.

An object may be traveling at hundreds of thousands of kilometers per hour and yet in motional equilibrium everything will appear at rest.

It is a grand paradox that we can know possibly what happened to a distant star ten billion years ago, but we cannot know what is happening to that star ten billion light-years away at this very moment.

It is most likely that the Universe is both infinite and eternal, though it has never ever had the same disposition consistently forever. We know this intuitively and by logical deduction by the dynamic principles that govern instantaneous energy transactions in the universe. However large a system we may imagine, that system of finite size will be part of a larger super-system that I call meta-system, within which its environmental interactions are governed by these energy transactions. Because we cannot imagine this never to be the case, therefore the Universe must be open, infinite and non-zero (eternal) state. It is continually forever changing.

If all the matter in the universe were collected into a huge ball, perhaps this ball might constitute zero percent of a total open and infinite universe of zero state.

Imagine all the grains of sand and all the rocks on earth—however numerous of finite number, and yet no two are exactly the same, each unique, across the multiple dimensions by which we may describe the specimen and other different specimen as "rocks" or as "grains of sand."

The paradox is that if the universe is open and infinite, then probably there are infinite numbers of rocks and grains of sand in that universe, no two of which are exactly identical upon its several dimensions of description. Each of an infinite set, would still be unique unto itself as a system or a product of a larger system.

An infinite set can still be a small subset of a much larger infinite set. Perhaps we can only express and describe this relationship between infinite sets and relative subsets on a percentage basis or as a dynamic ratio, except that we cannot know how large either set or subset really is. In fact, an infinite number of subsets may be contained within a larger super-set. In such a manner we can speak legitimately of infinite infinities.

An infinite universe is without edge, without center, without beginning and with no ending. A dynamic state universe is one that is ever changing from one state into another, but it remains forever infinite. Presumably, at a cosmological scale, there are no preferred motions or directions or larger orientations. In this manner perhaps we may speak of the universal relativity of an infinite universe.

The truly grand paradox of an infinite universe is that it may be infinite in an infinite number of different ways. We may speak of the universe occurring infinitesimally microscopic, or small, occurring on an infinite number of levels of size. We may also speak of a universe or "poly-verse" that is cast in an infinite number of higher dimensions.

The truly grand paradox of such an infinitely infinite "meta-verse" may be that for all its mysterious endlessness, all systems within it are finite and all systems have a beginning and an end, even if these systems constitute in the large and the long run infinite sets.

An infinitely infinite universe therefore can accommodate an infinite amount of matter and still remain for all intents and purposes mostly infinite space.

It may come as little surprise that humankind has now discovered multiple stellar systems with many different arrangements of planets and moons around one, two or even three or more gravitationally unified star systems. Perhaps it may actually come as little surprise to find living systems quite prolifically upon these different exo-planetary systems, and that, somewhere, very far away, living systems will have evolved other intelligent life forms capable of symbolic and scientific technological civilization. They may just be so far away that we cannot directly communicate with them except in the past tense. If nothing else this must speak for the fundamental sense of isolation of humankind upon earth, and therefore for the fundamental preciousness and potential fragility of the earth as a unique system within a larger universe.

The molecules and elements of the earth could only have been forged in some previous stellar furnace that had long ago become radioactively cooled off and that much longer ago became extinct as an active star.

That we find a large range of the atoms of the periodic table represented in the mineral content of the earth, suggesting that the typical earth type composition, presumably commonplace in the Milky Way, came originally from a common type of star system. We perhaps do not understand very well how this may be the case.

Gravitational dynamic? Perhaps universally gravity and gravitational systems follow certain paradigmatic and inviolable laws in which all objects are in a state of motion but seek a state of absolute rest that can never be achieved. The most that is achieved is a relative state of gravitational equilibrium, whether single body or multiple body systems.

Can we imagine the possibility of space-time itself being thicker in its intrinsic flow the stronger the gravitational field, and thinner where gravitational fields are weaker?

From the standpoint of gravitational dynamics, it is not just that the sun and earth and other astronomical bodies are in perpetual motion until disruption or collision, but also that single body systems like the sun or the earth produce internally their own heat as a result of unending gravitational pressures and forces impinging on a single discrete point that in larger black-hole formations becomes a singularity. Can we imagine the possibility of the systematic and instantaneous conversion of gravitational energy by some unknown pathway or mechanism into heat and light energy that in an object the size of the sun, becomes nuclear

Auto-Anthropology

plasma, while in the earth, becoming liquid or even gaseous heavy elements?

I suspect our Sun has output in its lifetime far more energy and nucleonic material in terms of net mass than was originally contained within the Sun itself. It is possible its total output of energy and mass to match its own mass occurs in much shorter cycles than we may think. In short, the gravitation of the sun is so great that it not only replaces its own mass in shorter, fairly even cycles, but during that cycle outputs far greater total net mass and energy than is available through fusion/fission reactions within the Sun.

Undoubtedly the Sun creates an extremely stable and almost endless system of energy production. Such a solar system maintains its own gravitational equilibrium as such gravitational pressures serve to resist the expansion of the star, maintaining a rather stable size and configuration. It strikes me that, as a star may grow older, it becomes gradually hotter at its core, such that early nuclear reactions that fused hydrogen/helium into variations of lithium, nitrogen and oxygen, later resulted in the fusion of these nuclei into heavier and heavier elements.

There emerges thus a small very dense core of high atomic number matter but the overall system is less massive than before and is in retrograde. Such a solar system perhaps will lose proportionately a significant amount of its own mass and with diminishing gravitational pressures begin rapid expansion of gaseous and less heavy nucleonic material in its pen-ultimate phase such that its nuclear reactions become largely expired, though it remains radioactively hot for many "half-lives" to come.

At this stage, perhaps, most of its lighter hydrogen-helium fuel that is not bound up in heavier molecular-mineral structures, however molten or gaseous, becomes lost into the surround manifold of space, perhaps the majority of this lighter material blown off in a final massive explosion that produces a smaller, denser and solid core as a stellar remnant.

A small heavy element core at the center of a Sun-sized star may gradually grow in size in relation to the outer lighter element layers. High gravitational pressures found to increase toward the core might permit the fusion of heavier elements.

Self and Society

It is power that speaks loudest that always does the final talking--that carries the day. Power rules as much as it corrupts.

Sense of self cannot be gained outside of some sense of society. Self and society go hand-in-hand and as symbolic constructions reinforce and contextualize one another. Without sense of self, society is an insect colony, a living dystopia. Without sense of society, self is nothing but an unfinished monster, a perpetual child pretending to be an adult.

Power always carries the day, even if in the long run it is the powerless that prevail.

Sense of self is many different things at many different times, all brought together by a single name and a single sense of continuity of experience we call life.

The self always sits in ambiguous and potentially conflicting relationship with the society within which the self is situated. It is presumed that the healthiest sense of self is most symmetrical to the social identity prescribed by the society to the individual, or that is achieved by the individual as a course of appropriate and conventional institutional interaction within that society. But we must somehow account for the possibility that not all societies are not only not equal, but most are also maybe not equally healthy or adaptive in their human development institutionalization and socialization. What I mean goes something like this:

In an insane society the healthy person will appear at odds with the society.

In a sane society an unhealthy person will be at odds with the society.

How do we measure the relative healthiness of a given society? Any such measure must of course be relative to the value systems normatively promoted by such a society, but science provides us with at least one kind of solution. Certainly what would be healthy in the context of Mainland China under communist rule would not be considered altogether healthy in the context of Great Britain or the United States society, and vice versa.

Can my chosen field of anthropology provide a panhuman normative solution to this kind of complex dilemma of values and outcomes? Can we look more broadly to related fields of psychology and sociology for further support?

We can presuppose certain basic principles common to all humankind in spite of their ethno-national and ethno-cultural diversities. All people are of a single species, Homo sapiens, and thus are more or less the same on a general continuum of inherent human variability.

Self and society interact from birth to death in an existential dialectic. Self externalizes itself as an identity construct of the society, while Society internalizes itself within the Self primarily through the process of socialization as a sense of super-ego and character.

Ego is the result of this dialectic, and if healthy will be defined by its sense of equilibrium and balance between self-orientation and social orientation. We expect a consonance, a resonance and a constructive interaction that we call symmetrical and balanced.

Both internalized character and social identity are constructs of this dialectic between self and Society.

Auto-Anthropology

Science & Systems

In terms of the elaboration of systems, there seems yet a place for the philosopher in the elucidation of our world, and it is clear that without philosophy, the sciences are normally narrow-minded and shallow in their range.

Philosophers ask new questions of reality, while scientists mostly seek answers to problems already posed. There are many questions, it seems, that scientists fail to ask and many problems philosophers have failed to pose.

Philosophy is more relevant today than at anytime in the past—the main problem seems to be that we lack a philosophy of complexity that the modern world presents to us at every turn. The Ancient Greek Philosopher's who reasoned so clearly about their world would find the mansion of modern philosophy a candy-shop for children's delight and imagination.

The final answers to the universe and our shared reality will not be discovered at the end of a telescope, but realized from the seat of a philosopher's armchair, for only the human mind can see beyond where light or direct experience cannot reach.

We must live with several grand paradoxes—we are always prisoners of our own minds, and we cannot ever hope to escape this prison state except by the exercise of our imaginations.

Though our imaginations are necessarily blind, it is only by means of our imagination that we can see beyond the boundaries of our own mind.

We can never hope to see beyond the boundaries of our own minds, or to know more than what our minds may know, except by means of our imaginations.

To crush a child's imagination is to stem and cut-short the development of all that is highest and greatest about being human.

To say "human being" is a bit of a misnomer, rather it is more apt to say: "human becoming."

The greatest human virtue is rooted in the most basic of human vices-- for only honesty allows us to see the world without illusion, as it really is, and honesty is born of the acknowledgement and awareness of the possibility for dishonesty and prevarication.

Human intelligence is rooted in our capacity to tell lies in a way so convincing that we even fool ourselves.

Scientists are normally strong in their methods but just as often weak in their theories. Scientists are taught more to act according to the standards and strictures of their specific fields, as experts, than to think in an independent manner.

Independent thinking is the only form of thinking that conceives new ideas and creates new theories. Independent thinking is based upon independent living and acting. The mind cannot be truly independent if the body is made a slave of the whims of others.

Auto-Anthropology

Science normally falters and fails at the edge of the unknown—the trouble with the edge of the unknown is that its boundaries and configurations are not known.

Much that today passes for truth and fact will tomorrow pass away as fiction and fantasy, and much that passes today as fiction and fantasy will tomorrow become the true and factual reality.

Science seeks normally symbolic closure on its world just as if it were a religion—that closure will not be had until science fully embraces general systems theory as the rational extension of science. But science cannot answer these religious questions without becoming an ideology: i.e., a pseudo-science in service of close-minded, self-perpetuating interests.

Systems is more than just about technological application of scientific knowledge to real problem sets, especially those problems that are super-complex, multivariate and without finite solution sets.

Humankind may adapt as a species better to the global future of the Hominid Era of Earth if and when people learn to think more adaptively in terms of systems solutions to common problems confronted by humankind.

This is happening anyway but not in a manner coordinated. Systems are neutral, they are value free, and they apply equally well or poorly for all interested customers. Systems permit planning a future that we have never before known—the possibility of logical sustainability and perpetuity, as well as the prospect of a "more for less" fundamental energy revolution.

To think in terms of systems is to think laterally rather than linearly, and to act diagonally rather than in a purely horizontal or vertical manner.

Just because we cannot see it doesn't mean it isn't there, especially if the reason and logic of our knowledge tells us it must be so. Science has developed more on the basis of the invisible truth than on the basis of the visible untruth.

The entire universe, objective reality as we can see, infer and understand it, seems entirely constituted by systems at every level, section and scale of our observation.

Systems appear to occur naturally as a result of stochastic self-organization, and account for both the order and chaos of our natural world.

In fact, from a scientific standpoint there is nothing we can see or touch that is not a part or a product of some kind of system, not just of a system, but more importantly of systems within systems constituted by other systems and all somehow working in coordination, or otherwise, to produce observable effects.

Life and Philosophy

Death is the mother of beauty—tragedy is the godparent of Life

---

Life is a big distraction, but better a lifetime of distraction than an eternity of oblivion.

Life is learning to make the most of what death gives to us.

The world disdains a realist, but hates an idealist. There is no corner or quarter left for the hapless idealist. What the world loves best is the illusionist, however short-lived the effects and long lasting the consequences.

Death is the price we must pay for life. It is only tragic when it must be paid up front, too early. The death of others in the world, and other beings, always reminds us of our own mortality and our own final appointment with our fate.

If death is the mother of beauty, it must be the case that life is the mother of all philosophy. It was Socrates who stated that a man is either happily married or else he is a philosopher. Perhaps philosophy is what we resort to when life doesn't work out as expected.

Anthropology and Humanity

Better the enemy you know than the friend you don't know.

The human propensity to the abuse of petty power always prevails in the construction of every circumstance—the challenge is for us to recognize, and deal by ourselves, this propensity, as it exists in others.

I have no friends, and no enemies. I have only many acquaintances who might at one moment are a friend and at the next, become an enemy.

It is not a question of loving or hating anyone in the world, but only of learning how to deal effectively with them in spite of our feelings one way or the other.

Keep one's friends at arm's length and one's enemies embraced.

Humanity is a double-edged word—humans are both good and bad. It is always important to find the good in people, in spite of their bad points, but it is more important never to forget the possibility of their bad sides in spite of their best traits.

I had one true friend once, but I can hardly remember his name any longer.

Auto-Anthropology

It is not so much that other people disappointment me, but that I disappoint myself in having too high expectations of others and not high enough expectations of myself. I think these things go hand in hand--how we see others is often the mirror image, of how we see ourselves.

It is as important to always forgive, no matter what, as it is never to forget what the mess was in the first place.

We, as a human civilization, no matter the ethno-nationality, will always need a military to protect us from the foreign aggression of others, and a constabulary to protect others from ourselves.
It is always better to forgive than to forget.

It took me at least sixty years to figure out the value of forgiveness—For most of my life I carried on the back of my shoulders a cangue of my own device, a resentment of past wrongs without justice, blaming others for its design and function in my life. I have only now myself to blame, casting off the cangue from my shoulders. It is never too late until we are passed finally.

Art

There is no portrait that is not an artist's self-portrait. It is no one detail of the face, but all the details of the painting put together that gives away the true sense of self.

Style is the gestalt of the hidden, silent, subconscious self.

Skill in draftsmanship or in formal design does not make a great artist-- great art comes from the soul of the self and reaches for the souls of others.

Art is the visual language of the subconscious self—it is a window upon our dream world.

A life without art is a life bereft of sublime meaning or true purpose--it is a life lived in the shallows.

I do art for the saneness it brings to an otherwise seemingly insane world.

My art need make no sense to anyone but myself—as long as it makes sense to me it seems appropriate to call it "art."

My art has expressed itself in many forms throughout my life, through my painting, my woodworking, my gardening, and my writing. Nowhere

Auto-Anthropology

has it been better expressed than through my family and through learning to deal well and gracefully with others in the world.

Composing and executing a painting allows me the private time and space to put back together a myriad range of feelings and experience otherwise shattered upon the rocks and shoals of our everyday world.

A life without art is an empty life, a hole in the soul, a sense of spirit bereft of a sense of self.

I no longer seek reasons for my art, or to justify my art except to say that is what I do and why I do it.

The art of political extremism, either right or left, is propaganda of the ugliness of humanity—it is art for politics sake, and politics for art sake.

An artist is deprecated in the modern world for the stereotype of disconformity, poverty and isolation. The general deprecation of the artist is a measure of how far we yet need to goo to achieve civilization, as at the heart of the matter we are all artists beneath our clothes.

Education and Development

The child is the reflection of the parent, and the parent is the reflection of the child: the teacher is the reflection of both. To the student, the teacher is a parent--to the parent, the teacher is still a child.

Formal education is the bureaucracy of knowledge; Educational administration is the bureaucracy of the bureaucracy of knowledge. One should not look for new and fresh talent in the gated alabaster cemetery of old ideas.

State education is a large siphon of a redistributive economy--it trickles in small amounts down to the individual teacher alone in the classroom, after having passed through many hands and pockets.

A mentor is elected, not selected. Selecting a mentor is sort of like planning to be spontaneous--it just doesn't come off the right way.

Serendipity and curiosity go hand-in-hand in a life of learning—a willingness to take chances, to try new things and to expose one weakness to the unknown and untried entails an openness to new experience and open-mindedness to new ways of seeing the world.

In life, by far, we are our own worst enemies, and, hopefully, our own best friends. It is a case of striking a peace accord with one's own nature-- making allies of potential adversaries, and learning to live with one's sketchy track record.

Reading is the key to all knowledge—literacy, whether traditional or digital, forms the foundation for civilization. Reading unlocks the treasure chest of knowledge and the acquired experience and accumulated wisdom of the ages.

I've been a student all my life, and as a teacher, I am still my own best student. I will learn to be a good teacher just about the time I'm ready to retire and step from this mortal coil.

Development proceeds inexorably upon its own timetable, whether we wish it to or not—it does not wait for the lazy or the sleepy. Time coerces all of us in the same way, and it is really the only resource we have to share in the world.

The greatest gift we can give to others is the gift of our time--it is most important that others not take this gift for granted, as has happened so much in the past, but to try to make the most of that gift for yet others in the future.

In a digital knowledge economy, students must teach the teacher, who are invariably too slow to catch on before it all changes yet again. This is what the information revolution really means, besides students who are bored with traditional teaching methods.

I have found little satisfaction, and even less happiness, in being a teacher. The pay is poor, the hours on one's feet long, and the respect non-existent.

It is good to learn by our own mistakes, and to allow someone the freedom to learn by their mistakes, but it is even better to learn by other's mistakes and to allow them the discipline to be taught by those mistakes.

No one can be a better teacher to a person than that person oneself. The openness to learn by our own mistakes, to be taught by our own life lessons, is what defines us as human, and what separates us from the rest of the animal kingdom. In this regard, a teacher is more a facilitator than an instructor.

Environment & the World

We have come in the first decades of the 21ˢᵗ Century to more acutely and more commonly realize our vital natural attachments to the world and its natural environments.

There are few if any pristine, untouched natural or primordial environments left on earth. Human dominance has meant that what remains of nature is being increasingly shaped into human dimensions.

We are living in the biological age of the 7ᵗʰ known mass extinction, truncating millions of years of speciation and evolution into a few millennia of drastic change, global habit disruption and loss, witnessed by the rise of human cultural civilization on a global level.

This may well be the final mass extinction upon earth, after which life on earth recedes into hidden nooks and crannies of a depleted earth.

Until humankind organizes globally as a single species amongst all the other species of life on earth, life on earth, including life of Homo sapiens, has little chance of long-term survival.

It would be tragic beyond all proportion for the whole universes indeed, for our grandchildren too have to bear with the final destruction of life on earth, including the destruction of human civilization.

Why do we take our own future so much for granted; perhaps because we take our lost history so much for granted.

History & the Past

Peace is the pursuit of war by other means. War is the pursuit of peace by other means—war and peace are the teeth and tail of the same creature that chases its own tail never to catch it.

History lessons from the past are the epitaphs on forgotten gravestones, unless they can be applied meaningfully to the present in anticipation of the future.

Those who repeat the mistakes of history are bound and determined to forget those lessons along the way.

In history, the winner always takes all, and the loser is bound for the anonymity of the forgotten grave.

No history is complete or finished as a story of the past, only ever part true. History lessons are just forgotten, their reminders only archaeological remnants in the drifting sand.

History is an inveterately human affair. Recording and retelling history is a preoccupation of humankind alone in the larger cosmos.

FINI

Indie Alternative Anthropology

Auto-Anthropology
Auto-Anthropology (1992-1998)
A Room In China (2000)
It Makes a Difference (1990)

Anthropological Essays
Anthropological Aesthetics, Rationality,
Ideology & Humanity (1982-1992)
Essays in Anthropological Knowledge (1995)
An Anthropologist in the Larger World (2017)

The Anthropology of Knowledge
Anthropologos & Anthropologia (1992)
Cultural Cybernetics (1996)
Cultural Cognition & Cybernetics (1996)

Archeological Anthropology
Digging the Past (2002)
Relativity & Relativism (1992)
Southeast Asian Sources (1993)

Ethno-Cultural Studies
Ethnoculture: Ethno-cultural Studies (2005)
Boat People (1986)
The Jetty Chinese (1995)
The Overseas Chinese (2005)
Peranakan (1991)
Nonya (1993)

Symbolic-Linguistic Studies
English & Education (2000)
Language and Culture 1
Language and Culture 2
Language and Culture 3

<u>Lewis Micropublishing Series</u>